D0013189

The Origins of the Jump Shot

Eight Men Who Shook the World of Basketball

John Christgau

University of Nebraska Press
Lincoln and London

© 1999 by the University of
Nebraska Press
All rights reserved
Manufactured in the
United States of America
⊗
Library of Congress
Cataloging-in-
Publication Data
Christgau, John.
The origins of the jump shot :
eight men who shook the world
of basketball / John Christgau.
p.   cm.
Includes bibliographical references.
ISBN 0-8032-6394-5 (pbk. : alk. paper)
1. Basketball—Offense.   2. Basketball
players—United States—
Biography.   3. Basketball—United
States—History.   I. Title.
GV889.C48   1999
796.323'2–dc21   98–37508
CIP

Contents

Photographs

Introduction

"Basketball," the *American People's Encyclopedia* says, "may dispute baseball's claim as the national game of the U.S., because [basketball] is the only such game that is wholly American in origin."

Since James Naismith invented the game with peach baskets in Springfield, Massachusetts, in 1891, the introduction of the jump shot stands as one of the game's most important changes. Where did the remarkable shot come from? Who were its originators? Who were the pioneer players who had the courage to depart from the rigid conventions of the game and leap into the air to shoot?

In January 1996 I set out on what I thought would be a short search with a quick answer. I first interviewed Myer "Whitey" Skoog, the earliest jump shooter I had seen during my boyhood in Minnesota. From there the investigation moved steadily back in time, with earlier and earlier practitioners. Along the way were false leads, sudden turns, dead ends, then new and surprising discoveries. I read in the May 1929 *Athletic Journal* about a mysterious player from Washington State, described only as "Endslow," who was "adept at . . . making a jump, one-hand shot." An equally mysterious left-hander named "Finnegan" from North Dakota also turned up. Another very early and exciting player hailed from somewhere in Wisconsin, but nobody could recall his name. I was told about a tiny player from Hawaii named Itsu. And there were other candidates with improbable names, like Garland Pinholster and Tennessee Slim. It became a search that threatened to expand with infinite possibilities.

A year later, after traveling to ten states and interviewing more than a hundred players, coaches, and fans from the past, I identified eight players, most of them long forgotten in basketball history, who I was satisfied were among the earliest pioneers.

Somewhere toward the end of my search in November 1996, the NBA celebrated its fiftieth anniversary and announced the fifty greatest players ever. The press bitterly criticized some of the choices; other great players who had been overlooked were remembered and lionized. Across the country old fans and students of the game argued furiously in letters to the editor over who had been able to do what and how well on a basketball court. What was lost in the argument were the connections between those great deeds and the past; what was lost was the connection between basketball and life.

For hours I had sat listening as my pioneers and those who had known them told me stories about what had shaped and molded them as young basketball players. I had expected to hear tales of nip-and-tuck battles and last-second heroic shots, and in that regard I was not disappointed. But beyond that, I heard tales of hardship, sorrow, fierce independence, and triumph. The more I listened, the more I knew that arguments about who was the quickest or the strongest or the most acrobatic and fluid on a basketball floor became a meaningless discussion as long as it was divorced from lives and history. What for me had begun as a story on the origins of the jump shot became just as much a story on the origins of creativity itself.

Glory be to God for
All things counter, original . . . strange
Gerard Manley Hopkins

Let us honor if we can
The vertical man.
W. H. Auden

Fire, Myer!

When the boys from the Brainerd, Minnesota, basketball team gathered at noon that overcast winter day in 1944 for the long bus ride north to Bemidji, the war news was that Allied bombers were pounding the Japanese stronghold at Rabaul. It was Friday, January 14, and a winter snow cast a blue-gray haze across the northern landscape. For a week the nights had been clear and cold, with daytime temperatures in the low thirties. That particular morning the temperature had been only twelve degrees. By noon the air had warmed to twenty-four degrees, and the roads were clear except for icy spots and occasional frost heaves.

Brainerd coach Kermit Aase hustled his players onto the bus. Just twenty-five years old, Aase had a boyish face and thick hair that he swept straight back. In the team picture taken that year for the school yearbook he might have been mistaken for one of his players had he not been wearing a sleeveless T-shirt that showed off arms too long and muscled to be adolescent. The second oldest of seven children in a Norwegian family from Kenyon, Minnesota, Aase had been a pitcher for the University of Minnesota's Golden Gophers baseball team. Eventually, his pitching talents took him from the Big Ten to several farm teams in the Washington Senators organization; that was before he threw out his arm and wound up as a coach in Brainerd.

Despite his youth, he had no trouble exerting leadership with his players. After he boarded the bus, he stood like a general beside the driver and counted heads, down one side, then up the other. A dozen boys, he verified. They were all there.

By the time the Brainerd Warriors arrived in Bemidji, the two-ton, eighteen-foot-high statue of Paul Bunyan standing with his back to Lake Bemidji was only a dim outline in the winter dusk. In 1937, Bemidjians had positioned the cement giant, dressed in a colorful mackinaw, to guard the town.

At Bemidji, "the first city on the Mississippi," the then north-flowing river made a graceful loop to the east before it turned south. *Bemidjigumaug*, a Chippewa word meaning "river or route that flows sideways," was shortened to Bemidji by the early lumber industry settlers. It was the lumber industry, with its accompanying heroic myths, that shaped the town's character as it became a popular north-woods recreation center. "Set like a jewel in the billowy folds of nature," newspaper ads in the Twin Cities proclaimed that Bemidji was "where devotees of angling and hunting . . . find surcease from the humdrum annoyance and turmoil of everyday life."

The road trip was the Warriors' only overnight game of the year, and it offered the team a chance to stay in the grand Bemidji Hotel. Meanwhile, the game also was a critical contest in which more than just basketball was at stake. The rivalry between Brainerd and Bemidji was intense; the towns were too similar—like jealous siblings. Beyond whatever basketball rivalry they might have felt was the issue of what *town* was superior. Twice that week in banner headlines the *Bemidji Daily Pioneer* had ballyhooed the Friday night contest. A full house of three thousand fans would pack the huge Memorial Hall to watch a battle that the *Pioneer* said would "decide many things."

Memorial Hall of Bemidji State Teachers College had been the largest WPA project in Minnesota. The hall was a masterpiece of art-deco architecture. It sat on a bluff overlooking Lake Bemidji, with its blind columns, fluted marble, and series of bas-relief athletes over the entryway; the middle figure was a basketball player in a crouch, swinging an underhand free throw. The bleachers were solid oak planks affixed to polished marble steps that rose up on either side of the gym floor. Vents that were cut into the marble at frequent intervals poured heat directly onto the feet of fans who had trudged through the snow to attend the game.

An icy wind was blowing off the lake, straight onto Memorial Hall, when Coach Aase led his Warriors off the bus. Like a file of obedient cattle, they all leaned forward into the cold and followed Aase through the crowd of fans who had already arrived. When they reached the locker room, Aase began his pregame pep talk. "Boys, concentrate on your free throws," he told his players after they were dressed. "Our free throws could be the difference."

Next, he turned to the subject of whom the starters would be. All week he had avoided reporters who pressed him to reveal the names of the chosen. But he hadn't been sure himself.

After opening the Central Eight Conference season with two easy victories against Wadena and Alexandria, Aase's overconfident Warriors had been soundly thrashed by Crosby-Ironton. Now they were 2–1 in the Conference, good enough for a second place tie with Bemidji, behind undefeated St. Cloud Tech. In practice that week Aase had tried to correct what had gone wrong in Crosby-Ironton. "We haven't scored but twenty times this season on plays," he complained. He had had them spend the early part of the week rehearsing plays. The defeat at Crosby-Ironton had also been because "the boys lacked fight," or so Aase felt, and he announced on Tuesday that there would be lineup changes, only he left it a mystery as to what those changes would be.

None of the starters he eventually selected was even six feet tall. At one forward position would be the promising but inexperienced sophomore Marv Bollig, who at midseason had suffered what the *Brainerd Dispatch* called a "slump." The other forward would be junior Jack Hoffman, who also lacked experience. On court Hoffman wore wire glasses that made him look like a bookworm. He seldom took shots, and that bookish look made him seem to lack confidence. At one guard position would be co-captain Johnny Benson, a baby-faced senior and the team's second leading scorer. The other guard would be diminutive Chuck Warnberg, nicknamed "Little Torpedo" because of his aggressive style of play. He was a pure shooter and "as cool as an Eskimo on a cake of ice" when the pressure was on.

Finally, Aase announced his center-pivot man and star. His name was Myer Upton Skoog. At only five-eleven, with snow-white hair as fine as cornsilk and a face that remained utterly expressionless during the heat of play, he seemed an improbable star and an unlikely center. He appeared no match for Bemidji's towering Phil Feir, who was the perfect embodiment of the town's lumberjack myth. At six-five and two hundred plus pounds, he dwarfed Myer Skoog.

"Side guard him," Aase told Myer, "to keep the ball away from him. If he *gets* the ball," Aase added, "slide behind him." He glanced at his forwards Marv Bollig and Jack Hoffman. "If you can, sag off your men and help Myer." Bollig's eager nodding failed to conceal how anxious he felt as a rookie sophomore facing a manly giant.

A year earlier Brainerd's quickness and speed had been behind the Warriors stunning upset of an undefeated Bemidji squad. Now Aase looked at his two guards, baby-faced Johnny Benson and Torpedo Warnberg. "Move the ball quickly," he instructed them. "They don't have our speed."

By the time Aase got to his last concern in his pep talk, his players could hear the Bemidji band playing and the full-house crowd whooping in anticipation of tip-off time. The energetic cheering hardly seemed the right backdrop for Aase to tell his players with confidence, "This is Bemidji's fourth game in a week. They'll be tired. So don't get discouraged in the first half. Keep at 'em!"

Those bleacher vents positioned to warm the cold feet of fans poured heat into Memorial Hall. Even before the game had started, Myer Skoog broke a sweat as he practiced the one move he hoped to be able to use against Bemidji's towering Feir. Back to the basket, he faked right and then pivoted back the other way with a long step that would get him away from Feir's Bunyanesque reach so that he could shoot his one-hand push shot as he soared sideways.

While the two teams warmed up, Aase and Bemidji coach Glenn Barnum met in front of the scorer's table to negotiate a critical point before tip-off. Over the last decade basketball had changed from a slow game that had even featured a player known as a "standing guard," who seldom moved and never took a shot. It was instead becoming a speedball game with furious action and racing players. One result was livelier fans, but another was more fouls as players crashed into one another. Game rules requiring disqualification after only four fouls were proving impractical. In the Central Eight Conference, a balance had been struck. With the agreement of both coaches before game time, five rather than four fouls would decide disqualification.

Kermit Aase favored the additional foul. Given his team's speed and scrappiness, they were likely to foul more often. And in every game so far Myer Skoog had gone right up to the edge of disqualification in an effort to stop taller players. "No disqualification until the fifth foul," Aase told Glenn Barnum. Barnum was nearly as young as Aase. He looked athletic and courtwise, and he was convinced that provisions for an additional foul did not favor his squad. With their height advantage, they could slap shots away almost without leaping. "No," Barnum had vetoed Aase's idea. "We'll stay with the four-foul limit."

Barnum informed referees Jim Witham and Jolly Erickson, and at exactly 8:15 P.M., they blew their whistles to start the game. Myer Skoog shook Phil Feir's hand before they both stepped into the jump circle. The sight of Skoog gazing up at Feir produced isolated catcalls over the pathetic mismatch. But once Jolly Erickson had thrown the ball up, Myer was at the peak of his jump, tipping the ball back to Johnny Benson before Feir even left the floor. The boys on the Brainerd bench whooped, but it was short-lived enthusiasm. Benson promptly raced into the forecourt and threw the ball out of bounds.

Bemidji came down the floor and set up slowly, moving the ball on the perimeter from one stationary player to the next. No one moved except Feir, who slid back and forth across the key, his long arms calling for the ball in between pushing Myer off his side. They called it the "key" because the narrow lane lines that ballooned to the free-throw circle resembled the keyhole in an old door, and Feir's teammates finally got him the ball as he slid through the heart of the keyhole. With Myer on his right side, he turned left to shoot. Myer scrambled behind him, but Feir already had the ball up and over his head for the shot when Myer hooked him.

Foul, Skoog!

Feir's slow, awkward underhand free throw might have been the model for the bas relief on the Memorial Hall entrance; awkward or not, he made both shots.

0–2, Bemidji.

That brief opening exchange seemed to draw the lines for the contest: headlong, errant Warriors versus slow but steady Lumberjacks. What followed during the next minutes reinforced those battle lines. The pesky Warriors traveled and then missed two field-goal attempts, in between which the steady Jacks loped to their spots and scored twice from the field.

0–6, Bemidji.

Bollig missed again for Brainerd, and in a repeat of the first score, Feir drew his second foul from Skoog as he turned in the heart of the key for a shot. Again, he made both free throws.

0–8, Bemidji.

The two teams exchanged several missed field goals. Brainerd's last was a long, bulletlike set shot by guard Jack Hoffman that ricocheted off the backboard into the hands of a surprised Bemidji defender. He was alone at nearly midcourt and could have turned to break for an easy layup if he hadn't been hidebound by Bemidji's plan. He waited for everyone to flow past him before he slowly dribbled the ball into the front court where they scored again on another play that had taken almost a minute to unfold.

0–10, Bemidji!

The huge crowd roared its approval. Kermit Aase could not get anybody's attention for a time-out until Johnny Benson's feet came pounding down the sidelines as he dribbled past his own bench where the entire team waved its arms.

Traveling, Benson!

During the time-out, Aase tried to shout over the deafening noise of the band and the crowd that had suddenly been ignited by the lopsided score. Aase's head bobbed as he shouted for his players *just to settle down, settle down, it was* OK, *they'd be all right.* His lips moved, and the veins stood out on his neck, but when the buzzer sounded to end the time-out, not one of the players could have repeated Aase's instructions. His last words were shouted into the conch of Myer Skoog's ear. "You've got two fouls! Be careful!"

After Bemidji inbounded the ball, they set up slowly and tried once again to get the ball inside to their giant. But now Myer was using his quick footwork to dance from one side of Phil Feir to the other, and every time a Bemidji player seemed about to push a pass to Feir, one of Myer's arms became entangled with Feir's. Finally, one of Bemidji's guards let go a long set shot and missed. Johnny Benson grabbed the rebound and raced up the floor. This time there were no distracting calls by the Brainerd bench for a time-out, and he scored an easy layup.

2–10, Bemidji.

On Bemidji's next possession, Feir missed a field goal and then fouled Skoog on the rebound. Myer dipped and swung the free throw, his chin lifted and pointing at the backboard as if to signal the intensity of his concentration. But the boos were deafening, and the shot rolled the rim and dropped off. Bemidji's Quinn missed another long field goal, thrown up in frustration over not being able to get the ball past Skoog to Feir. Angry at himself over the miss, Quinn hacked Torpedo Warnberg on the rebound.

Warnberg also missed his free throw and then picked up the wrong man as Bemidji came back down the floor. Jack Hoffman raced to cover Bemidji's open man and crashed into him for a foul. While the players took up positions along the lane, Kermit Aase substituted senior Bob "Buster" Brown for Chuck Warnberg, whose torpedolike court fury had resulted in a wild pass, a missed field goal, a missed free throw, and now a defensive lapse.

After Bemidji made good on its free throw, the scoreboard flashed *2–11, Bemidji,* still a lopsided rout that kept the Bemidji crowd whooping and bellowing as Brainerd rushed down the floor and Buster Brown promptly drew a foul. Only a week earlier Brown had confided to Coach Aase that he had decided to join the Army Air Corps. Now he stepped to the free-throw line twice distracted—by the immediate mayhem of a screaming crowd *and* the uncertainties of his future. He too missed his free throw. The crowd roared its approval as Bemidji set up slowly for the last shot, but a rifle pass to Phil Feir sailed out-of-bounds.

Brainerd raced to beat the clock that would end the quarter. Only seconds still showed when two Bemidji defenders surrounded Jack Hoffman. His glasses knocked crooked, he pivoted repeatedly in a frantic effort to find somebody open to whom he could pass. He seemed hopelessly bottled up when he suddenly managed to poke his head out from the tangle of arms around him and push an awkward bounce pass to Myer Skoog at midcourt.

Myer took one long step that launched him into the air. None of the Bemidji fans would have seen the parallels, but the soaring was the same as if he had taken off again from the Boom Lake ski jump in Brainerd, where he liked to practice ski-jumping in the silence of a snowy night. At the peak of his leap, he hurled the ball with a lunge that twisted him in the air. The desperate shot headed straight for the basket and looked sure to be one more grand achievement for Brainerd's quiet star.

Myer's father had emigrated to the New World at the age of fourteen from the island of Rolla off the coast of Norway. It was the same rugged fjord region of Norway from which Viking Norsemen had set out on explorations that would eventually take them across the Hudson Bay and into the lake country of Minnesota. Five hundred years later Myer Martin Frantsen had also arrived from Norway, bringing with him a love of skiing and ski jumping and a determination to succeed in the New World. Obliged to take the surname of brothers and sisters who had preceded him to America, he changed his name to Skoog, meaning "Little Community," and he worked as a crew cook for lumberjacks logging the great forests around the north shore of Lake Superior, whose inlets and shoreline reminded him of the fjords of Norway.

The roughness of a logging camp life soon proved too much for Myer Martin Skoog, a man of deep religious faith. After two years he went to work selling sewing machines and later life insurance before he enlisted for service in the Great War. On a battlefield in France, where he served as a doctor's aide, he was gassed and then eventually discharged to return to Minnesota. He settled on a dairy farm north of Duluth. In time he met Nora Nelson at the Lutheran church in Duluth. Myer Upton Skoog, their fourth child, was born in 1926.

Myer's earliest recollection was of returning home after church to find their farmhouse engulfed in flames. After the fire the family moved to a Norwegian settlement near Randall, Minnesota, where Myer's father continued farming. Following the example of his parents, who led the children in Norwegian grace before meals, Myer spoke only Norwegian as a child. Over and over his mother bounced him on her knee and recited Norwegian rhymes whose rhythms stuck in his mind long after he could remember what they meant. Christmas featured candlelit trees and hymns from the Homeland. Even the Fourth of July celebration was a bizarre mix of American cap guns and Norwegian chatter.

Winters were bone cold, and Myer walked to the one-room school-house bundled up like an Eskimo. One day in the first grade his teacher gave him a note as he stood wrapped for the walk home. "Make sure your mother and father read this," she told him. He carried the note home dutifully, wondering if it was praise or censure for his schoolwork.

His mother read the note while Myer unwrapped himself beside the stove. "If you want your son to be an American," the note warned, "you're going to have to start speaking English at home." It was a sudden awakening for his parents. Secure in their pocket of Norwegian friends, they had enjoyed all of the opportunities of the New World while preserving the culture of the old. Now, a change was clearly in order, and English became the rule of the day in the Skoog household. Still, Myer's father clung to the ritual of leading all of the children with their friends on cross-country skiing expeditions in the dead of winter, their breath making steam like a locomotive. He taught them all the same long, classic stride he had learned as a boy in Norway.

Their adventures were interrupted suddenly when Myer's father became ill. He had seldom talked about his war experiences, or any of his experiences for that matter. It was neither false modesty nor shyness but rather an expression of his Norwegian Lutheran conviction that the self is not the center of the world. Now, however, it was clear that he was suffering from the lingering effects of the gassing he had suffered in the Great War, and he spent months recovering in the veterans' hospital at Ft. Snelling in Minneapolis, leaving Nora Skoog and her children to manage the farm.

In 1933, after Myer's father recovered, the family moved to the town of Little Falls, Minnesota. Still more Norwegian than American, young Myer struggled to appreciate the peculiar form of American idolatry that the town heaped on its homegrown hero, "Lucky" Lindbergh. It was fame that seemed at odds with the quiet selflessness of Norwegian character, at least as Myer saw it in his father.

In 1936 the Skoog family had moved to Brainerd, Minnesota, where Myer's father accepted a position as manager of the town's Singer sewing machine outlet. Once a railroad, farming, and timber center, with prosperity Brainerd also had become a recreational center for fishing and hunting in the surrounding lake country. Although townfolk now, the Skoogs remained committed to their pastoral habits, and the family continued its cross-country skiing expeditions, gliding across frozen lakes, then stopping in the woods to build a fire and have lunch.

It wasn't until the fourth grade in Brainerd that young Myer Skoog experienced his first contest, the Brainerd city marble championships. For a long while he had merely watched opponents draw a circle in the dirt, then work to knock one another's marbles out of the circle. Once he took it up himself, his aim proved deadly. In a Brainerd park in the summer of 1938, he easily defeated one opponent after another until the boy with the snow-white hair was declared the overall city champion. His picture appeared in the *Brainerd Dispatch*.

Meanwhile, Myer had barely heard of the much larger world of basketball. But the excitement of competition was in his blood, not just against others but against himself. He was testing his own limits. Recognizing that the spirit of American competition was beginning to captivate his sons, Myer Martin Skoog outfitted the boys in long skis with three grooves for jumping. Then after supper one night he drove them out to Boom Lake on the edge of town. The old wooden ski jump stood silhouetted in the winter moonlight like a prehistoric beast. There, he taught them all the balance and timing of ski jumping. It came as quickly to Myer as flicking a marble with his thumb, and he found that his strong legs catapulted him off the lip of the jump and gave him the exhilarating sensation of floating.

Now Myer began to take an interest in other competitive sports that gave him a chance to exercise his coordination and skill. Still in junior high, he managed to earn a spot on the eighth-grade basketball team, but the beginning was rocky for him. His ski-jumping instincts for leaping and soaring were frustrated by his coach, who admonished him that, except for rebounding, *in basketball you kept your feet on the floor*.

Even on the free-throw line his instincts seemed at war with the rules, and one day in a game, almost without thinking, he lifted his arms to his chest and shot a one-hand free throw. His coach's disapproval was immediate. "Skoog, you hot dog!" he shouted. "You're gonna sit down until you learn to shoot free throws correctly!"

From then on, even though his one-hand floor shot was as deadly accurate as his marble game, he shot his free throws underhand with both hands. It was better than risking another embarrassing insult. That would have violated not just a code of basketball, but the deeper traditions of his Norwegian heritage: you never, *ever* called attention to yourself or indulged in showmanship. To avoid even a hint of theatricality, he adopted the habit of keeping an absolutely expressionless, stoic face when on the court, especially when he scored on one of his one-hand push shots. It was all consistent with an unflappable Nordic demeanor.

In the winter of 1940, Brainerd Junior High held its annual Winter Sports Day, and Myer Skoog added yet another success to his championships: he became Brainerd's junior high ski-jump champion. In recognition of his talent, he was crowned "King of Winter Sports Day," and again his picture appeared in the *Dispatch*.

The following fall Myer entered the tenth grade at Washington High. High school seemed to promise nothing special, but eventually, on the strength of his accurate one-hand push shot, he earned a starting position on the B basketball team. Still, he drew little attention to himself. Finally, in a post-season contest between graduating "Hasbeens" and upcoming "Hopefuls," he scored a meager six points. It hardly suggested a legend in the making.

Things began to change, however, on Saturday afternoons the spring and summer before his junior year. A spiral staircase led down to a small gym with a low ceiling in the basement of the old Northern Pacific Railroad YMCA in Brainerd. There, he and other hopefuls played for hours on end. A support post in the middle of the floor provided what they all jokingly called a "natural screen" that they used to shake their defender while dribbling. Two or three dribbles past that post, Myer would pick up his dribble, take a long step, then use the same, explosive leaping ability he had developed on ski jumps to launch himself high into the air for a running, one-hand shot. Even if his defender hadn't been screened by the post, the shot was too explosive and quick for anybody to block. Where did such an unusual shot come from? What were its antecedents on basketball's evolutionary tree?

The year 1922, just four years before Myer Skoog was born, saw the birth of Walter E. Meanwell's book *The Science of Basketball for Men*. Meanwell's "little black book"—the cover was coal black—went through four editions immediately after its publication and became the bible for basketball in the United States. Meanwell, who died in 1953, was born in England and never played basketball himself, but "The Little Doctor," as he was known, was a professor of physical education and the varsity basketball coach for twenty years at Wisconsin. There he won four Big Ten titles and was described by Knute Rockne as "the final word on basketball."

In a chapter entitled "Basket Shooting," Meanwell described what in 1922, thirty years after Dr. Naismith had invented the game, was still the standard shot in basketball. That shot was the "Two-Hand, Underhand Loop Shot," which began just below the waist, with feet spread. Meanwell also described "The Overhand Loop Shot," which was thrown from the chest with two hands and did *not* require the player to leave the floor.

Meanwell described several less popular shots in his little handbook. He must have anticipated how difficult it would be for later generations to visualize the peculiar contortions that characterized those early shots, so he included photographic plates as illustration. The figure pictured in the "Two-Hand Cross-Body Shoulder Shot" resembled the twisted configuration of Myron's statue of Discobolus, and no matter who was shooting it, the eventual shot surely crashed against the backboard like a discus.

Meanwell's little black book also included a short discussion of "The One-Hand Push Shot," made from a standing position. Meanwell wrote that while executing the shot, the player should jump toward the basket. Common points of error in the execution of the shot, Meanwell said with British pride, were to "neglect to English the ball, and to broad rather than to high jump."

Not long after the appearance of Meanwell's valuable book, a monthly publication called *The Athletic Journal* began appearing throughout the country. In one of the journal's earliest issues, devoted entirely to basketball, Forrest "Phog" Allen explained in his article on the "Anatomy of Basketball" that the three fundamental shots were: the free throw, the two-hand push shot, and the one-hand English shot from the same standing position that Meanwell had described. "The one-hand English shot is not used so much as the other two," Allen wrote.

An illustration for that rare, one-hand English shot showed the player holding the ball in one hand off his shoulder but in his eyeline. Meanwhile, players trying to understand Allen's discussion of the more popular two-hand shot had to read: "The flexing pronators are attached to the internal condyle of the humerus [and] the supinators and extensors are attached to the external condyle." No wonder that some players began experimenting with new, less difficult shots. By 1925 Ralph Jones, coach at Purdue, argued for more freedom in shooting. As a case in point he recalled that one of his best scorers "made the most goals while running away from the basket, jumping in the air, turning and throwing from just over his left shoulder with two hands."

It was a shot that could only have been executed by the Flying Wallendas. And despite the argument for more freedom in shooting, the "Underhand Loop Shot," with both feet solidly on the floor, remained the orthodox shot. Then in January 1927, J. Craig Ruby (who played for Walter Meanwell at Wisconsin) wrote that a variation of the loop shot, the "Two-Hand Poised Chest Shot," required the player to "jump or hop off the floor as part of the follow through." The same article demonstrating the "One-Hand Short Shot" provided a series of illustrations, one of which was labeled "The Jump." Just as Meanwell's description of the "One-Hand Push Shot" had done, Ruby's article encouraged players to leave the floor during the shot.

In May 1929, H. O. Page described the team strategies and individual player techniques of the Indiana State High School Basketball Tournament of that year. "The high arch push shot was common around the thirty foot zone," Page wrote. But he noted that "the coming shot when closely guarded seems to be either the one-hand push-up or hook shot, *going at top speed.*"

It was the first discussion in print of the running one-hander, and by January 1933, W. L. Bowers, a high-school coach from Cumberland, Maryland, acknowledged: "Many of the so-called set shots in basketball do not really belong in that category." His reasoning was that the shooters were not set but *moving*, because from fifteen feet or more, it was necessary for the sake of impetus that a player "leave his feet and continue in the direction of the shot." So the popularity of the running one-hander was growing. In May of the same year an article in *The Athletic Journal* on state high-school champions from around the country took note of a Bismarck, North Dakota, player named Finnegan, a left-handed forward whose "one handed shooting and speed were amazing."

The exact moment of the popularization of the running one-hander was December 30, 1936, in Madison Square Garden, during a basketball double-header featuring New York University versus Georgetown in the first game, and in the second, Claire Bee's hotshots from Long Island University, riding a string of forty-three straight victories, versus Johnny Bunn's Stanford Indians, led by the little-known but high-scoring Hank Luisetti.

A 1934 graduate of Galileo High in San Francisco, Luisetti promptly enrolled at Stanford. Modern writers who have not read Walter E. Meanwell's little black book or *The Athletic Journal* credit Luisetti with beginning the running one-hander. But he was only popularizing a shot that had been emerging for years, and the day before the double-header in Madison Square Garden in December 1936, the New York papers reported: "Every one of the amiable, clean-cut Coast kids [fires away] with leaping one-handed shots." Still, City College of New York's legendary Nat Holman remained unconvinced that a shot predicated on a "prayer" was smart basketball.

Stanford won handily that night, ending the long winning streak of LIU, and the running one-hander was suddenly respectable. Immediately, hundreds of players throughout the country began trying to learn to run and leap and shoot. In time, one of those was Myer Upton Skoog in a small basement gym in Brainerd, Minnesota.

Myer and his friends had played that night until the gym closed at nine. Myer's mother whacked him when he got home for skipping supper, but it was a small price to pay for the confidence he was gaining on a basketball court. There *was*, after all, a place in the game for his instincts, perhaps not shooting one-hand free throws, but surely using his quickness to rebound and score.

Myer's junior year at Washington High in 1942 was his first playing varsity basketball; that same year Kermit Aase began his coaching career in Brainerd. Before Aase even set eyes on Myer Skoog the first time, he had heard about the white-haired junior with explosive jumping ability and an uncanny flat shot, developed in the low ceiling of the town's YMCA.

Myer became one of Aase's starters. He could score, he could dribble, he could rebound, and Aase was sure he had a star in the making. The only question was where to play him; he moved him from forward to guard, then back to forward again, and finally toward the end of the year to center position, where he could utilize his jumping ability to tip the ball until he could control the rebound.

Assessing the team's chances in the Central Eight Conference, *Dispatch* sportswriter Pat Keith noted: "Skoog gives the Warriors a very dangerous weapon—the one-handed shot." By midseason Myer was one of the team's leading scorers.

For Myer, the most satisfying moment of his junior year had come in late February with a stunning upset of "mighty Bemidji, scourge of the Central Eight Conference," as described by the *Dispatch*. Riding a seventeen-game winning streak, which included their earlier pasting of Brainerd, the overconfident Lumberjacks had been swept off their feet in front of a packed house in the Washington gym as Myer repeatedly stole rebounds over Bemidji's junior giant Phil Feir. "Skoog was exceptional," Pat Keith wrote, "his best game of the year by far."

Meanwhile, Coach Kermit Aase had a ready excuse for those who felt he had a special ethnic bond with his tow-headed Norski star. "Hell, I think *everybody's* Norwegian," he laughed.

Summarizing Warriors basketball at the end of the season, the *Dispatch* noted that Myer Skoog, who had been selected to the All District team, still had another year to play. "We shall hear more about him next year," they wrote.

As soon as the first deep snows fell that next winter of 1943–44, however, Myer returned to ski jumping. Skiing enthusiasts had fixed up the old jump at Boom Lake, equipping it with lights at the top and bottom. Now Myer would walk home from basketball practice, eat quickly, throw his skis over his shoulder, and hurry out to Boom Lake in order to get in three or four jumps before they turned off the new lights.

To get to the top of the fifty-foot-high jump, he ascended a rickety staircase, then fastened his bindings under the single floodlight illuminating the start platform. When it was his turn, he slipped to the edge of the platform, his skis half out in space, then lunged forward and headed down the ramp.

He concentrated on holding his crouch until the last possible moment. The wood railing stiles of the jump began shooting past on the edge of his vision as he gained speed and raced toward the lip of the jump. Leaping off that lip at exactly the right moment was critical. To jump too soon would set back his takeoff point and shorten his jump. Too late, and he'd already be airborne without the extra push of a leap. Finding that exact moment was not a matter of deliberation, or even thought. It was pure instinct, followed by the exhilaration of floating in the air, of holding himself balanced and frozen while everything seemed to be going at triple-speed at the same time it went in slow motion.

He experienced that same feeling of floating-forever after he leaped to take the final shot in the first quarter of that fourth game of the season in Bemidji's Memorial Hall. While he was still in the air, the Brainerd bench stood up. A last-second, lucky shot would turn things around. It would take the wind right out of Bemidji's sails. Renewed and confident, the Warriors could gather themselves between quarters and begin their comeback. Myer Skoog's miracle basket would be the first step.

It was not to be. The shot hit the backboard, corkscrewed the rim, and flew off as the buzzer sounded.

2–11, Bemidji still.

They had managed but one field goal. And Kermit Aase was right. Free throws were proving to be the difference—*the wrong difference*. Brainerd had missed three straight throws, while Bemidji hadn't missed in five times at the line. Meanwhile, Myer Skoog already had two fouls, and Bemidji's fans, still stinging from Brainerd's upset victory of the previous year, smelled a payback rout. Their cheering again made it impossible for anybody to hear Aase's second-quarter instructions, whatever they were. And when the already weary-looking Warriors dragged themselves back out on the floor to start the second quarter, they were the ones who looked fatigued and already defeated.

Myer controlled the tip again to start the second quarter, and sophomore Marv Bollig was hardly across half court when he threw up a foolish, dead-on, twenty-five-foot shot that slammed off the backboard and caromed through.

4–11, Bemidji.

Bollig's shot had all the earmarks of luck so blind and invincible that it even ignored stupidity. Meanwhile, it also served to remind the Brainerd bench that luck was all they had at the moment.

Bemidji worked the ball patiently over the next five minutes, trying to get it inside to Phil Feir, who scored twice during the interval.

4–15 Bemidji.

On successive Brainerd possessions, Jack Hoffman traveled, and Johnny Benson missed another free throw. Meanwhile, Kermit Aase substituted junior Eivind Hoff for Jack Hoffman. Hoff had a long, narrow face with a sharp jaw and deep-set eyes. On court he wore a look of fierce determination and carried himself in a wary crouch, like an animal ready to spring. Pat Keith called Hoff "the most determined player ever to perform for Brainerd," and he was hardly in the game a minute before his dogged defense prompted Bemidji to miss twice. On the second miss, he wrestled the rebound from Feir, threw the ball to Johnny Benson, then sprinted to catch up with his fast-breaking teammates, who finally returned the ball to him so that he could plunge through a knot of Bemidji players and score.

6–15, Bemidji.

The rest of the quarter was seesaw combat during which Brainerd could not close the gap. Then with still more than a minute left in the half, Bemidji began holding the ball for the last shot. The crowd fell quiet and watched as Bemidji's guards stood at midcourt, hoping to open up the key for an easy pass into Feir. But Brainerd lay back and waited. A full minute passed, and no one on the floor moved. An occasional hoot, directed at Brainerd for refusing to play into Bemidji's hands, punctuated the silence. Kermit Aase held up both palms to signal that his players were to *lay back, still, lay back!* None of his players noticed, and with ten seconds on the clock, the Bemidji guards inched forward. Seduced, Brainerd tightened. Aase jumped to his feet and used his palms again to try to push his players back into a gaggle that could surround Phil Feir.

Still, no one was watching him, and with just two seconds left, only Myer Skoog stuck to the Bemidji giant as the ball came to him on a rifle pass that he caught high over his head on his right side. Positioned on Feir's left side, Myer tried to slide behind him, but Feir turned quickly and scored easily as the buzzer sounded.

14–23, Bemidji.

In the bowels of the locker room in Memorial Hall, while the noise of Bemidji's band sounded as faraway as if across a lake, Aase enjoined his players at half time, "Give a little bit more. So they don't get the ball into Feir." Finally, in a soft voice that seemed squeezed and restrained, as if he was trying to keep his own fever in check, he tried to deliver a pep talk that would send his boys out on the floor ready to stage a comeback.

Yet there was no exuberant whooping from his players when he was finished. It was as if each of them knew that some games had a will of their own which defied whatever coaching strategies were brought to bear. Bemidji *would* tire, but not because Coach Aase happened to see it coming. Brainerd would shake their wet spirits and catch fire, but not because Kermit Aase had tried to say something inspirational to ignite them. It would come down to a close game. Their faces were already filled with apprehension over the struggle ahead. Thank God, it would probably all hang on their star, Myer Skoog, whose face was as calm as ever as he walked out on the floor for the second half.

Wiser now after two center jumps, Bemidji stole Myer Skoog's control tip to start the second half, and Keith Hoberg scored immediately. On the return possession Brainerd lost the ball on a bad pass, and Hoberg scored again.

14–27, Bemidji.

Delirious with the prospect of an avenging rout, the crowd cheered so loudly after Hoberg's score that no one in the house heard Jolly Erickson's whistle blow when Phil Feir fouled Myer Skoog. Myer had gotten the ball with Feir pressed behind him. He had faked left this time, then whirled back to his right around Feir, who recovered too late and could only snag Myer's arms as he tried to get off the shot.

Jolly set everyone in place for Myer's free throws. Meanwhile, despite the will of a game, Kermit Aase began looking down his bench for the right substitute for Chuck Warnberg, who had his defensive hands full trying to stop the hot shooting Keith Hoberg. Meanwhile, Myer made only the second of his two free throws.

15–27, Bemidji.

During the second attempt, Eivind Hoff had jumped up at the call of his name and trotted down the bench and seated himself next to Aase, who was too busy delivering rapid instructions to Hoff to notice that Feir missed a field goal attempt that allowed Torpedo Warnberg to score on a pell-mell drive.

17–27, Bemidji.

"Who scored?" Aase had to ask.

"Torpedo," Hoff answered.

They both watched as the furious action continued. Skoog scored, Feir walked, and then in less than a minute, Torpedo Warnberg, who had come within a hairbreadth of being yanked, scored two more baskets without an answer from Bemidji.

23–27, Bemidji.

With Eivind Hoff still beside him, Aase sat back and watched. He had come dangerously close to sticking his nose unnecessarily into the workings of game fate. For several sorties, as the crowd roared and cheered, Bemidji surrendered its Lumberjack pace to the frenzied will of the game. The two teams raced up and down the court. The results were a disaster: bad passes, walking, foolish shots taken while careening wildly, and finally only one free throw by Bemidji's Keith Hoberg to show for their efforts.

23–28 Bemidji.

And one free throw by Myer Skoog.

24–28, Bemidji.

Again, it was Feir who had fouled Myer, this time, after Myer had turned to face the Bemidji center, who had lifted his arms to block what he thought was Myer's shot. Instead, Myer had ducked under Feir's arm, which had dropped like a guillotine. It was Feir's third foul. One more and he was gone. Bemidji called a time-out to make defensive adjustments. Meanwhile, Kermit Aase could only thank God and his lucky stars that Glenn Barnum had insisted on staying with the four-foul limit.

After the time-out, Bemidji managed to reassert its will and plodded through a play that unfolded slowly. This time, however, when Phil Feir finally turned to shoot, Myer Skoog leaped with both hands high and swept the ball away cleanly.

The crowd's booing to protest a foul was just dying out when Brainerd pushed the ball straight into Myer, who pivoted to face Feir. But Feir had cautiously retreated a half step and stood with his hands high again, calling the attention of everybody in Memorial Hall, and especially the officials, to his defensive innocence. Meanwhile, the Bemidji guards had collapsed on Myer from behind. One of them was trying to reach around Myer and slap the ball when Jolly Erickson's whistle blew.

The crowd booed again. Feir raised his hands even higher in mock innocence. The crowd fell silent in the confusion over who had committed the foul. It was one of the collapsing guards, not Feir. Still, the Bemidji fans continued booing as Myer dipped slowly and made the free throw.

25–28, Bemidji.

Again, Bemidji lumbered through a deliberate play that ended when Marv Bollig, eager to intercept an obvious pass, crashed into Bemidji guard Dick Laurence.

Foul, Bollig.

The missed free throw bounced high. Myer Skoog jumped to tip it from the long reach of Phil Feir. The ball bounced twice along the end line before Myer himself pounced on it, then shoveled it to Johnny Benson. Advancing down the floor, Myer glanced at the scoreboard.

3:20 left in the third quarter. 25–28 Bemidji.

Once he had reached his own free-throw line, Myer turned his back on Phil Feir and set himself at the corner of the key. All night he had not only felt Feir pushing back against him, but also heard Feir's labored breathing. Now, however, there was nothing. Unable to take his eyes off Johnny Benson, who had pulled up off a quick dribble and was pivoting desperately to get free for a pass into the key, Myer put his hands behind his back to feel for Feir. Still nothing.

Myer backed closer to the basket until he finally felt the solid wall that was Feir. Then Johnny Benson's wild pass came a good two feet wide of Myer, who stepped to catch it and in the same motion pivoted to face the basket. Feir retreated a half step, his hands high again to parade his innocence.

Myer looked up at him, and the thought formed quickly: *I am not gonna take a dribble to him.* But what then? Giving it no more thought, he crouched quickly and then jumped.

It was as if he had lifted off the lip of a ski jump, and now there was that familiar Boom Lake sensation of both triple-speed and slow motion. At the edge of his vision, instead of the wood palings of the ski jump flying by, he could see the colorful trails left by streaking jerseys. Meanwhile, despite the noise in Memorial Hall, he was in a cocoon of silence and floating.

The eventual shot was awkward. Afterward, he would remember only that at the peak of his jump, his whole body, and not just his arms, had convulsed in some way to set the ball on its flight. By the time he began dropping to the floor, even before it was clear that the shot would be way short, he was stricken with the conviction that he had done something wrong. Just as soon as he landed, the shot's strange forces, like the buck of a cannon, sent him sprawling backwards onto the floor. In that second he was on the floor, another thought flashed: *Hot dog!* The shot had been pure show-off. He glanced at his coach. Aase stared back, his face as unreadable as Myer's.

That night, lying on his bed in the Bemidji Hotel, Myer tried to sort out which of the two critical moments of the game had been the high point. Was it that third-quarter leaping shot that came from the same reservoir of grace and instinct that permitted him to fly off a ski jump and had made him feel like such a hot dog? Despite how beguiling it was to hang in the air like a ski jumper, on a basketball court it was wrong. Yet, if it had truly been a flashy shot, his unassuming coach would surely have said something. But he hadn't even mentioned it, probably, Myer decided, because Aase had been too overwhelmed by the other, more dramatic shot.

It had come in the last seconds, and Myer lay on his bed reliving it: After that third-quarter shot, he had picked himself up off the floor and sprinted to catch up with Feir, whose next shot he blocked. On Brainerd's possession, Chuck Warnberg's hot hand had delivered again, and he had scored his fourth field goal of the quarter. Fouled on the shot, he stepped to the free-throw line with a chance to tie the score. But the free throw rolled the rim twice and spun out.

27–28, Bemidji.

With two seconds left in the third quarter, Myer had rebounded a missed Bemidji free throw and hurled a long pass to Bollig, who had been fouled at the buzzer. Time gone, he had remained on the floor alone and missed the free throw that would have tied the game.

The entire Brainerd team had surrounded a confident Kermit Aase during the huddle at the bench. Bemidji had tired, just as he had said they would, and Brainerd was only one point behind. It was their game to win. But once the Warriors had taken the floor again for the fourth quarter, the lead seesawed back and forth, as if the *game* couldn't decide how it wanted to resolve itself.

Myer had again faked and ducked under Feir's arm.

29–28, Brainerd, their first lead.

Feir had countered with two free throws after Myer had committed his third foul.

29–30, Bemidji back on top.

The two teams had traded bad passes and missed field goals. Then Bemidji's Hoberg added another free throw to their lead.

29–31, Bemidji.

Johnny Benson missed a free throw, and with three minutes left and a three-point lead, Bemidji had begun stalling. With two minutes left, the pass went into Feir, who stood holding the ball high over his head. Myer jumped and tipped it out of Feir's hands. Feir and Skoog scrambled for the loose ball. Jolly Erickson blew his whistle. Every player on the court froze. Was it Skoog, whose face was stonier than ever? Or Feir, who was frozen with his hands high? They both already had three fouls. Whoever the guilty one was, he would be gone.

Kermit Aase glanced at Glenn Barnum. Why hadn't he convinced Barnum to raise the limit to five fouls? Because he hadn't, there was a good chance that the Warriors were going to have to pay a steep price. Jolly Erickson slipped through the sweaty players and found the culprit. Feir dropped his hands in defeat.

His play had been solid. He had held Myer Skoog to just three baskets. The boos and shrill whistles for his disqualification had risen higher and higher through the time-out Bemidji took to figure out what to do. They were still booing when Bollig stepped to the free-throw line and quickly made the free throw.

30–31, Bemidji.

Again, this time with one minute left, Bemidji had tried to stall. But with twenty seconds on the clock, a long cross-court pass had sailed out of bounds. Kermit Aase stood up and made a T with his fingers. Because of the pandemonium, only Myer had noticed him and called time out.

In the Brainerd huddle, Aase had to shout at the top of his voice to make the simple play outline heard. Jack Hoffman would in-bound to Johnny Benson, who would dribble the ball down the right side. Everybody else was to stay left. Aase had looked at his star. "Myer, set up in the left key. When Johnny crosses half court, swing out to receive the pass from him." He did not have to finish. What Myer did next, and at what pace to beat the clock and score, had been left up to him.

Racing down the sidelines, Johnny Benson had whirled twice to escape defenders before he crossed the half-court line and then looked for Myer, who had had to swing all the way out beyond the top of the free-throw circle before he was free to receive the pass.

Remembering it on his bed, Myer wasn't sure if he had dribbled once, twice, or not at all before he took off with the same one-footed, high-arching leap of the earlier desperation shot he had missed. All he could remember was that the angle of the twenty-five-foot shot, slightly off a dead straight line to the basket, meant that he could have either banked the shot or gone straight for the rim. In a split second, again more instinct than thought, he had chosen the latter.

The shot had been like a low-line drive in baseball. It had caught the back of the rim and made the net fly forward as it ripped through the basket.

31–30, Brainerd.

Despite the locker-room victory celebration, Kermit Aase had insisted on an eleven o'clock curfew. He'd be making a bed check, he had warned. And now Myer Skoog lay in bed with the lights out, wondering if his coach would finally come to tell him that, despite his last-second heroics, the strange leaping shot in the third quarter had been pure circus. It had been a vain violation of the traditions of basketball. It had been a cocky departure from everything Myer Skoog had been taught about basketball and life.

"I'm gonna put *that* shot away," he told himself. "I'll never do it again!"

There was a soft knock on his room door. He sat up. It had to be Coach Aase, making his promised bed check. And maybe coming to chastise him for the foolish shot. But Aase only stuck his head in the door and flicked the light switch. "I see you're in bed."

"You said curfew was eleven."

Aase smiled, only a slight corner-curl of his lips. "Myer," he said softly, "you're the only one in bed."

Myer Skoog did not get immediate credit for the last-minute heroic shot that beat Bemidji in early January 1944. Bemidji sportswriters, numbed by the loss, reported incorrectly that it was Brainerd's Marv Bollig who had scored the winning basket. Back in Brainerd the *Dispatch* reported with equal inaccuracy that Chuck Warnberg had been the hero. It wasn't until a week later that the *Dispatch* apologized for the confusion and reported correctly that "Myer Skoog, Warrior center, was the lad who tallied the winning bucket in the fading seconds." Lost in the confusion was any memory, except Myer's, of his spontaneous, third-quarter leaping shot, which had come out of a game situation so powerful that it had overridden the reserve of his character and the traditions of the game.

In June, Myer Skoog graduated from high school, heralded as "one of the all time greats of Brainerd High." He then served two years in the navy, during which time he played basketball with a base team in Florida. Just nineteen years of age, and a pasty white that reflected both his Scandinavian fairness and north-woods winters, he picked up the nickname "Whitey" from teammates who were deeply tanned by the Florida sun. Meanwhile, that extraordinary, one-time jump shot still lay buried deep beneath his Norwegian reserve.

Discharged from the navy in 1947, he enrolled at the University of Minnesota without benefit of an athletic scholarship. "I never really thought of going anyplace else," he would shrug and dismiss it later before incredulous professional teammates who had enjoyed generous college scholarships.

It was December of his sophomore year in 1948 before he tried that leaping shot again, this time at the preseason Corn Bowl Fiesta at Drake University in Des Moines, Iowa. It came as spontaneously as that first shot in Bemidji had come, but now without the sense afterward that he had done something only a hot dog would do. Playing guard for the Gophers, he had the ball at the top of the free-throw circle and began to drive left in a wide curve toward the baseline.

"I had my man beat," he explained later, "except, on the baseline, still fifteen feet from the basket, the big six-foot-seven center from Drake stepped right in front of me. I was thinking I was going all the way, but I would have charged. I only had one alternative: to stop and go up. I was almost behind the backboard. I jumped and sort of hung for a split second until the Drake center started downward. Then I came out with the shot with my right hand."

This time the shot was good. It stuck in the memory of those sportswriters who saw it and later incorrectly identified it as Whitey Skoog's *first* jump shot. Meanwhile, Whitey began refining it in daily practices in cavernous Williams Arena under the watchful eyes of his coach, Osborn "Ozzie" Cowles, a native Minnesotan who had won ten letters in three sports as a young man at Carleton College in Northfield, Minnesota. In 1942 he had taken his Dartmouth basketball squad to the finals of the NCAA tournament. Now, in only his third year as head coach for the Gophers, Cowles had a cherubic face with neatly parted hair, he was short, and he always wore a bow tie for games. His practices were choreographed, punctual affairs that began with a half hour of warm-up shooting on the elevated floor of Williams Arena, while he stood to the side studying his players and holding a white slip of paper with a practice outline.

Whitey Skoog's jump shot might have seemed in wild defiance of that sense of order, yet Cowles was only bothered by Whitey's daredevil ski-jumping, which he continued to pursue in the Twin Cities as he had in Brainerd.

"Now this . . . *ski-jumping* you do," he took Whitey aside and told him gently. "It's not a good idea." Then, after watching Whitey use his jump shot more and more in Big Ten games, Cowles took Skoog aside again. "Here's a move I'd like you to learn," he said and then demonstrated a stutter step. "It'll be more effective for you."

Having scouted the Gophers and Skoog, Big Ten opponents were adjusting their defenses to take away his preferred baseline drive. Now, the stutter-step could take him *either* toward the baseline or into the middle of the court, where he could stop dead before defenses collapsed and go up for his new shot.

"What you do, Whitey," Cowles explained and demonstrated, "is you take this little stride forward. If your defender doesn't move back, you've already got half a step on him, so you take another quick full step and you're *gone*."

It became the move by which Whitey Skoog gained All America honors at Minnesota in 1950 and 1951. His snow-white hair, now kept in a neat crew cut, his jump shot, and his stone face in the midst of rip-roaring competition—they all marked him as one of the most remarkable players in the country. Yet no one knew *how* remarkable: he was the son of Norwegian immigrants, once sent home from school with a note warning his parents not to let language and nationality set him apart. Now, suspended in the air by the buoyant cheering of eighteen thousand enthusiastic Minnesota fans, his was the ultimate assimilation.

Still, you could read none of that in his impassive face. "The young man simply will not be flustered," explained Ozzie Cowles of Whitey's icy calm. "You couldn't rattle him if you tied him to railroad tracks in front of a train."

Once Gopher fans had gotten used to the incongruity of such a foot-loose shot from such a deadpan player, they began chanting "Fire, Myer!" every time he got the ball. The chant rising, he would take that short stutter-step repeatedly, then the long, quick second step, followed by one, two, or three dribbles, until he got to an open spot on the floor, where he stopped dead and then leaped to shoot.

In time, there were variations. Wally Salovich, the Gopher's rugged, six-five center-forward with a cotton-soft hook shot, would back out toward Whitey and then bend over, offering his wide body as a screen. Or, once nervous defenders had retreated too far out of respect for Whitey's quickness, he would suddenly pull back that first stutter-step and go straight up from far out, with the deafening chant of "Fire, Myer!" seeming to propel him into the lights.

Newspaper pictures of Whitey taking the shot, distorted because the cameras were aimed from beneath the elevated floor of Williams Arena, showed Whitey's knee caps at the level of his defender's eyes. One Big Ten coach complained, "You've got to gun him down with a plane." Then one day a reporter from the university's radio station called him. "Why do you kick your legs on the shot?" the reporter wondered.

"Well," Whitey groped, "it's a matter of *protection*."

The reporter accepted his explanation, although even Whitey wasn't sure what he meant, or what he was "protecting" himself against. Then two university film students came out to record the shot for coaches trying to teach it around the state. Once Whitey saw on film what he was doing, he wondered if the instinctive kick of his legs wasn't to keep his balance. Or, it occurred to him, maybe he did it to prevent a repeat of that first time in Bemidji, when the shot's recoil had pitched him back on his "duff."

After Whitey became the territorial draft choice of the Minneapolis Lakers in 1951, he began letting his legs hang straight on a jump shot that helped the original Lakers continue their incredible streak of NBA championships. The 1952–53 season featured Whitey as a starting guard; the first NBA superstar, George Mikan, credited Skoog with "the greatest jump shot I ever saw." Yet, one cold night in 1957, in a Philadelphia train station after a game against the

Warriors, Whitey bent over to pick up his suitcase and snapped something in his back. It was the end of his professional career.

After graduate study back at the university, he began a long coaching career, first basketball and then golf at tiny Gustavus Adolphus College in St. Peter, Minnesota. Ironically, for the man whose gift had been leaping high into the air and then hanging—off ski jumps and hardwood courts—it was in teaching golf, the one sport where you *never* left the ground, that he enjoyed the most success. His Gusties won sixteen conference titles, and he coached nine college All Americans in golf.

One warm spring afternoon in Minnesota, one of those All Americans was practicing iron shots on a green sward up on "the hill" of the Gustavus campus. All the glories of Whitey's college and pro career were long behind him. Yet as he drove by and spotted his star, he could not help smiling at the dedication of this young golfer for whom glories similar to his own lay ahead; Whitey beeped his horn in approval.

Half an hour later, Whitey answered a knock on his office door. It was his All American. "Coach, I gotta tell you something. For the last half hour out there, I hit every ball right on the groove. Even *before* I went out to hit, I knew I was gonna hit the ball well. How do you explain that?"

Whitey nodded. "I know what that is," he said and remembered when he could hang high in the air and know a shot was good before he let it go. "For lack of a better name, I sometimes call it *Nirvana*. There's some mysticism connected with this. All those things that go to make us up—our mind, our physiology, our psyche—all those things are in harmony. Things that could disturb us are not even a factor. Afterward, we want to get back there, to that state of harmony. But we can't stay there. It's like being on a mountaintop. You have to come down. You can't build a house up there."

The Mouse of Grattan Playground

In the fall of 1942, fears of a Japanese invasion were rife in San Francisco, and the city did what it could to prepare itself. In early September a new and stronger "Victory Siren" to warn of attack delivered test blasts that penetrated the dead spots of the old siren and "practically lifted people off their seats," acccording to the *San Francisco Chronicle*. Dim-out procedures required that windows and doors be shaded, streetlights shielded on top and seaward, and car headlights covered with dark cellophane. A driver who had sped through a dim-out zone with lights ablaze was jailed for ten days. Despite the regulations and the strict enforcement, on clear nights the city's irrepressible Gold Rush spirit suffused the horizon with an orange-yellow corona, and anxious Marin County citizens looking across the Bay to San Francisco warned that the glow was as good as a silent homing signal for Japanese bombers.

San Franciscans were already pulling their shades and dimming their lights early the evening of Thursday, October 8, when sixteen-year-old John Gonzales finished the last of his homework. He told his mother where he was going—to the Japanese branch of the YMCA across town on Geary Street—and not to expect him home before eleven. For a school night, he was keeping late hours, but she had grown so used to his comings and goings to dozens of different basketball leagues that she merely nodded agreement and watched him leave, his equipment satchel swinging at his side.

Once outside, he walked the half block from his stucco row house on Lincoln Way across from Golden Gate Park to the streetcar stop at the corner. It was only a short wait before he boarded the No. 7 car of the Market Street Line and began the half-hour ride to the YMCA. He sat at a window seat and looked out at the gnarled, wind-twisted Monterey cypress trees that lined the park. Just beyond Kezar Stadium, the car screeched and wailed as it jogged left onto Stanyan, then right onto Haight Street. It headed straight east along the Panhandle, the long green finger of the park that ran up the valley between Twin Peaks and Lone Mountain.

At the intersection of Haight and Fillmore, John transferred to the Fillmore line that ran north toward Geary Street. Again at a window seat, he watched in a half daze as they passed the drab row houses and apartments of the Hayes Valley and the Western Addition, their black window shades drawn.

For weeks, headlines had hammered home news of fierce fighting in the Solomon Islands, German advances to the outskirts of Stalingrad, and Rommel counterattacking in Africa. However faraway these places seemed, no one failed to make the connection between victory there and lights properly dimmed in San Francisco, or a pound of scrap metal donated, or war bonds bought. Along with the rest of his friends, John was convinced that the war would be over long before he was old enough to have to go, even if soldiering was in his blood.

His Spanish ancestors had been soldiers for Coronado's expedition to the new world. But four hundred years later, when John Joseph Gonzales started school in Bakersfield, California, he was not much bigger than a toy soldier. He spent the weekends and summers at his grandparents' small bungalow on Marsh Street on the outskirts of Bakersfield. The house was always filled with his grandparents and six young uncles and their friends, all of whom came and went at all hours of the day and night. "Junior" Gonzales slept on a hide-a-bed in the living room, and the constant activity made him irrepressible and wild. Word around the hectic household was, "Don't turn your head for a second on Junior, or he'll be gone."

It was his grandparents who watched over their first grandson the closest, cranking up their old Durant limousine with wooden spoke wheels and letting him ride alone in the back seat while his grandfather, who dug ditches for the water company, drove to the neighborhood market with a regal stiffness.

His grandparents were "Mamma" and "Poppa" to everybody in Bakersfield, and Mamma taught her grandson the satisfaction of work and the pride of finishing a job. She would let Junior dust the furniture or stand on a stool at the sink so that he could wash the cobwebs out of the mason jars before she sterilized them for canning. As he got older she let him peel the chilies she had baked and then soaked before canning.

When Junior Gonzales was seven, his mother and father were divorced, and he and his mother moved to Fresno. But the attachment between Junior and his grandparents was so deep that for four years he returned to Bakersfield during summers. Their bungalow beehive bristled with the activity of uncles marrying and moving in with their spouses while they looked for work during the hard times of the Great Depression.

By 1938 John's mother had remarried, and his stepdad, Ed Burton, moved the family from Fresno to Lincoln Way in San Francisco so that he could pursue a law degree at Hastings Law School. Still, John kept the name Gonzales, and for two more years he spent the summers in Bakersfield with Mamma and Poppa. Before he returned to San Francisco at the end of each summer, his father would buy new school clothes for his tiny son, who was smaller even than the smallest girl in his class at San Francisco's Jefferson Elementary School.

As John prepared to enter Lowell High School in San Francisco in the fall of 1940, one of his uncles in Bakersfield wrote his mother that it would not be wise to send Junior there for summer vacations anymore. The sudden separation from his grandparents rocked him. Their affection and the constant activity of the Bakersfield bungalow had made him talkative and friendly. Despite his size, he had a mosquitolike quickness that older boys admired in touch football contests, and his inclusion in those games gave him an ease and affability around athletes. But now occasional periods of silence around his new San Francisco friends prompted them to remark, "Oh, he's in one of his moods."

He didn't bother to explain why. How could they ever appreciate what it had meant to him to be lifted to a stool and given the enormous responsibility of peeling the chilies? Or which of them would ever understand the joy of riding alone in the back seat of a spoke-wheeled limousine as he was chauffeured to the market? How would they be able to understand why it had crushed him to have that come to an end?

He hadn't snapped out of it until one of his first days at Lowell High. Not yet five feet tall, and weighing less than eighty pounds, he was in a long line of students standing on their numbers in physical education, waiting for their instructor to take roll.

The instructor was the legendary Benny Neff, himself no bigger than a peanut. Neff had close, gnarled hair that came to a widow's peak that served as an arrow between his already intense eyes. He had been the varsity basketball coach at Lowell for ten years, and neither his size nor the nearly laughable stiffness of his archaic two-hand set shot diminished his authority on a basketball court. Practices on Saturday featured two hours of running plays during which no one took a shot or dribbled. Whoever ignored his cries for "bounce passes, bounce passes!" or succumbed to the temptation to shoot, thereby stopping motion as intricate as the wheels turning inside a clock, had to dodge Neff's whistle as it was whipped across the floor by the sling of its lanyard. "Dogmeat!" his gruff voice filled the gym. Or worse, if you made the same mistake twice, "Catmeat!"

Yet whether he was overseeing his players' clockwork movements at practice or bent over at courtside during a game time-out to slide five pennies on the floor to improvise a play, no one who ever played for Benny Neff doubted his affection or felt like a mere coin or a cold clock spring. It was the way he aimed that widow's peak and his eyes at you, the way he never forgot your name, even if you were just "catmeat" from one of his PE classes. It was the way he would take you aside and fix his eyes on you and reminisce about great players from the past at Lowell, measuring one against the other—"Richie Hay was the greatest"—as if the opportunity to share these recollections with you privately put you on the same pedestal in his life. In spite of his gruffness and intensity, it was the affection of his players and students that really mattered to Benny Neff, even if he could claim proudly in 1942 that three of the five starters from Stanford's National Collegiate Athletic Association (NCAA) championship team had played for him at Lowell High.

Benny Neff's authority and reputation were well known even to those new students who had never met him or played on one of his teams, and now under Neff's imperious eye John Gonzales stood at attention. Braced like a soldier in Coronado's expedition, he was still only half the size of the students flanking him. But his size hardly seemed as onerous as the real adversity of his life, which was the fact that he still hadn't gotten over the separation from his grandparents.

Neff scanned the uneven line of raw-boned, knobby-kneed students. He fixed his gaze on the tiniest one. Then he raised one hand and pointed at him.

"I'm gonna make *you* a basketball player."

It could have been a comic parody of the Uncle Sam poster, and John hardly knew what to think. *A basketball player?* He wasn't even five feet tall or a hundred pounds, and he was smaller even than the Chinese and Japanese students at school, who at least had very strong muscles in their small bodies. Why wasn't he singling out one of them for a miracle transformation?

The Asian Americans at Lowell were among the benefactors of the city's exponent system for basketball competition. Assigned "exponent" points based on age, height, and weight, players could enjoy the democracy of a system of basketball competition that eliminated towering players. The 110s were the smallest, bony freshman or sophomore weanlings who somewhere along the way might have skipped a grade. Next came the 120s, with innocent faces and baby fat still. These "Neffmen" of the tens and twenties played for Benny in the fall. Or in the winter, there was thirties competition for those upperclassmen whose permanently stunted growth seemed to consign them forever to the artificial world of exponent basketball.

The younger exponent players could at least cling to the hope that they would one day graduate to the real world glories of varsity basketball. But John Gonzales was too small even for lightweight basketball. If there was a game for him, it was not basketball, but baseball, where quickness and sure hands made up for his size. Anson Orr, who had once played professional baseball and now ran the summer baseball programs at Big Rec in Golden Gate Park, had recognized John's quickness and sure hands and told him, "I'm gonna make you a second baseman."

At first, it seemed to make more sense than Benny Neff's pledge. Yet it was clear to John, as he watched Neff pick out two or three other mites from the line of young students in his PE class, that their basketball prospects depended not on their size, but on Benny Neff's will. And in that moment John Gonzales began to focus on something hopeful and promising rather than the disappointment of the permanent separation from his grandparents. He began practicing basketball regularly on the playground courts of nearby St. Anne's school, or Jefferson Elementary. Then, as if chance was in league with his own determination to immerse himself in basketball, he met Bill Calhoun.

Calhoun was two years younger than his freshman classmates, but boyishly handsome, with blue eyes and blond hair. In the eighth grade Calhoun's youthful and clear soprano voice singing "God Bless America" at assemblies had earned him the title of "Best Male Singer" at Grattan School in the hills of the Buena Vista district, and he had appeared with a youth chorus in the San Francisco Opera House for a performance of Sibelius's *Finlandia*.

Bill Calhoun wound up seated next to John Gonzales in the soprano section of the Lowell High School chorus, filled mainly with girls. At six feet, Calhoun was also a promising freshman string bean in basketball, and through their common interest in the game, Bill and John became close friends. After only a few weeks in the class, however, Calhoun's voice began to crack and slide away from its soprano clarity as he also continued to shoot up like a beanstalk.

"I shouldn't have taken this class," he confessed one day to John Gonzales. At the end of the semester, he was finished with the Lowell chorus.

Meanwhile, John Gonzales remained half the size of his friend Bill Calhoun, and he failed to make the fall lightweight 110 team of Neffmen at Lowell. Still, Benny Neff continued to encourage him in PE and taught him moves and fundamentals that nourished the hope that he could one day play team basketball; he spent his freshman year practicing in the San Francisco fog at the outdoor courts at St. Anne's or Jefferson, or hanging out with Bill Calhoun and others at the Grattan playground on upper Stanyan Street, waiting for the older, bigger players to give up the courts for three-on-three competition.

The dedication paid off, and by his sophomore year John Gonzales was issued his first basketball uniform as a member of Benny Neff's 110s. Calling himself the "umpteenth man," he played little, and during time-outs could only watch as Benny Neff moved pennies on the floor, none of which, John Gonzales thought, would ever represent him. In the yearbook pages that featured team members in one-on-one matchups, he was almost dwarfed by his muscular opponent in a picture captioned "Gonzales guarding; Fujita with ball."

Then after Pearl Harbor in December, Fujita, Aizawa, Mochizuki, and dozens of other Japanese students from nearby Japan Town were gone, sent to relocation centers in the interior. Other than black-out provisions and vague invasion fears, the war seemed remote to John Gonzales and his friends, who told each other, "We'll finish this fast."

Basketball, not war, was at the center of their lives, and despite the fact that Bill Calhoun's promise as a basketball player seemed to have been cut short by a heart murmur that prohibited him from competing at Lowell his sophomore year, he kept his friendship with John Gonzales, and he went right on playing basketball away from school at every opportunity. The two met now and then at Ninth Street and Irving to ride the rear cow catcher to the "N" tunnel, where they rendezvoused with other friends and walked to Lowell. Or they hung out on Saturdays at Grattan playground, where Calhoun brought John Gonzales into his circle of taller, more experienced, and older basketball buddies.

"This is my friend, John," Calhoun made the introductions, and the two standing side-by-side like Mutt and Jeff were an improbable pair, the one growing like a weed while the other remained a runt. Included in Calhoun's circle of friends was Ken Leslie, a well-built, all-around athlete whose major contribution to the friendship— beyond his enormous basketball talent—was to provide appropriate nicknames for everybody.

He looked John Gonzales up and down. It took him only a second to come up with a nickname—"Mouse!" It stuck immediately, along with all the other nicknames he had coined. By adding a "D" to the end of Calhoun's name, Leslie had already hung the nickname "Hound" on him. And even as a professional basketball player years later, Frank Kudelka carried the nickname "Apples," the name Leslie had given him because he was so fond of apples.

So Apples and Mouse and Hound, along with "Red" Lilja, who would one day play with the Canadian Olympic team, and Kevin O'Shea, who everybody knew was a pro prospect, refined their talents with fierce "dime-a-time" three-on-three games on Saturdays at Grattan playground, with a panoramic view of the city beneath them and to the north.

"If you just get *in* a game," John told himself, "it means you're starting to get good."

It was beginning to come, the feeling of naturalness on a basketball court, the feeling that it wasn't an isolated step here or a quick cut there but that whatever move he executed was only part of a larger flow of action orchestrated by Benny Neff. By the fall of 1942, as he entered his junior year at Lowell, he had graduated to the 120s, and Neff himself was praising John's quickness and coordination.

Somewhere in his legs of wire, John was also beginning to discover that he had the ability to jump. Still, he remained a bench substitute, not the "umpteenth man" anymore, but not a starter yet either. Then in a phone call one night that fall, he received an invitation to join a team called the "Sunset Junior Optimists," and at a stiff ceremony in a garage on Judah Street, a host of players including Mouse and Hound and a friend named Rene Herrerias, who wasn't much bigger than John, received blue satin reversible jackets with the word "Sunset" in gold script on the back.

For John, it meant that he was now out three, sometimes four nights a week, playing in pick-up games or recreation leagues. But no number of nights out late—which his mother indulged with a patient smile because she was happy to see him at last connected to something beyond the memory of his grandparents—no amount of practice practice practice could overcome the fact that in every gym and in every game he was still the smallest man on the floor, smaller even than Rene Herrerias, who was so proud of his flashy Sunset jacket that he laughingly told everybody he was sleeping in it.

The only relief from basketball that fall had been in early September, when a call went out the first week of school for high school wartime volunteers to harvest crops. The entire student body of Lowell had gathered in front of the school to sign up for the hard work. The next day a picture of the eager student volunteers had appeared in the *San Francisco Chronicle*. It was a sea of two thousand faces, and Mouse and Hound and their basketball friends, proudly dressed in their blue satin warm-up jackets, were right up front in the picture, looking up and waving confidently to the camera. The war was lasting longer than anyone had thought possible, but John remained convinced that it would be over long before he was old enough to serve.

For the time being, the important thing was basketball. He would not be able to enjoy the artificial world of exponent basketball forever. Sooner or later he'd have to play with the big boys. Then what? At Grattan, when he did get in games, he found that with his speed he could easily drive to the basket; once there, however, the taller men slapped the ball away effortlessly. If he stayed outside, he could hit his set shot, but only if he could get clear.

If he could get clear—that was the issue. And when he finally got off the streetcar at Fillmore and Geary that Thursday night in October 1942, getting clear was the main thing on his mind as he walked two blocks west on Geary to the gym inside the Japanese branch of the YMCA.

Since 1918 the Japanese branch of the San Francisco YMCA had operated out of an old mansion on Sutter Street. The mansion's attic had been converted to a gym with a ten-foot ceiling that sloped to five feet at the court sidelines. It meant that the first Japanese youth who played basketball there all had flat shots which caromed off the backboards like cue balls.

In the early 1930s the industrialist John R. Mott, whose humanitarianism eventually earned him the Nobel Peace Prize, pledged to pay for half of the cost of a new building if the Japanese community raised the other half; by 1935 the new Japanese branch of the San Francisco YMCA at 1530 Buchanan was finished. A gray stucco building with social halls upstairs and a spacious gym whose high ceiling was supported by curved laminated wooden beams, it was a glorious improvement over the old Sutter Street mansion. Besides social activities, there were recreational basketball leagues and a varsity team of Japanese players called "the Greyhounds," in honor of their speed and quickness.

Among the Greyhound players was a five-foot-two-inch playmaking guard named Fred Hoshiyama, who was one of four brothers born of Japanese immigrant settlers in the Yamato Colony, the first successful settlement of Japanese in the United States. Located just outside the city limits of the San Joaquin Valley community of Livingston, which in the 1920s posted "Japs Keep Out" signs, the colony was a settlement by necessity. "We will not compete with you in any way," the colony leaders assured the nearby Livingston community, and although one of Fred Hoshiyama's best friends was the son of the Livingston police chief, the colony knew its segregated place and kept it.

In 1929 Fred and his family moved to San Francisco, where the Hoshiyama brothers became active in the Japanese branch of the YMCA. By the fall of 1941 Fred had been selected as "Boys Work Secretary" for the new Buchanan YMCA building and was responsible for the branch's youth fitness programs. He set up basketball leagues with round-robin tournaments, recruited group leaders and volunteers, and took special pride in caring for the new gym floor, which he periodically sanded, lacquered, and then waxed to a high shine.

On Sunday, December 7, 1941, to celebrate his twenty-fifth birthday, Fred Hoshiyama took a young woman from the Japanese community in the Buchanan neighborhood to a movie at a theater on Market Street. Walking home afterward, the couple heard the news of the Japanese attack on Pearl Harbor.

Fred was stunned. "What does this mean?" he wondered aloud. He was a citizen by birth. His parents, however, were aliens, denied the right of property ownership or citizenship. What would this news mean for them?

For weeks, wild rumors of what it might mean flew through the San Francisco Japanese community. To maintain rumor control, the YMCA's Buchanan building became an information center, and daily Fred and his colleagues typed English and Japanese versions of a newsletter that was mimeographed and then distributed in the streets. Meanwhile, Lincoln Kinai, the branch's executive secretary, kept liaison with government authorities who had set up operations in the Whitcomb Hotel, to plan what to do with the Japanese community.

Despite the efforts at control, rumors of relocation, imprisonment, or deportation circulated. Then in February, authorities from the Immigration and Naturalization Service and Federal Bureau of Investigation swept into the enclave of Japanese aliens at Terminal Island in Los Angeles and removed them all with only twenty-four hours' notice; the San Francisco Japanese community braced itself for the worst.

The worst came on February 19, 1942, with Franklin Delano Roosevelt's signing of Executive Order 9066, providing for the "resettlement" from the West Coast of "all persons of Japanese ancestry." Martial law was declared, strict curfew regulations enforced, and the telephone poles in San Francisco carried news of the impending mass evacuation of 110,000 Japanese to relocation centers in the interior.

What it would eventually mean for the Japanese branch of the YMCA, no one was quite sure. Still, since the community it served and depended on for money would soon be gone, Lincoln Kinai and his staff prepared to close the branch. FBI agents came and confiscated the two Japanese-character typewriters at the branch, but the rest of the office equipment was boxed and moved to the basement crawl space for storage.

On March 28, 1942—the day before they were directed to report for evacuation—Lincoln Kinai and his staff, including Fred Hoshiyama, and community leaders gathered for a farewell ceremony in the upstairs social room of the Buchanan branch.

"We're sorry this is happening to you," they were told by the sympathetic general secretary of the San Francisco YMCA. "We'll do the best for you. We'll return your building as soon as we can."

Refreshments were served. The small, solemn group exchanged handshakes. Fred Hoshiyama turned over the keys. Before leaving, he took one last, proud glance at the gym, in whose polished floor he had taken so much pride. Then he went outside and watched from the streets as the downtown officials turned out the lights and locked the doors.

The building had sat empty and dark for several months before YMCA officials leased it to the United Service Organization as a center for black soldiers headed for the South Pacific. Daily announcements in the *San Francisco Chronicle* listed the club's activities, including finger painting, evening jam sessions followed by dances, pinochle classes, movies, and badminton.

The gym with its highly polished floor was also the occasional site of a city-sponsored recreational basketball game for boys still too young for the war. An October twilight chill had settled on the hills of the western addition and Pacific Heights that Thursday night when Mouse Gonzales arrived. He turned down Buchanan Street and bounced up the steps to the building.

As gyms went—and he had played in too many different ones over the last months even to count—the Buchanan Y was one of the better ones, with a high ceiling, good lighting, and a shiny but elastic floor. Meanwhile, it seemed strange that in a body so small as his there could be extremities that were slow to warm to the heat of exercise, but no matter in what gym—especially the colder ones— John Gonzales's hands were always the last things to get loose. So his first concern as he cut across the floor toward the dressing rooms was that the gym seemed cold, and his hands felt like ice cubes.

He noticed a few players already dressed and on the floor shooting as he disappeared into the small locker rooms. He changed quickly into a ragtag uniform that was at odds with itself. The only thing that pulled them all together as members of one team was the blue, slick grace of their satin jackets.

Once on the floor, John hardly noticed who else had shown up for the game. He had played enough recreational basketball now to know that any night's roster usually depended upon the unpredictable circumstances of parental permission, homework, transportation, and the vagaries of each player's mood. For those who did show up, what mattered was that there were at least four others, to avoid the embarrassment and disappointment of a forfeit.

From week-to-week the coaching was as checkered as their uniforms. Whoever from the Sunset Optimists showed up to take charge merely appointed a starting five and then made periodic substitutions. What few plays there were gave way to instinct and flow. It was the perfect crucible for personal experimentation, and between warm-up shots, John huffed into his cupped hands as if he had just come in from a blizzard.

His hands were still icy when action began, and he felt himself disappearing into a flow that even a game as unstructured and disorganized as this one generated. Then, somewhere in the midst of action that subsumed him, he found himself dribbling across the half-court line, then cutting through retreating players. He lifted his head. Up ahead in the key, he spotted those towering figures again, waiting to knock his shot away. Beyond the free-throw line, still too far out for any shot except a long set shot that would be all body lunge, he found a hole free of players, and he stopped suddenly. By the time he had planted both feet and crouched to jump, the hole was already beginning to collapse. He leaped quickly and rose straight up.

What is this? he wondered as he went up.

It wasn't only that he had separated himself from the floor. "Bounce passes, bounce passes!" Benny Neff's shouted directions had made it clear how critical that floor was to the game. But John's sudden leap was a disconnection from the flow. He had separated himself from the game, and he held one clear thought as he rose above the arms reaching up for him: *This is stupid!*

Try as he would immediately afterward, he could not visualize exactly what he had done, or how he had managed to raise the ball over his head and release the shot. Somehow, it went in, and retreating down the floor, somebody snarled at him, "Lucky shot!"

What the hell did I do? he still wondered. Riding home on the streetcar, it was clearer. *You got up there and nobody bothered you.*

Despite the fact that he still couldn't visualize the mechanics of the shot, he remembered the arms clawing up after him, and the principle sat in his head like a billboard: *I'm a little man in a big man's game. But now I have a shot nobody can touch.*

Early the next Saturday morning he went around the corner and straight to the outdoor courts at St. Anne's schoolyard and experimented by himself. Beneath the long morning shadows of the church's mission-architecture bell towers, he tried again and again to reconstruct the mechanics of a shot that had seemed to have come more by accident than by design.

The problem was finding the timing. He could not make the independent act of grasping the ball flow into leaping straight up in the air. Then moving his arms against the direction of his leap was awkward. Rather than liquid movements, they seemed artificial and disconnected, no more related to each other than the old trick of circling one hand on your belly while you tapped your head with the other. Maybe they became graceful and connected, he thought, only when you were immersed in that mysterious game flow.

Then, one day while he was waiting with his team to take his turn against the winners up at Grattan playground, he watched one of the big men snatch a rebound and then jump back up and hang for a second before he pushed the ball softly off the backboard.

That's the way to do it! he told himself.

For weeks he practiced it daily by himself, until he was confident that it wouldn't be dismissed as some desperate, lucky shot if he took it in a game. That winter, after the 120s season ended, he began to feel the rhythm of the shot and focused on the finer details of execution. He called them his "shooting keys." First, the thumb of his shooting hand had to be straight out, at an exact right angle to his index finger. Second, together his two hands had to form a cup that cradled the ball like a huge pearl as he raised it over his head. Third, the elevated ball had to be centered off his nose before he dropped away his left hand and released the shot.

By the summer before his senior year in high school, John Gonzales had passed the five-foot mark and finally weighed more than one hundred pounds. It was just about as big as he would ever get, he was convinced, but he knew he had a shot now where his size didn't matter. *I don't have to run all over the court trying to get clear*, he realized. *If I can't shake my man, I've still got a shot that nobody can touch.* He even grew daring enough to drive straight at the taller players, until he was almost under their noses before he stopped and jumped. *They can't get to me*, he quietly told himself. *The closer I get to them, the better it is. They're either gonna foul me, or I'm gonna make the shot.*

In the dime-a-time, three-on-three games at Grattan playground, Mouse learned to hold his own against taller players like Red and Apples and Kevin O'Shea, and even the Hound, whose heart murmur had disappeared. At six-three now, he was expected to be one of Lowell's varsity leaders.

"That's a pretty good shot," the Hound conceded. And it wasn't long before he was experimenting with it, trying to meld it into his own repertoire.

John Gonzales remained too mouselike even to hope for a Lowell varsity spot his senior year. But practicing at Grattan all that summer, he made it his personal crusade to get good enough with his new shot to earn a starting berth on the 130s the following winter. That came easily, and he became one of the team's leading scorers in the run for the city's 130s championship in 1944. What proved more difficult was recognition that with his unusual shot, Mouse Gonzales had a future in basketball. His thirties coach, whose specialty was football, not basketball, hardly recognized that the shot was a departure from the traditions of the game. While there was a plus side to that—at least he wasn't so hidebound by basketball tradition that he prohibited it—the downside was that he did nothing to encourage Mouse to believe that he could someday graduate from the world of miniature basketball and hold his own against the big boys.

In January 1944, in the championship thirties game against Washington High at Kezar Pavilion, on a floor as resilient as a trampoline, Mouse Gonzales soared high in the air again and again with his new shot, and the Lowell team might have been city champs if the other starting guard hadn't had to play wearing a clumsy catcher's mask. The night before the game he had broken his nose in a fight on Market Street with one of the thousands of sailors headed for the war.

Among other things, the episode served as a reminder that the war still hadn't gone away. And by the end of June 1944, three weeks after the news of the D-Day invasion, the army drafted John Gonzales as part of the huge call-up of men who would be needed for the push across Europe to Berlin. After advanced infantry training in Texas, John arrived in Le Havre in February 1945 as part of the replacement force for troops lost in the Battle of the Bulge.

Combat veterans joked that the fresh troops were nothing but cannon fodder, but despite news of high casualty rates as the Allies fought across France, John spent his first night in Southampton in a huge mess while Tommy Dorsey's band played its classic rendition of "Marie."

Marie, the dawn is breaking . . ., Dorsey's soloist Jack Leonard crooned the lyrics.

In John's own life, a dawn was breaking; he was eighteen years old, but in his mind no longer embarrassingly small. Basketball now seemed a part of some distant past. Like his ancestors before him, he was a soldier in a great expedition. "This war's not too bad," he told himself as he enjoyed a delicious hot meal and listened to the song.

The green recruits were loaded into narrow "forty-and-eight"

French boxcars that held either eight horses or forty men packed so close together their feet overlapped. At Liège, the recruits were told, "We wanna give you more training."

The next morning, after an hour firing .30-caliber machine guns, they were told, "Pack your gear. You're going to the front." That night, attached to the 104th Infantry Division outside the village of Düren, west of Cologne, John and another rookie were led out by a veteran on a night patrol to make contact with another company. It was pitch dark and ice cold, and two hundred yards outside their own lines the three soldiers stumbled onto two Allied tanks on fire from direct hits.

"We better get the hell out of here!" the patrol leader whispered. They broke at a run through the dark for their own lines and suddenly came face-to-face with a startled German soldier. Confronted by the three infantrymen, the German tossed his helmet and rifle into the snow. They marched him back to their company command post. The other nervous rookie kept his rifle pointed at the German's head. "This son-of-a-bitch isn't gonna get away!" he swore.

Once back to what they thought was the safety of their company command post, rapid Nazi artillery fire began exploding around them. John dove into a bomb crater. As he dug into the side of the crater with his entrenching tool, he heard the deeper sound of his division's outgoing artillery. After a terrifying night in the bomb crater, at dawn the entire division began moving east, slugging through the *bocage*, punching through Germany's vaunted Siegfried Line. By April they were inside Germany in mop-up, house-to-house fighting against Germans retreating for a final stand in Berlin.

One day in late April, John's rifle company began advancing at dawn through central Germany. At 3 o'clock in the afternoon, they halted beside a small pond off the central square of a German village west of Halle. John and his squad searched civilian houses to confiscate weapons; then John hunkered in the courtyard of a small house and ministered to his blistered feet.

Shortly, the call came to resume the advance. John slipped on his boots, snatched his rifle, and headed for a choice seat behind the turret on the last tank in a small column brought up to accompany their advance. However, three rookie squad members had already beaten him to the spot, so he took a seat behind the turret of the next tank forward.

He had no sooner settled in than a thunderous explosion rocked the rear tank. A body came flying forward and landed in a heap at John's feet. He grabbed his rifle, with pieces of flesh stuck on it, and with two other squad members raced for the cover of a small shed in a nearby courtyard. The two other squad members, wounded by shrapnel, huddled beside him. In the dark shed, he could feel that he was covered with blood.

I'm OK, he told himself. *It's not my blood.*

When it appeared the shelling had stopped, John told them, "You guys stay here. I'll see what's going on." Sprinting through the courtyard strewn with casualties, he noticed one soldier face-down with the meat of one buttock blown away. The wounded soldier lifted his head and groaned, "I'm OK."

Once he reached what remained of the column of tanks, John was told what had happened. It hadn't been incoming enemy artillery at all, but a defective shell that had exploded in the barrel of a tank destroyer at the rear of the column, the muzzle of its cannon hanging just over the spot where John had tried to sit. The three unlucky soldiers who had beaten him to the choice spot were gone, and the pieces of flesh stuck to John's rifle were all that was left of them.

Of the dozen members of John's squad, only three survived. His company captain eventually found John sitting in a blood-soaked jacket at the foot of a tree.

"Are you all right?"

John nodded.

"Here, take my jacket."

John stripped his off and threw it away. "Jesus," he muttered. I could have been *gone*."

It was the second "dawning" he had experienced in less than six months, this one even more deeply felt. Those three men who had disappeared—did they have families? What unfinished business and regrets did they leave behind? It was too late now for them to redo their lives, but not for John, for whom the sudden importance of family sat like another billboard in his head.

After VJ (Victory in Japan) day, despite having earned the Combat Infantryman's Badge and two battle stars, John still hadn't earned enough points for discharge, and he was assigned to the Ninth Service Command at Ft. MacArthur in southern California. Immediately, as a reflection of how important family had become to him, he took the surname of his stepfather, and as the Most Valuable Player for the Ninth Command Basketball Tournament at Ft. Ord, he was no longer Mouse Gonzales but "John J. Burton, hard-hitting forward."

At only five-nine and 135 pounds dripping wet, he still wasn't much bigger than the mouse of Grattan playground. And basketball was still an unfinished chapter in his life. Could he play college basketball like the very same big boys against whom he had developed his deadly jump shot at Grattan? They were all beginning their successful college careers. Ken Leslie was at San Diego State. Kevin O'Shea had been recruited by Notre Dame and would soon establish himself as an All American. Apples Kudelka was at St. Mary's. Little Rene Herrerias, who had once been so proud of his Sunset Optimists' jacket that he had slept in it, was one of the starting guards for a University of San Francisco (USF) freshman squad that would eventually graduate to a National Invitational Tournament (NIT) championship. And Bill Calhoun had gone straight from high school to the Rochester Royals, who would become NBA champs before he quit. They were all on their way to becoming stars. The only question was whether John J. Burton could follow in their footsteps.

Only one major college had inquired about him. After the tournament at Ft. Ord, recruiters from Santa Clara had sought him out. "How would you like to have a scholarship to play basketball for us?" they offered.

"Sure!" he answered eagerly. It was a sudden, surprising offer, but it seemed legitimate.

They asked him for his San Francisco address. "After your discharge, somebody will be in touch with you."

On June 29, 1946, exactly two years after being drafted, he was discharged. The Santa Clara recruiters called immediately. "Come on down. We'll show you the campus."

He spent half a day visiting the beautiful campus with palm trees and mission architecture. Afterward, they took him to the gym, where Coach Ray Pesco sat watching impassively as other prospects scrimmaged. Within minutes, John was on the floor with them, trying quickly to get into the rhythm and confidence of his uncanny jump shot. But the gym was cold, his hands felt like ice sculptures, and afterward Pesco told him politely, "Well, thanks for coming. Keep in touch."

The disappointment was only temporary. After all he'd been through in combat, just being alive was worth celebrating, and that fall he eagerly enrolled at tiny San Francisco State College, a small, liberal-arts campus, neatly packed into a few square blocks on Buchanan, just across Market Street from Old Mission Dolores.

Dan Farmer was the Gator's coach. At six-four, 230 pounds, Farmer had once played at Chico State in the northern Sacramento Valley. He had coached the Gators to fourteen straight winning seasons, a credit, the papers said, "to genial Dan's talent for spotting likely hardcourt players roaming the halls of the Buchanan campus."

For the next two years, the newspapers used dozens of different adjectives, including "frail," "small," "little fellow," "Little John," "diminutive," and "mighty mite" to describe John Burton's electrifying performances for San Francisco State's Golden Gators. Against the taller players, he had learned now to turn his body to protect the ball as he went up, and Farmer claimed the adjustment made his jump shot "unstoppable." The Gators played in the ancient Kezar Pavilion, whose floor was more like a trampoline than ever, hurling John higher and higher for his jumpers. The only uncertainty was the smallness of his hands. They were still the last things to get warm before game time.

One cold night at Kezar, Burton suffered a particularly disastrous first half, his shots "as wild as a blind man," the school's paper reported. While his teammates warmed up at half time, John sat on the bench and complained, "My hands are freezing. I can't control my shot." Blowing into his cupped hands failed to warm them. Finally, it was Gator manager Joe Heath who suggested, "Why don't we get a hot water bottle?"

It was worth a try, John felt, and Heath ran off to find a hot water bottle. It proved to be the answer, and John scored twenty points in the second half. From then on he never tried to play without first sitting on the bench with his icy hands buried in the hot water bottle, which the newspapers characterized as the Gators "sixth man."

For such a small school, the Gators drew large crowds to Kezar. According to Farmer, they came "to watch the little fellow outplay the big men." One night while John sat warming his hands in the water bottle, he spotted the familiar short figure of Benny Neff approaching along the Kezar sidelines.

"How are you, John?" Neff asked.

He hasn't forgotten my name! John thought as he shook Neff's hand.

Neff disappeared into the bank of fans rising up into the Kezar darkness, and John sat down and buried his hands again in the hot water bottle, whose heat summoned up memories.

It had been almost seven years since Mouse Gonzales had stood on his number in PE and faced Neff the first time at Lowell High. John remembered Neff's stare as he sized up the line of students. It had been the hard, cold stare of somebody measuring candidates for survival in a world filled with Grattan playgrounds where towering legends gathered to clash like Titans. Or worse, it had been as if Neff were measuring you for your ability to survive on a battlefield showered with incoming artillery that could make you vanish in a flash.

It was a world with no place in it for a mere mouse; yet Neff had picked out Mouse Gonzales and pointed at him. He wasn't just an imperious Uncle Sam who wanted conscripts, *any* conscripts, for the great battle. He wanted *you*, no matter how wee and insignificant you were. Because what carried the battle in life as well as on a basketball court wasn't monumental size or the strength of Hercules. What mattered most was heart and fiery spirit.

During two-and-a-half years at San Francisco State, John Burton's heart and fiery spirit and jump shot were indomitable, and he became the first Gator ever to score more than a thousand points. In the forties, the Bay Area had produced dozens of players from Grattan playground and elsewhere, including Bill Calhoun, Frank Kudelka, Ken Leslie, Kevin O'Shea, Don Barksdale, Cappy Lavin, Fred Scolari, Stu Inman, Rene Herrerias, Joe McNamee, and Hemie Feutsch. They had all gone on to greater glories in college or professional basketball, products of what some writers would later call, notwithstanding the achievements of USF in the 1950s, the "Golden Age of San Francisco Basketball." Those same writers and coaches called Jumpin' John Burton one of the finest players of that Golden Age.

In February 1948, Gator manager Joe Heath, who had figured out how to warm up John's hands, also found the answer to warming his heart. One night at a San Francisco State College dance, Heath introduced John to Virginia Amaral. A year later, after a game at Southern Oregon, he took a Greyhound bus back to San Francisco. From the station on Mission, he walked over to Market to pick up a new suit. Then he bought a black-and-yellow tie that his friends would later call "the damnedest looking tie you ever saw in your life."

He and Virginia were married the next day in a short ceremony in a San Francisco church. Not long after, they were expecting their first child. In an effort to prepare for his new family, he got up daily at 4 A.M. to deliver two morning paper routes. At the same time, he struggled to keep up a remarkable scoring pace with the Gators.

One morning he woke up and could not get his breakfast down. Then the muscles in his stomach began cramping, and he feared an appendicitis attack, or worse. The couple had no money for private medical attention, so bent over like an old man, John checked himself into the Veterans Hospital in San Francisco. In the middle of the season, he was hospitalized for a week. The doctors could not tell him what was wrong. Meanwhile, sportswriters made note of the diminutive star's hospitalization and temporary disappearance from the world of Gator basketball, but Dan Farmer never visited or phoned to check on his star.

Family is why I exist, John told himself. *And if this is the "family" of basketball,* John lay in bed wondering, *I'm finished with it.*

Once his mysterious ailment disappeared, he never went back to the Gators. Instead, fully recovered, he took his pioneering jump shot to an even higher level, playing Amateur Athletic Union (AAU) basketball in front of huge crowds, again at Kezar Pavilion.

On March 10, 1950, while playing at Kezar for the San Francisco Olympic Club that he experienced what he called the "final chapter" of his basketball career. At stake was the championship of the Pacific Association league and the right to go to Denver for the annual AAU championship. Kezar was packed for the semifinal game, featuring the Olympic Club, with Jumpin' John Burton, versus Stewart Chevrolet, coached by Hank Luisetti and led by George Yardley and Stu Inman.

It was a lopsided game from the start, John and his Olympic Club teammates being no match for the talented, taller Stewart team, which had won the Pacific Association championship the previous year. Still, John was everywhere during the game, stealing balls, racing the length of the floor, then pulling up to shoot his patented jump shot.

"They can't stop you!" one of his teammates told him during an early time out.

Eventually, he scored nineteen points, mostly on his jump shot. With two minutes left in the game, and the outcome no longer in doubt, his coach took him out. Every fan in Kezar rose to cheer for the mighty mite. "Although Stewarts won," the *Chronicle* noted the next morning, and although the game featured players with national reputations, "the crowd reserved its handclapping for diminutive John Burton . . . who was completely dwarfed by George Yardley and Stu Inman."

The standing ovation lasted and lasted. It wasn't just cheering for a tiny but mighty David against the Goliaths of the game. It was cheering for a shot so unique that the *Chronicle*'s awkward description of it as a "jump, over-the-head push shot" belied how graceful and quick it was.

Meanwhile, that cheering crowd had no way of knowing how far John Burton had come, not just from his days as "Mouse" on the playgrounds of San Francisco, shooting the first jump shots anybody had seen on the Coast, but from that nearly shattering combat dawning he had experienced. For this young man whose distant ancestors had been professional soldiers, family, and not basketball, was now the center of his life. And even as he sat on the bench listening to the cheers rise higher and higher, his heart beating in triple time, he knew that the promises of his family outweighed whatever future there was for him in the game of basketball.

The Leader of the Class

It was a small item on page three of the *New York Times* on September 1, 1936. A tropical storm of full-hurricane force, the *Times* reported, was whirling northward over the Atlantic Ocean. But it was a nameless and distant force, some two thousand miles off the Florida coast, no more threatening to North Americans than the news that same day that General Franco's rebel forces in Spain had driven to within eight miles of the fortress city of Toledo.

With no satellite eyes to track the hurricane, it was a week before the *Times* reported that the storm was now three hundred miles northeast of the Lesser Antilles. Described briefly as a "cyclonic disturbance of unknown intensity," it remained too vague and distant a threat for the weather bureau even to issue storm warnings.

On Wednesday, September 16, at his home in Princeton, New Jersey, fifteen-year-old Bud Palmer began packing the clothes he would need for his enrollment that Saturday as a freshman at the prestigious Phillips-Exeter Academy in New Hampshire. As he packed, the last thing he worried about was the news that the hurricane was now south of Bermuda and moving slowly north-northeast. "Because of the great distance of the storm from the American coastline," the *Times* quoted weather officials as saying, "there is no cause for alarm in the United States."

By Friday no one could ignore the huge storm. Six hundred miles wide and carrying winds of ninety miles per hour, it slammed into the Atlantic Coast from Beaufort, North Carolina, to the Virginia Capes. Then it turned north and began ripping Washington DC and heading for the Jersey coast. In Baltimore the strong winds blew the water out of Chesapeake Bay, and yachts at their docks keeled over in the mud. Eighteen-foot waves rolled over breakwaters and bulkheads at Cape May and then broke like surf down waterfront streets. Hurricane signals sounded in New York City, and the weather bureau issued storm warnings for the New England coast. The only hope for saving New England from storm ravages, the weather bureau noted, was a high-pressure area moving eastward from the Great Lakes. If it arrived soon enough, like a blocker in football it would "intercept the great windstorm and veer its course east" out to sea.

Meanwhile, roads throughout the Northeast were flooded, thousands of cars were stalled, powerlines downed, and it was foolhardy, if not suicidal, for Bud Palmer and his mother to head for New England. Yet, early Saturday morning, chasing the trail edge of the hurricane as it moved north, they set out for Exeter, New Hampshire, in Blanche Palmer's twelve-cylinder Lincoln Zephyr. Blown-down trees lay across the road, and Blanche drove hunched over the wheel, trying to see the road ahead through the driving rain. Her son also leaned forward to watch ahead, not out of fear, but rather anticipation. Phillips-Exeter would begin another new, exciting chapter in his life, and the howling hurricane weather, however menacing, did not alarm him. Excitement and turbulence were nothing new in his life. After all, he was the son of Lefty Flynn.

Lefty's full name was Maurice Dennis Flynn, and he was the strapping son of a tough Irishman who had made a small fortune at the turn of the century in the New York City construction business. Lefty's mother was a frustrated operatic soprano who rode around the city in a chauffeured limousine and struck melodramatic stage poses. Meanwhile, she could only watch with envy and alarm as her son, blessed with perfect pitch and a deep, clear voice, seemed to be squandering his talent in noisy barrooms, which fell immediately silent whenever young Lefty began singing verse after verse of Irish ballads and folk songs.

"He's the greatest natural basso I've ever heard in my life," a voice coach told Lefty's mother. The coach urged her to prepare him for the opera. But Lefty's greatest gift was for antic behavior, and as a prep-school boy at St. Paul's in New York, he delighted his classmates but infuriated his bluenosed schoolmasters by creating clever ribald lyrics for the chapel hymns. At graduation from St. Paul's he could recite verse after verse of rowdy railroad songs, but little of what he had studied had stuck in his mind, and he was denied admission to Yale.

His disappointed parents were forced to enroll him for a year's study at Pawling Prep School, outside Poughkeepsie. By then, Lefty Flynn was six-three and more than two hundred pounds; at Pawling, he was a man among boys. In 1910 he and two other athletic Pawling classmates came down to New York City as a three-man track team for an interscholastic meet. Lefty won all the dashes, the high jump, the pole vault, the long jump, and the shot put, and whatever academic deficiencies he still had after a year of half-hearted study at Pawling were overlooked by Yale in favor of his promise as a football player.

He played fullback for two years at Yale. He could punt the ball sixty yards and run line plunges with the force of a locomotive. "We thought we had a pretty good club at West Point," a cadet named Dwight Eisenhower recalled years later, "until we ran into Yale with a big fullback named Lefty Flynn." Unfortunately, Lefty Flynn was already a heavy drinker, who grew more affable with each drink. One night in the middle of his sophomore football season, he listened to the girlfriend of one of his friends spell out the sad story of her neglect and shame. With his heart turned to sentimental mush by alcohol, Lefty agreed to marry her. When the news broke on the Yale campus, he was immediately thrown out of school.

The marriage was quickly annulled, and Lefty enlisted in the navy. He was chauffeured to the Brooklyn Navy Yard in the family's Cadillac limousine, and his mother stood on the fender and called to her embarrassed son in a crowd of enlistees, "Oh, Mory . . . *Morrrrr-rrrrry*, darling, be a brave sailor boy!"

Maurice "Lefty" Flynn never forgot the embarrassment of that melodramatic farewell, and it was as if every two-fisted and irresponsible thing he did thereafter was meant to counteract that moment. Eventually, in search of something to straighten out his charismatic but wayward son, Lefty's father turned from indulgence to denial and sent him north to Canada to work on a construction gang. Unfortunately, opportunity and excitement seemed to seek Lefty out, and he soon found himself as a laborer on the Canadian set of a silent film featuring Wallace Beery. At one point in the script the action called for Beery to knock a stunt man off a cliff in a fistfight. But looking down over the cliff at a raging river below, where pick-up boats were waiting, the stuntman balked. Desperate to get their cameras rolling, the crew looked around for a replacement.

"Hell," Lefty peered over the cliff and then offered, "that doesn't look so bad."

"You'll do it?"

"Sure, I'll do it." Then he turned to Wallace Beery. "But let's not just fake this fight. Go ahead and really hit me."

While cameras rolled, Beery knocked Lefty off the cliff and into the raging river. When he finally woke up in the recovery boat, a circle of faces told him, "God, that was terrific, Lefty! If you ever think of going into the movies, come on out to Hollywood."

Lefty Flynn met Blanche Palmer, the daughter of a New York City physician, at a party in Manhattan, and they were married in 1916. They were polar opposites, she settled but unforgiving, he restless but warmhearted. Despite the arrival of their daughter Barbara a year later, no one gave their marriage much chance of survival.

Resorting now to a hybrid of indulgence and deprivation, Lefty's father did his best to isolate his son from the temptations of glamour by setting the young married couple up on a cattle ranch on the desolate high plains outside Craig, Colorado. Ranch life had just the romance and toughness of a railroad song, and Lefty might have stuck it out if the forty-below winters hadn't been too much for Blanche. In 1920 the young couple moved to Hollywood.

They bought a small, two-bedroom bungalow on Poinsettia Drive just off Hollywood Boulevard. Lefty began doing bit parts and daredevil stunt-man scenes in the silent movies. Unfortunately, his womanizing and carousing proved harder for Blanche to endure than the cold Colorado winters she had fled, and by the time their son John Palmer Flynn was born in 1921, Lefty and Blanche had separated and divorced.

Seduced in a milder way by the glamour of Hollywood, Blanche took her breakfasts in bed, wearing a sheer peignoir. Weekends she opened the bungalow for huge buffets attended by her new Hollywood friends. Meanwhile, Lefty had graduated to more substantial roles in more tawdry films. In one production the action called for Lefty to make a deep-sea dive with a dagger in his teeth, to rescue the heroine caught by a giant clam. The script also called for Lefty to be entangled during the rescue in the tentacles of a horrific but dead octopus. At six o'clock the morning of the shoot, Lefty stumbled onto the stage, hung over from the night before. After two cups of coffee, he stripped, bit down on the dagger, and disappeared beneath the water. It was an agonizing minute before he popped to the surface and shouted at the crew, "Are you sure that son-of-a-bitch down there is dead?"

Preparing himself for his role as the world heavyweight champion, he sparred against Gene Tunney, who told him, "Honest to god, Lefty, you ought to go into boxing."

The deep-sea rescues and the blandishments from heroes did nothing to curb his appetite for adventure, and he drank harder, caroused more, and eventually took his third wife—this time a silent screen heroine named Viola Dana.

With the advent of sound films, it was the deep, resonant voice of Lefty Flynn, and not his brashness, that made him a promising actor. No matter that his pictures got better, Blanche's unforgiving nature kept her vindictive and bitter, and she told her young son again and again that despite all of Lefty's swashbuckling daring-do, he was at heart yellow. "At Yale," she said, twisting the truth of his football prowess, "he went into the line *backwards*."

Lefty ignored the bitterness and rancor so that he could bring Tom Mix or Hoot Gibson by the Poinsettia bungalow to meet his son, whom they all called "Bud" because he was such a small, budding version of his huge father. Or Lefty took the boy to Will Rogers's

Santa Monica ranch, where Will himself lifted Bud into the saddle of one of his horses. At the Santa Monica Beach Club, Joel McCrea loved to toss a beach ball high into the air and then bet that little Bud couldn't catch it. That he always did—while McCrea laughed over losing his bet—was early proof that the boy loved athletic challenges.

There were visits to the sets during filming and introductions to other luminaries—Bill Tilden, Douglas Fairbanks, a young prop boy named David Selznick—but they meant little or nothing to little Bud Flynn, who was busy proving that his own courage would never be called into question.

At six, he and Benny McCaffery, his streetwise next-door neighbor, devised a makeshift boxing ring in Benny's backyard, then staged fights against boys from around the neighborhood. Whoever cried first was the loser, and the spectators had to pay to watch. The winner-take-all purses ran as high as a $1.50.

Benny McCaffery was eight and an experienced boxer. Managing Bud for his first fight in the six-year-old division, Benny told his protégé, "Everybody thinks this is sort of fun, so the kid you're fighting will dance around. You dance around, too. But then you do this." Benny demonstrated what he wanted by faking a left jab. "But then come up with a nice right hand and hit him in the nose. He'll bleed and start to cry and you'll win."

Afterward, a victorious and wealthier Bud, reflecting the warm-heartedness of his father, treated everybody to sodas at the local drugstore. It might have gone on for months had the mothers of the defeated boys not marched upon Blanche Flynn.

"What is going on?" they demanded to know.

The boys of Poinsettia Drive had to find other recreation then, and that was basketball on the playground of Gardner Junction Elementary School in Hollywood. Bud and his school friends scrambled and scrapped and fought with the same fierceness they had used as boxers. And despite the deftness Bud had developed catching beach balls tossed to him by Joel McCrea, he was too small and weak still to get a heavy basketball to the hoop without launching it with a leap. Whatever his future might hold—the excitement and courage of Lefty Flynn's life, he hoped—the game of basketball seemed to promise little.

Lefty's Hollywood life wasn't all that it appeared, however. Yes, he had that resonant, magnificent voice, and the new swashbuckling talkies were the perfect dramatic vehicle for his voice and his bravado. But halfway through the action of each film, he would disappear from the set. Once, they had to search for him for days. They finally found Lefty drunk with a friend in a sailboat floating off the coast of Mexico.

It took little more than Lefty's unpredictable behavior, and the bitterness that it continued to cause in Blanche, to convince her to get as far away from Hollywood and Lefty Flynn as she could. Enticed by the strength of the European economy, as well as a wealthy boyfriend in Europe, in 1929 she moved to Switzerland with her two children. After her boyfriend invited her to tour the continent with him, Blanche enrolled her daughter in a private girls' school in Switzerland. And persuaded more by Blanche's good looks than the merits of her young son, the headmaster of an exclusive private school for young boys, called Le Rosey on Lac Léman, just south of Lausanne, accepted Bud Flynn.

At eight, he was the youngest and smallest boy at Le Rosey. He was also among the least polished. As a homesick transplant he knew little about life beyond makeshift boxing rings and Hollywood excitement. Meanwhile, the school was filled with well-born students—his roommate was the young brother of the Shah of Iran—and he fought two and three times daily to defend himself against taunting. But he mastered French quickly, acquired a taste for caviar, and adopted other refinements of his schoolmates. When Blanche arrived after the first year to take him on tour during vacation break, she hardly recognized her own son. He met her at the train station wearing a tie and a rose blazer with the school's crest, white flannels, black shoes, and a jaunty cap. That night at dinner in a pension, she was startled to find him positioning the chair for her to be seated.

The source of the change was Madame Carnal, the wife of the headmaster. A large, strikingly attractive woman with impeccable manners, she would move quietly through the dormitories at night, listening for weeping boys and signs of sadness, ministering to the homesick and the lonely. She had special affection for the smaller boys, particularly those who, like Bud Flynn, were trying so hard to be brave. She showed no sympathy for the bigger boys who complained about Bud's frequent fighting. "What is the matter with you?" she chided the bigger boys. "Can't you defend yourselves?"

Bud Flynn remained at Le Rosey for four years. Each summer he vacationed in Colorado Springs at the home of his great uncle Eugene Parsival Shove. Despite the fact that Uncle Gene was from Blanche's side of the family, and presumably responsible, for Bud the vacations were a return to the excitement and drama of Lefty Flynn. Uncle Gene was a tough and adventurous early Colorado pioneer who had been the first mayor of Gunnison and had established its first bank. He bought his gin by the keg and had it shipped from Scotland to Colorado, where he stored it in his basement liquor cellar. There, in the cold dark, he tutored Bud on how to start the siphon to run the 180-proof gin into a crystal decanter. As Bud stumbled back up the cellar stairs, holding a mouthful of gin, Uncle Gene told him, "Swallow it!"

Back in Europe, several suitors sought Blanche Palmer Flynn's hand in marriage, but she refused their offers and continued to cultivate the bitterness she felt for Lefty Flynn. In 1934 she returned to America with her two children and rented a home in Princeton, New Jersey. Meanwhile, Lefty was too irresponsible and unreliable even for Hollywood, and he had moved to North Carolina, where he ran a peach ranch and raised horses.

For Blanche, leaving Europe to return to the fold of America's more flamboyant character was one thing, but continuing the pretense that she was in any way connected to the mercurial character of Lefty Flynn was another. Her first act back in New Jersey was to return to her maiden name Palmer. She encouraged her children to do likewise, but Bud balked at such wholesale rejection of Lefty. "Look, Mother," he told her, "you married him. I didn't. He's my *father*."

Eventually, Blanche won out, and her son acquired a new name to add to the transformation of character he had experienced at Le Rosey. But even as the polished John Palmer, he could not shed the deep affection he had for Lefty. Over Blanche's objections, Lefty would drive his son to New York City where they were usually the first ones to arrive at Yankee Stadium, because Lefty Flynn wanted to observe the spontaneity of players joking with each other as they warmed up by stretching and jogging.

Once, Babe Ruth stood with the tip of his bat in the dirt so he could lean on it while waiting to take batting practice. The looseness prompted Lefty to jump to his feet. "Hey, Babe! *Babe!*" he called. It stunned Bud to see the great Babe Ruth turn, then shamble over toward their seats.

"Hey, Lefty," Babe said. "How are you? Is this your boy?"

"This is Bud."

The Babe shook Bud's hand. "Son," he smiled, "if I get one today, it's for you."

In the late innings, he smacked one a mile, and making the turn at third base, mincing his steps to make sure he tagged the base, he pointed to Lefty Flynn's son, as if to say, "That was for you!"

The episode reminded Bud Palmer who he was. Despite his European manners, despite the shedding of his name, he was still Lefty Flynn's son, bound for something far greater and more theatrical than Blanche Palmer might ever have wanted. It was at a private boarding school named the Hun School in Princeton that he began to get a sense of what that might be. There, at age thirteen, he played organized basketball for the first time in his life. Because of his European schooling, he was more adept at soccer than basketball, where he still had to hurl himself at the basket to launch the ball. But he had inherited Lefty Flynn's flair for dramatic action, and the frequent scoring as well as the opportunity to race up and down the floor offered vague promises of success.

Those vague promises began to become clearer one night in the winter of 1935 in a Hun School basketball game. As had been the case for him in Switzerland, he was among the smallest boys in the school, and the sight of him on a basketball floor inspired underdog sympathies rather than any heroic expectation. But just before the game in question ended in a tie, an opponent elbowed him in the mouth. Cut and bleeding, and weak in his knees, he had to be set in place for a single free throw.

He stepped back from the line so that he could hurl the shot with his body. The lunge drove the ball at the basket like a line drive. The ball clipped the front rim, then bounced straight up and rose above the backboard. When it finally dropped, it bounced once, twice, three times on the rim before it fell through the basket.

Neither the awkward mechanics of the shot nor its incredible bouncing luck should have been cause for his confidence. But the praise of his teammates as he left the floor was real. And it dawned on him that a basketball court offered the same genuine excitement that had once prompted Lefty Flynn to insist that Wallace Beery really hit him.

I can play this game, Bud told himself afterward. *I can* play *this game!*

In the spring of 1936 Bud met Dr. Louis Perry, headmaster of Phillips-Exeter Academy in New Hampshire. Dr. Perry had come down to Princeton on a mission to recruit promising students from the Country Day School, whose rigorous academic setting was the first step toward enrollment at Exeter, both on the long prep-school road to Princeton University.

Since his return from Europe, Bud had made several new friends from the Country Day School, and now he sat with them as they listened to Dr. Perry promise them that at Exeter, "You will be a community."

For months afterward, listening to his friends talk of their plans to attend Exeter, Bud wondered if it wasn't where he should go, too. Money was not an issue. Ever since his mother's divorce, the two of them had been well taken care of—by Blanche's wealthy father, by Lefty Flynn's father, who was still indulging the mistakes of his son, even by Lefty himself, who blamed nobody but himself for the failed marriage. Nor were academics an issue. At the Hun School Bud had distinguished himself in the hands of one of the school's toughest teachers, an English instructor who liked to stand before the entire class of frightened boys and make an embarrassing example of one of them by slashing his paper with the tip of his pen because of a single run-on sentence. It had turned out to be Bud's favorite subject, because he had a knack—or call it another legacy from Lefty Flynn—for writing and speaking as if he had a dagger between his teeth, going right to the heart of the matter without wasted words or hesitation.

Dr. Perry's promise of "community" convinced Bud that Exeter was for him. Meanwhile, his mother was solidly behind the idea, not only for the academic promise of Exeter, but to separate her son from Lefty Flynn, who had married a fourth time and whose occasional rendezvous with Bud she did her best to prevent.

Whatever anger Lefty felt over his ex-wife's vindictiveness, he kept to himself. "You owe everything to your mother," he wrote Bud before his departure for New Hampshire. "I love seeing you. I'm your father. But I was a pretty bad guy when you were growing up. If it upsets your mother too much for you to see me, I'll understand."

By the time Blanche and Bud arrived in Exeter, the hurricane had been pushed out to sea by that Great Lakes low pressure area that moved east like a football blocker and left behind a muggy, dark stillness in New England. As Bud struggled to his room with his luggage, the voices of other boys arriving echoed with a strident harshness in the marble foyers, and that feeling of Exeter community that Dr. Perry had promised was as palpable as the hurricane mugginess. The red brick walls, thick with ivy, the vaulted doorways, marble stairwells with moons worn in the steps—the effect of it all was monastic brotherhood without the silence. It was exactly the place for him, he was certain, and he hugged his mother goodbye, then raced to join his fellow freshman buddies from the Country Day School in a game of touch football on the huge green playing fields on the edge of the campus.

At 7:45 A.M. on Monday, dressed in ties and jackets, the young students of Exeter began to take their seats for required chapel. The freshman "preps" filled the first rows of the chapel beneath the ornate rotunda with a skylight. Up front, and bathed in the morning sun of the skylight, the preps felt exalted and privileged, surpassed only by the school officials and Dr. Perry, who sat on an elevated stage in rich leather chairs with brass brads.

At exactly 8:00 A.M., a volley of bells sounded, the high doors at the rear of the chapel were closed, late arrivals were turned away, and Dr. Perry took the podium to address the boys of Exeter.

There was no need for him to be introduced. He had a rotund face and eyebrows that arched to accompany his playful moods. "This morning," he began abruptly, "I'd like to present you with another chapter on the human condition, this one drawn from our local newspapers. It concerns a wealthy eccentric who kept his money squirreled away in a shopping bag."

Chuckles and horselaughs arose from the upper-class boys in the rear, who settled in for what was obviously a regular ceremony. Dr. Perry smiled and waited until their chuckling had subsided, then positioned his pince-nez and began reading the newspaper item:

Time and again, the friends of the wealthy eccentric had urged him to put his money in a bank. For years he refused. Finally, he acceded to the urging of his friends and headed reluctantly for his local bank. "What can I do for you?" the teller inquired. The eccentric was so frightened he could hardly muster a whisper. "I wish to put my money in your bank." While a line of impatient customers formed behind the eccentric, the teller carefully counted out the money, filled out a deposit slip, and handed a receipt to the eccentric. "Is there anything else?" the teller inquired politely. "Yes," the eccentric could still only whisper. "How do I get the money out?" "That's quite simple, sir. You just write a check." While the line grew still longer, the teller gave the eccentric a brief lesson in check writing. Then he asked, "Sir, how much do you wish to take out?" "All of it," the eccentric replied.

Dr. Perry's daily readings on the "human condition" were met with applause and laughter. For Bud Palmer, that first day in the Exeter Chapel was like a rallying cry. He had gone from Hollywood backyard prize fights to defending his honor with fisticuffs at Le Rosey. At the Hun School, his instructors had slashed at student papers like violent fencers. Through it all there had been his mother's un-relenting rancor over Lefty Flynn. Now, here was this benignant Exeter headmaster who wanted his charges to appreciate that life was amusing.

Not that Bud Palmer had slipped his past entirely. At five-feet-four-inches and only 104 pounds, he was dubbed the leader of Exeter's "underprivileged, undernourished class," and his name was always at the top of the list of undersized boys that was occasionally posted as a reminder that at Exeter you were supposed to develop mind *and* body. For that development, the school had magnificent athletic facilities—manicured green lawns for lacrosse and soccer, indoor baseball diamonds and training tracks, a modern gymna-sium—that were better than most colleges, and Bud threw himself into year-round recreation. Unfortunately, he was still too thin and frail to compete with any distinction. In cross country, his knobby knees knocked against each other until they were raw and bleed-ing. Sent off-campus on training runs in the late afternoon, he often got lost and had to be picked up by his anxious coach who came searching for him in the dark by car headlights.

Where there weren't official school teams for the preps to com-pete on, they created competition of their own. At night, the boys of his dormitory set up tenpins in the corridor and then bowled them down with a rubber ball. Meanwhile, an intramural freshman bas-ketball league featured weekly games among players who were not that much bigger than Bud Palmer. Despite his knob-kneed run-ning up and down the court, and his ludicrous lunging shots, it was the one game which he still felt held out a vague hope that he could excel. It had more to do with who he was than the nature of the game. There was something in him, or so he sensed each time he picked up a ball, that seemed to be perfectly suited for the game of basketball. But what that something might be, beyond the childhood deftness he had shown catching beach balls, he still wasn't sure.

Then one day in Bud's second year at Phillips-Exeter, Lefty Flynn appeared out of the blue to visit his son. They met in Bud's room, and Lefty was as animated and stimulating as ever when he deliv-ered the first lecture Bud could ever remember from his father.

"Let me tell you something, son," he began. "This is the real thing." He rapped the table between them with his index finger, as if he might have been talking only about the reality of the table. "I started this sentence . . ." he continued and then paused to let several seconds pass, "ten seconds ago." He leaned forward. "You'll never see those ten seconds again. They're gone in your life. And this," he repeated and rapped the table again, "this is the real thing. This is not a dress rehearsal. So don't ever go to your grave with a lot of ifs."

Lefty's speech about living fully went a long way toward explaining his own excesses. Yet in the eyes of his son Bud, it was exactly the inspiration Lefty had intended, and Bud resolved that he would do nothing thereafter with half a heart.

The first opportunity he found to put his new dedication into effect was in the Phillips-Exeter gym. It was as big as any university field house, with one long court and three additional courts laid sideways. On Saturday nights the gym was the site of feature-length films, with most of the Exeter boys seated on folding chairs arranged on the basketball floor. The movies were usually madcap comedies or swashbuckling adventures, only slightly less unreal than the silent movie adventures of Lefty Flynn. Meanwhile, because of Lefty's influence, invention and spontaneity were already a theme in Bud's life. Now, the same Exeter stage where Hollywood actors performed every Saturday night became the perfect place for Bud to begin inventing with a basketball.

Years later, when he looked back on the Exeter period of his life and tried to remember the exact moment he had discovered the jump shot, he could not identify it. He could remember being dismissed from his last morning class and then racing over to the gym every day exactly at noon. He could remember coming up the stairs from the dark, steamy, subterranean locker room, and then alone in the gym, because everyone else was at lunch, practicing in only the soft light that came through the churchlike rosette window at one end. He could remember shooting by himself at one of those six side baskets while the Exeter varsity, which he still hadn't made, ran full-court drills.

He could remember playing lacrosse and disobeying one of its commandments, which was that you shot only with your strongest arm, and he could remember with perfect clarity telling himself, "Well, hell, why can't I shoot from *both* sides?" and then immediately doing it. He could remember that basketball suffered from strict commandments, too, commandments which weren't for him a cause of frustration. Instead, they were a departure point for the spirit of originality that kept whispering in his ear with a deep voice like Lefty Flynn's. It kept telling him, "Bud, it doesn't *have* to be that way."

He could remember growing suddenly like a weed somewhere during that Exeter period, until he was six-three and 180 pounds, one of the tallest boys on campus. He was a far cry from that frail shrimp who had once carried around the vague sense that there was something latent in him that was right for the game of basketball. He was no longer just a budding image of his father. He was the finished form.

He could remember every detail of a trip from Exeter down to Connecticut one weekend, when a husky friend of his mother's told him, in almost the same words she used, that Lefty Flynn was yellow, and then Bud challenged the man to step outside, because, "Nobody's gonna call my father yellow."

He could remember specific moments in specific classes, his English class, for instance, ten or fifteen boys around a huge oval table, arguing and dissecting literature, and the day he had handed in what he'thought was a great essay until his instructor D'Arcy Curwen asked him to write the whole thing on the blackboard for the other boys to critique. While he did so Curwen stood to the side and drew a picture of a faucet with water pouring out of it, to make it clear the entire essay was maundering drool.

He remembered vividly spending Christmas vacation in Colorado Springs with his Uncle Gene, and his mother arranging for him to get tutoring in basketball from the coach at Colorado College, who would occasionally let Bud join his scrimmages. He remembered making the varsity basketball team at Exeter his junior year and then his senior year playing against the freshman team from Dartmouth with a six-eight center. He remembered warming up before the game and not missing a single shot, and then once the game started, faking one way against the six-eight center and going the other until he stopped and jumped and shot, basket after basket.

His senior year at Exeter he was awarded the "Yale Cup," given to the outstanding scholar-athlete, and he remembered thinking, "I have proved something to my mother."

He remembered the sense of community and absolute equality at Exeter, nobody being better than anybody else, even if they did have a rich father or a famous uncle. He remembered things as trivial as smells, the same ones writer John Knowles, class of '45, would remember and describe in his famous novel *A Separate Peace*, which talks of the locker-room smells at Exeter, "of paraffin and singed rubber, of soaked wool and liniment . . . and of the human body after it has been used to the limit."

He could remember the exact thought that preceded his discovery of the jump shot, which was, *If I dribble, and stop, and jump, I will have an advantage*. But the day, the hour, the exact minute and circumstances, the exact smells and noises and light of that first shot, he could not reconstruct, if indeed there had been a first one. In all likelihood, there had been no single moment of discovery. For him, it was a shot without a flashpoint. It was a shot that went all the way back to his childhood lunges on a playground in Hollywood, just so he could get the ball to the basket, and then developed by increments that couldn't be fixed to a specific moment any more than the growth of a tree could.

Bud Palmer graduated from Exeter in 1940 and enrolled at Princeton University, where he played the post for three years in a set offense that gave little opportunity for him to execute his jump shot. In 1943 he enlisted in the navy and was sent to preflight school in Chapel Hill, North Carolina. Eventually, he piloted a B-26, towing target sleeves for fighters in what he joked was "The Battle of Miami."

"I was one of the most shot-at soldiers in World War II," he told people after his discharge in 1946.

One day in the fall of that year, he traveled to New York City to see the Knicks play in Madison Square Garden in the newly formed Basketball Association of America (BAA). Half a dozen of the players in the game were men he had played against, at Princeton or in the navy. As he sat watching, his father's table-rapping speech kept running through his head: "Don't ever go to your grave with a lot of ifs."

After the game, he went straight to Ned Irish, president of Madison Square Garden and a cofounder of the Knicks. Irish was surrounded by a crowd of admirers, and Bud had to push his way through the crowd. "Mr. Irish, I'd like to try out for your club," he said.

Irish looked Bud up and down, then screwed up his face. "Who the hell are you?"

"Bud Palmer."

"Never heard of you."

Then a lively voice in the crowd spoke up. "Hell, I know you, kid. My team played against you down in Princeton. You damn near beat us. We couldn't figure out your defense."

Bud turned to face the man. With sharp cheekbones, a smile a yard wide, and huge ears, there was no mistaking the face. It was Joe Lapchick, one of the original New York Celtics and the former coach of a St. John's team that had won the NIT but nearly lost to Princeton in Bud's junior year. Lapchick remembered Bud's unusual jump shot and convinced Irish that Bud deserved a tryout.

In December 1946 Bud signed his first pro contract for twenty-five hundred dollars. But Lapchick's approval of Palmer meant little to Knicks coach Neal Cohalen, who had coached at Manhattan College before agreeing to lead the Knicks.

From a huge Irish family in New York, Cohalen smoked a pipe and owned a liquor store. He had a wide circle of friends who enjoyed his pipe-smoking amiability but were often startled by his bluntness.

"What the hell kind of shot is that?" he shouted and called Bud out of his first scrimmage after three missed jump shots.

"It's my shot," Bud answered.

"Who told you to do that?"

Bud shrugged. "Nobody. I've had it . . . for as long as I've played."

"Well, sit down!"

For weeks Cohalen ignored Bud and his shot. Finally, Bud confronted him. "Damnit, Neal, let's sit down and talk about this."

The two men repaired to one of Cohalen's favorite watering holes, across the street from the Sixty-ninth Regiment Armory. Cohalen lit his pipe, and Bud ordered several drinks and then had to shout over the barroom noise. "Look, this is the reason I shoot the way I do. Nobody else is doing it."

Cohalen sucked on his pipe. "Nobody's shooting with a blindfold on either."

Bud ignored Cohalen's sarcasm. "I like to do it off a dribble."

Cohalen shook his head, as if the idea of trying to dribble and then shoot such a crazy shot was the ultimate absurdity.

"It gives me more velocity," Bud explained and stood up. "Look, if I just stand and jump," he continued and then demonstrated, "I can't get as high as if I run into it." He looked around quickly but was unable to find space in the crowded bar to demonstrate what he meant. "Dribbling into the shot, I've found that I've got the velocity to get up in the air."

"Well, what the hell you gonna do once you get up there?"

"I'm gonna *shoot* the damn ball."

Eventually, the wisdom of the shot, and Bud Palmer's accuracy shooting it, were impossible for Cohalen to deny, and Bud played with the New York Knicks for three seasons, from 1946 to 1949. Recalling that three-year "Knickerbocker period" of his life much later, it would come back to him only in disconnected vignettes and pieces, much like the Exeter period of his life.

He remembered that Knicks coach Neal Cohalen was replaced by Joe Lapchick, whose smile had seemed to stretch outside the vertical plane of his narrow face. Despite that easy, welcome smile, he remained "Mr. Lapchick" to Bud Palmer, whose European courtesies—acquired during his "Le Rosey period"—remained with him all his life.

Sportswriters considered New York college basketball so powerful during that period that the fledgling Knicks were second-rate by comparison. To prove themselves, the Knicks went to CCNY, where Mr. Lapchick warned his players, "There's gonna be a lot of pushing, a lot of shoving. Don't just take it." The Knicks eventual victory began to make professional basketball believers out of the New York writers.

He remembered that he was the pantywaist from an Ivy League school, the garrulous locker-room lawyer whom they tried to knock around until he made it clear that he was the protégé of Benny McCaffery, he was the Poinsettia Street boxing champ, he was the son of Lefty Flynn, who carried a dagger in his teeth.

He remembered gentle Tony Lavelli from Yale, who liked to entertain fans by playing his accordion at half time, and who once apologized to a defender after knocking him down. "Tony," Bud hollered at him, "don't apologize. *Step on him!*"

He remembered teammates Carl Braun and Lee Knorek and Harry Gallatin and Butch Van Breda Kolff and Sid Tanenbaum and Goebel Ritter and Ray Lumpp, and he remembered all of them being stranded in a snowstorm in Cleveland, and two of them—which two, it wasn't any longer clear—donning black coats and ties and blocked hats and speaking in fractured Polish or Russian or *something* foreign that convinced airport officials they were United Nations diplomats who needed an emergency flight back to New York.

He remembered rooming on the road with the great Sweetwater Clifton, one of the first black players in the NBA—a mountain of a man with sad eyes and huge supple hands—and having to tell a nervous Baltimore hotel manager, "Mr. Clifton is a gentleman. He's my roommate, and he's gonna stay here," and then after a few beers in their hotel room, Sweetwater telling Bud, "Damn, for a white boy, you sure can jump!"

He remembered starting one season full of energy and weighing 193 pounds and ending it at 168, hardly able to stand up; somewhere in between there was that one shot among the tens-of-thousands he realized he must have taken during his basketball career, a shot as fresh and clear in his mind as if he had taken it yesterday.

It had come during the course of a hectic, seesaw battle against the Baltimore Bullets at Madison Square Garden during a three o'clock afternoon game on Saturday, December 11, 1948. Officially, it was "Father and Son Day" at the Garden, and more than half of the 11,352 fans who had shown up were shrieking sons and daughters who had been admitted free with their parents. The lead had changed hands twenty-two times, and with each seesaw change of fortune, the young fans had exploded with exhilaration or slumped in despair. With less than a minute remaining, the Knicks were trailing by one point, and the fans had been whipsawed into such exhaustion that there was a strange quiet in the Garden when Bud Palmer got the ball at his right forward position and hesitated.

It was as if all of Madison Square Garden, Bud Palmer included, had stopped in the midst of the hysteria to think deeply and carefully about what to do next. Look for somebody inside? Find somebody open for a surefire shot? Or, take a time out? Get set up! Let Joe Lapchick get out a piece of chalk, bend his lanky frame to the floor, and plan, *plan* what to do next.

One thing was certain: for coaches and basketball strategists, the moment was already precarious enough without making it worse by taking some reckless, chancy, leaping shot that didn't even have a history or fundamentals. But for Bud Palmer, it was only a moment like that one, trying to shackle him with rules and restrictions, that invited defiance and audacity.

Suddenly, he faked driving the baseline. Then he dribbled left toward the free-throw circle. Eighteen feet from the basket, he picked up his dribble and stopped so quickly that his sneakers gave off a high yip. He remembered rising with the velocity he needed. He remembered holding the shot, holding it and holding it, until his desperate defender had dropped away beneath him, and then he started falling also. He remembered thinking that if there was one part of the shot he needed to change, it was his release of the ball while he was falling instead of hanging, because the eventual shot had no backspin and was not soft enough.

He watched the hard shot float away like a motionless knuckle ball. The cheering that exploded when it dropped through the nets was not just for the dramatic basket and the Knicks one point, come-from-behind victory. The fans were also celebrating the fact that there would be no more agonizing reversals to suffer through.

Nor was it the success of the shot or the Knicks' victory that would stick in Bud's mind. It was the way he had taken the shot, exactly his way, in defiance of a last-second circumstance that invited caution. It was exactly the way Lefty Flynn might have done it, in defiance of the rigid script of basketball.

Bud Palmer played three years with the New York Knicks, during which time he was their captain, one of their leading scorers, and always the garrulous locker-room lawyer, chatty with the press and as warmhearted as Lefty Flynn.

One day in the spring of 1951, just before the old Dumont Network's television broadcasts of the NIT, the Dumont announcer, also a New York sportswriter, wrote an angry article about Ned Irish and Madison Square Garden.

The first night of the NIT, Irish called up the station and angrily told them, "I'm not gonna let your guy into the Garden."

"Ned," the station protested, "he's announcing the game."

"I don't care. I won't let him in."

The station manager was desperate. "Well, who'll we get?"

"Get this kid Bud Palmer. He knows a lot more about basketball than your guy."

In no time, the voice of Bud Palmer, always with the resonance of Lefty Flynn, was on the airwaves throughout the East, doing play-by-play broadcasts of basketball.

In what little spare time he had, and using his own money, he drove up to Canada to St. Catherines, carrying a wire tape recorder which he used to transcribe his play-by-play account of the scrimmages of hockey's Toronto Maple Leafs. Before long, he was doing radio coverage of the National Hockey League, the Knicks, college basketball, the NIT, even dog shows and horse shows.

One night after the advent of TV coverage of hockey, Bud was high in the Garden press boxes doing radio coverage of a Rangers hockey game. For the first intermission, the TV broadcasters, also high above the rink, had planned a player interview at rinkside.

But with only a minute allotted for the interviewer to negotiate the stairs down to the ice, the idea of an interview had been scrapped.

Until Bud Palmer offered, *"I'll* do it."

He was still lean and fit, and obviously eager.

"We can't pay you," they told him.

"I don't care. I'll do it."

Soon he was racing up and down the stairs to do the on-camera interviews. The easy manners he had learned at Le Rosey, along with his flair for the dramatic, served him well. The only complication occurred one night during a Ranger hockey game. It was Bud's job to select the "Player of the Night," then three minutes before the end of the game—to give the player time to put in his teeth—he was supposed to call the Ranger bench and notify them who had been selected for the post-game interview. That night, with the game tied but with three minutes left, he had selected rugged Ranger star Doug Worthy. Worthy left the bench for the locker room to put in his teeth, but then with only thirty seconds to go, Andy Bathgate slammed in the Ranger's winning goal. During the subsequent interview of Worthy, whose teeth sparkled in the TV lights, there was no opportunity for Bud to explain to the booing fans the cosmetic rationale for his selection.

It was only a minor setback for a rookie broadcaster whose panache and ability to extemporize were perfectly suited for the new medium. It was spontaneity that went beyond broadcasting, and one night on the Knicks return flight to New York after a play-off game at Rochester, Coach Joe Lapchick was startled to see the pilot walking up and down the aisle, greeting some of his famous players.

"Hey, who's flying the plane?" Lapchick shouted out.

It was Bud, exercising the flying skills he had learned during "The Battle of Miami."

Bud Palmer's straightforward and unaffected media style stood in stark contrast to the deception and dishonesty that prevailed elsewhere. On television, Sen. Estes Kefauver grilled evasive and pugnacious racketeers. Even in Madison Square Garden, the citadel of healthy, honest sport, Bud watched with surprise one night during a broadcast when a ball-handling wizard named Eddie Gard from Long Island University repeatedly dribbled the ball off his foot.

How can he be doing that? Bud wondered and grew immediately suspicious.

It was no surprise to him when the news broke that a Columbia player named Jack Molinas had been regularly fixing games in the East. With a sudden crash as dramatic as a modern slam-dunk that shatters the glass, college basketball came tumbling down, and half-a-dozen Eastern college basketball programs were eventually affected.

The scandal did little to interrupt Bud Palmer's steady rise in sportscasting, and he began doing network broadcasts of professional golf, his smooth and steady chatter being a perfect tonic for the game's slow pace.

Then one afternoon, on a street corner in New York, a friend of Bud's introduced him to the actor David Niven.

"It's a great pleasure to meet you," Bud told Niven, who was at the peak of his fame. "You knew my father."

"Who was your father?"

"Lefty Flynn."

"My God," Niven smiled. "Did I know Lefty Flynn!"

Was it a reference to Lefty's promise, or his failure to realize it? Whatever, the bugbear of unrealized promise was never far from Bud Palmer's mind, and not long after, at a dinner in Hollywood, Bud spotted the movie mogul Jack Warner at a table across the room. Lefty Flynn had been one of the first actors ever signed by Warner, and Bud rose to go across the room and introduce himself.

"Don't do it," anxious friends at Bud's table told him. "Jack Warner doesn't like to talk to *anybody*."

Bud ignored the advice and headed for Warner's table. "Excuse me, Mr. Warner," he said. "I'm Bud Palmer."

Only some of the country knew who Bud was, but nearly all of it knew Jack Warner, and there was a brief moment of icy silence as Warner stared up at the tall figure looming over him.

"I'm Lefty Flynn's son," Bud added.

Warner smiled, came to his feet quickly, and hugged Bud. "That old man of yours," he finally said, "could have been the greatest actor ever."

Could have been. There it was again. The specter of unrealized promise. Bud remained determined that his own broadcasting career would never meet the same fate. Still, he remained unassuming, almost self-effacing, particularly concerning his basketball achievements. "I was never a star," he would insist. Then he would joke about leading the "undernourished" class at Phillips-Exeter.

One night at a Knicks game, some twenty years after Bud's playing days were over, an old Knicks fan introduced his grandson to Bud. "This is Bud Palmer, the first captain of the Knickerbockers, who shot the first jump shot." The grandson's eyes bulged.

It wasn't the only time somebody had credited him with being the first jump shooter, and for a second, Bud thought to correct the granddad. *Hell, I wasn't the first one*, he had always insisted. But now he stopped himself, his own heroic recollections of Lefty Flynn still in his head. *Well, that's OK*, he told himself as he shook the grandson's hand.

Not long after, advised by doctors that his father was dying from the ravages of cancer of the liver, Bud left his broadcasting duties and flew from New York to visit with Lefty Flynn for the last time. By the time Bud arrived, however, Lefty was unconscious, and he died within days.

It was several years later that Bud received a phone call from a man who introduced himself as "Bonomo the Great," a one-time friend of Lefty Flynn's in Hollywood. Bud remembered him immediately as a strong-man character who had appeared with Lefty in several productions.

"I tracked you down," Bonomo said. "Are you Lefty's son?"

Bud answered that he was.

"I did a serial once with your dad."

"I remember those old serials," Bud said and laughed.

Popular in the early years of filmmaking, the serials ran before the feature films and offered furious action and one hair-raising escapade after another.

"I don't remember how many episodes we did," Bonomo explained, "but it was a bunch."

"I used to have some of those old serial episodes lying around in their film cans somewhere. You should have them," Bud offered. "I'll see if I can find them."

Bonomo the Great died before Bud could turn up the old films. Once he did find them, the fragile celluloid had become powder in their cans. All the other silver-screen traces of Lefty Flynn's short and checkered acting career met the same, dusty fate, and as Bud Palmer continued to keep a broadcasting presence across the land, the legend of Lefty Flynn vanished like powder.

In 1974 Bud moved to the mountains of Colorado, which he had first learned to love as a boy visiting his Uncle Gene. From there, he continued to travel in order to do occasional broadcasts, especially of golf and the annual Bing Crosby Pro-Am at Pebble Beach.

One cold, windy, and wet day on the Monterey Peninsula, Bud was safely perched in a broadcast tower above the green of the picturesque seventeenth hole. On the fairway below, the passing golfers had donned rain gear and were leaned forward like mountain climbers as they approached the windswept green.

Late in the afternoon of the first day, Crosby climbed the tower to observe the action. "Why don't you play?" Bing said at one point. "I can arrange it."

Bud squirmed, for once in his life evasive. "Well, hell, I've got to announce," he said. "The network won't take kindly to me hacking around the course when I'm supposed to be announcing."

"I can make the arrangements," Bing offered. "I'll get you an early starting time. You'll be off the course in time to go on the air."

There was no use pretending. There was too much of the bold, open heart of Lefty Flynn in him. "Look," Bud admitted, "I don't really *want* to play. It's damn wet and cold down there."

Bing laughed. "I've had people offer me thousands of dollars to play. *Thousands of dollars*," Bing repeated. Then he shook his head in amazement. "Bud Palmer, you're the only one ever to refuse an invitation."

The Wheelhorse
of Steel City

He was born in 1922 in the boot-heel of Missouri, not far from the site of an 1811 earthquake so powerful that it twisted the course of the Mississippi River into the snakeline that marks Missouri's boundary with Tennessee. Christened "Davage" but called simply Dave, he was the only child of a tall black woman named Tommie McMorris, whose husband Amos Minor left her not long after Dave was born. Within two years, Tommie McMorris died of pneumonia, and her baby boy was left in the custody of her sisters Claudia and Louella and her brother Lincoln. They all regretted they had never finished high school, and they vowed not to marry until they had put their dead sister's child on the proper road to education and success.

The three of them set out with baby Dave for Gary, Indiana, where they rented a house for thirty-three dollars a month. Lincoln found steady work in the mills of Steel City, while Claudia and Louella took care of Dave. From the start the two women indulged him and taught him the importance of independence and enterprise. Claudia's life was a case in point, and what money she could save doing housework she invested in a three-bedroom home on Gary's Jackson Street that had a tiny bungalow out back. She rented out the back bungalow and then began looking for other properties in which to invest the rental income.

Meanwhile, the McMorrises were only the second or third black family in what a decade later would be an integrated neighborhood. Claudia, Louella, and Lincoln were too busy providing the best for young Dave ever to discuss with him how unique their position was in the community. He took for granted that he belonged in the neighborhood, and in many ways he even considered himself better off than his white friends.

Louella, the older and stouter of the two sisters, was the household cook and the firm disciplinarian for Dave. She insisted on good manners, kindliness, daily chores, and regular attendance at the Church of God and Christ, whose Sunday services ran from nine in the morning until one in the afternoon.

One Saturday, when Dave Minor was five, his aunt Claudia announced, "OK, we're going to Chicago and get Dave a suit." The two aunts flanked him in the back seat of their brand new 1927 Buick, while Lincoln sat alone up front like a proud chauffeur and drove them to Chicago to shop among the Jewish tailors on Maxwell Street.

Once they had settled on the proper tailor, it was Claudia who did all the talking, specifying the fabric and cut of the suit while Dave, who was already beginning to take a gangling shape that indicated he would be tall, stood like a stiff scarecrow as the tailor marked the sleeves with chalk.

"That's twelve dollars," the tailor told them when he had finished with the alterations.

"No, no, no!" Claudia wagged her finger at the tailor. "I could go right down the street and get it cheaper."

"Well, you go ahead," the tailor challenged her.

Claudia led the four of them out, but they were barely ten feet from the store when the tailor rushed after them.

"Wait a minute, wait a minute! How much will you pay?"

Claudia's back was arched with defiance. "We'll go nine dollars."

"All right," the tailor sighed. "The suit's ready."

When Davage Minor started Froebel School, through the encouragement and devotion of his aunts, he immediately distinguished himself in his studies. The school was a dark brick building with students from the first through the twelfth grades. Meanwhile, Claudia had married and borne a child of her own whom she named Preston. The two young boys from the same household—Dave and Preston—played together and were often mistaken for brothers.

But Preston was not as carefully trained and watched over as Dave had been. He could also be careless about his household chores, and Claudia told Dave, "I love you as much as I love my own son. Or even *better*," she added and smiled, "because you have a different heart."

Dave began to grow like a weed, and expeditions to Chicago to buy him tailored suits became twice-yearly affairs, with Louella pawning items of jewelry to pay for the suits. They even took him in 1933 to Chicago's Century of Progress Exposition, dressed in one of his smart suits, and he was escorted from one exhibition hall to another so that he could learn the history of enterprise.

One day not long after that trip, his Jackson Street and Froebel school friends told him, "We want you to meet a good guy, just moved here from Memphis."

Dave already had a wide circle of friends. He wasn't necessarily in search of new ones.

"His dad's a doctor," someone in the group said.

Dave shrugged.

"His mother's a teacher," someone else added. That should have meant *something* to Dave, who was always cozying up to his teachers. They called him a "math genius" because he was usually the first to finish his quizzes at Froebel. At home in the evening, he found himself around the kitchen table with Claudia and Louella, tutoring them in math for night courses they were both taking in order to earn high-school diplomas. He would even tutor his friends in math if they needed it. Now there was a new kid in the neighborhood who might be as bookish as Dave Minor.

Within days Dave met Edward James, whom they all called "Doc" because of his father's profession. Doc and Dave hit it off immediately. That Doc was also black figured little in the minds of Dave's friends who had brought them together. What mattered was that they were both indulged, they were both bright and yet affable, and they were both beginning to distinguish themselves among their peers by virtue of their athletic ability.

They began playing basketball together on Froebel's sixth- and seventh-grade teams. Dave Minor's first athletic distinctions, however, came in the eighth grade in 1936 as Froebel School's "95 Pound

Track and Field Champion," featuring competition in the pole vault, high jump, broad jump, hurdles, and sprints. Dave won a huge medal fixed to a blue ribbon and modestly credited his aunts and his uncle with having given him the inspiration to succeed.

It was one day before school in a crowd of his eighth-grade friends at Froebel that he said impulsively, "I believe I can jump over that fence." They were all just outside the fence in question, an iron enclosure almost five feet high with pickets pointed like spears. A few in the group laughed. Surely he wasn't serious. If he missed, he'd be impaled on the spear tips.

Doc recognized a kind of playful seriousness in Dave's eyes. "I wouldn't do that," he objected. "You'll hurt yourself."

He waved off Doc's objections and walked up to measure the fence. The sharp tip of the spikes came almost to his armpits, but the others saw that he was serious.

"Don't do it, man."

"You're gonna get spiked."

He backed up and crouched for the attempt.

"What the hell you doin'?" Doc screamed.

"Watch this!" he shouted back. He skipped once to start himself, then took three long steps. After his takeoff, he rolled onto his stomach as he cleared the fence and his shirt brushed against the spears. He landed on the cement in a half crouch, then bounced to his feet and waved to his terrified and speechless friends.

That summer Dave Minor shot up to six-two and 170 pounds, and the once gangling kid who had stood for his suit tailorings like a scarecrow now regularly leaped over that dangerous fence to entertain his friends. It was a fence that enclosed Froebel on all sides like a medieval barrier, and if jumping over it effortlessly symbolized anything, it was how easy it was for Dave Minor to vault any barriers between him and success.

Just as effortlessly—again without giving any thought to it—one day that winter on Froebel's freshman basketball team he brought the entire practice to a halt with what some described later as a "miracle move." It came during a scrimmage against the junior varsity. He was driving straight up the middle when he leaped for the shot with the same explosive spring that had carried him over the Froebel fence, except this time there *was* a barrier—a six-six JV hulk who moved in his path and jumped with him to block the shot. High in the air, his legs opened like scissors, Dave stretched his right hand to release the ball, but the long arms of the hulk stretched still higher. In a reflexive second, Dave realized there was no way to go over or through the stockade of arms. Instead, still floating through the air, he pulled the ball back down, switched it to his left hand, and came out with a sweeping shot that rolled off his finger tips and into the basket.

"Time out! Time out!" his coach Hank Mantz shouted.

Mantz was five-ten and stocky. Born and raised in Wisconsin, he had graduated from La Crosse Teachers College and then assumed his coaching-teaching duties at Froebel in 1933. He had beady eyes that he focused on a player like ice picks when he was angry. It was his "squinch face," his players joked, that betrayed his angry moods. With those ice-pick eyes boring in on him Dave worried the same as if his Aunt Louella had laid down a new household rule.

"Do you know what you did?" Mantz said without smiling.

"No," Dave stammered. Had he missed a cutter? Traveled before the shot? Hogged the ball? Mantz shook his head in disbelief and then blew his whistle to continue the scrimmage. Dave sweated and ran in double-time to overcome what he half suspected had been criticism for being unconscious on the floor.

Afterward, it was Doc who had to explain to Dave what he had done. "You really don't know what you did?" Dave shook his head. "That guy was gonna block your shot. You changed the damn ass ball from your right hand to your left. *While you were still up there.*"

"Well, I don't remember *what* I did. I was tryin' to make the basket."

"You sure as hell made it," Doc laughed.

The Froebel High School gym was an ancient sunken pit with a cracker-box floor and dim lights. Because there were no floor bleachers in the gym, spectators gathered on a round balcony that circled the floor, and the configuration of that balcony made it difficult for fans to follow any action in the corners. As a result all of Froebel's varsity games were played downtown at Gary Memorial Auditorium, and only the lowly freshmen were forced to play in the old gym, the balcony railing of which would still be scattered with fans eager to see what new, amazing shot frosh star Dave Minor would unveil.

While other players confined themselves to conventional two-hand set shots, or drove to the basket for easy lay-ups, Dave scored again and again from a distance on running one-hand shots. Whether he switched the ball in midair or not, his running one-handers, which he would execute from anywhere on the floor—sometimes after driving deep into one of those blind corners—were electrifying and unconventional. Those same legs that catapulted him over the Froebel fence sent him high in the air before he lofted up a soft shot and then alighted in stride.

On Thursday, December 9, 1937, a bone-chilling cold descended on Gary, Indiana. For Froebel basketball fans who gathered that afternoon in the tiny Froebel High gym to watch Dave Minor play, the icy weather was a distraction. "Forecast Zero in Gary Tonight," the headlines in the *Post-Tribune* read. All day, "icy gales whipped eastward across the United States," and by three o'clock that afternoon, when shivering fans began to gather again along the balcony railing, the temperature was at ten degrees and dropping steadily. It was, the *Post-Tribune* called it, "the worst cold wave of the winter."

That morning, Gary school superintendent William Wirt had reassured parents that school heating systems, which in past cold snaps had occasionally broken down, were working properly. Still, the old Froebel gym that afternoon seemed only a little warmer than it was outside, and it was a frigid atmosphere that hardly encouraged the looseness that would lead to anything extraordinary on a basketball court.

Beyond the stiff cold, Dave Minor had run into another obstacle that for the moment seemed as imposing as the wind-whipped cold or that iron picket fence around Froebel. Once he started on the likely course of one of his running one-handers, opposing coaches were designating not one, but two or three defenders to drop off their men and block his path. It didn't matter what right-to-left-hand acrobatics he might have been able to perform once he was air-borne, he couldn't get the speed or step rhythm even to take off. It was like making him stop every two steps to spin around bodies along the route of his running approach to the cross bar in high jumping.

Coach Mantz called a time-out. In the circle, Dave's teammates stared at him. He hadn't taken a single shot. But what the hell was he supposed to do? They were double, triple teaming him! He stared at Coach Mantz, who had on his "squinch face."

As demanding as Mantz could be, ice-picking holes in a player's face if he didn't perform, his "squinch face" disappeared suddenly, revealing that he was as confused and troubled as his star. The mechanics of Dave's running one-hander were strange to him. Beyond understanding that players had to have leaf-spring legs to get up for the shot, Mantz had never once expressed to anybody how you performed it correctly, let alone what adjustments you had to make when you couldn't even get it off.

They broke the huddle with nothing resolved, and eventually it was Dave Minor's instincts that once again prevailed. He received a pass at his right forward slot and immediately put a dribble down to go toward the baseline. But after one quick dribble, with his defender sliding to stay ahead of him, he crossed the dribble to his left hand and cut toward center court.

Ordinarily, it would have been two or three more dribbles, accompanied by giant strides, before he leaped for the shot. Now, however, he put on the brakes in a hole just short of the free-throw circle. Up ahead, two more defenders stood shoulder-to-shoulder like the picket fence at Froebel.

He planted both feet and jumped. It was an odd sensation, the feeling that he didn't have to soar *over* something—a crossbar or a hurdle or the sharp spear tips of the Froebel fence—but only rise higher and higher. It was a vertical leap that seemed in defiance of those icy gales outside, which were whipping eastward with such ferocity that they blew everything in their paths sideways. But wind or no wind outside, it was also a leap straight up in defiance of the lateral action of the game itself, back-and-forth, back-and-forth, with a seesaw flatness.

Dave Minor's first jump shot was also flat but true. He took it a dozen times more during the game. Before the game was over, other Froebel players, including Doc at center, tried to stop dead in their tracks off a dribble and leap from both feet for the shot—usually one that missed everything or slammed against the backboard like a rock. Hank Mantz finally jumped to his feet and screamed for a time-out.

"I don't want you shootin' that shot!" he told the players gathered around him in the huddle.

Dave Minor screwed up his face in puzzlement. It was the only way he could find to score.

Mantz's ice-pick eyes went around the circle of players. "No one shoot that damn shot!" he repeated.

Now Dave's eyes turned to ice picks.

"Except Minor," Mantz added.

Dave smiled.

"The rest of you shoot *two-handed*," Mantz finished.

In the locker room afterward, Mantz again grilled Dave. "You know what you're doin'?"

"I'm just tryin' to break free."

"But you're throwin' it flat."

Dave shrugged.

"That shot's no damn good," Mantz said.

The stubborn look on Dave's face—he might have been his Aunt Claudia dickering for a suit in Chicago—revealed that it didn't matter what Coach Mantz thought, or even what he, Dave Minor, thought. The shot came from instinct, not deliberation.

"Well," Mantz conceded, "if you're gonna shoot it, you should arch it."

Dave nodded.

"Meanwhile," Coach Mantz smiled, "I'm movin' you up to JV."

Before his freshman year was over, Coach Mantz had moved him up to the varsity, where he spent the rest of the season as a substitute, scoring occasionally on his new jump shot. Meanwhile, Froebel players tried secretly to learn the shot, on outdoor courts away from school where Mantz couldn't stop them. But the mechanics of it eluded them. Doc was especially lost trying to learn it, and he complained to Dave, "Man, I don't know what the hell you're doin'."

It was whining that invited Dave to be as tutorial as he was with his aunts in math. But he only shrugged. "I don't know either."

"Well, what are you *thinkin'*?" Doc pressed him.

"I just jump up and reach. I don't know *what* I'm doin'."

By his sophomore year, Dave Minor was a starter for the Froebel Blue Devils. With Doc James playing center his junior year, Dave led the team in scoring, executing that same flat jump shot he had discovered as a freshman. Still, again and again Hank Mantz told him, "That shot's no damn good. It's gonna be your downfall."

Whether it was Mantz's abiding irritation over the flatness of Dave's jump shot or childhood indulgence that had made Dave Minor at times headstrong, one day their two temperaments clashed in an episode that threatened to end Dave's basketball career.

It was at practice halfway through the season, and Dave and the starters were rehearsing plays that by then the defensive scrubs knew by heart. Again and again Dave's defender was beating him to the spot where he was supposed to receive the ball.

"For God's sake, Minor!" Mantz exploded finally. "Can't you get yourself loose?"

Dave struggled to catch his breath. "Coach . . . the defense knows where I'm goin'."

"Bullshit!"

"God-damnit, Coach," Dave's temper flared, "they're beatin' me to the spot!"

The rest of the players froze. In the hush Mantz walked over and stood nose-to-nose with his co-captain. Wearing his squinch-face, Mantz began in a shout, "I don't give a damn how good you think you are, Minor. I don't give a damn what kind of showboat shot you think you have. You're god-damn selfish, and you're loafing!"

For another two minutes, he stood point-blank with Dave, who was still trying to catch his breath, and gave him hell for loafing.

When Mantz was finished, he tooted his whistle and barked at the team to run the play again. Nobody moved. Mantz had clearly stepped out of bounds. Dave might have been indulged, but he was never a selfish showboat. Now, it was up to Mantz to apologize. Thirty seconds, a minute passed. Still nobody moved. Finally, Dave nodded to confirm that as far as he was concerned, the argument was irreconcilable, and he walked off the floor. The entire team followed him to the locker room. Without a word, they all began unlacing their shoes, pulling off their sweaty jerseys.

Dave Minor was staring at his locker, convinced he was finished with basketball, when in came Mantz finally. "Kid," he resorted to the affectionate nickname he often used with Dave, "I was wrong."

Despite the attention paid to him for his basketball exploits, it was in track that Dave earned the highest honors. For three straight years he was the sectional champion in the high jump. No one could beat him, and his teammates and friends who had once been deceived by the playful ease with which he leaped the Froebel fence began to understand that there was a competitive fire burning in him.

In his junior year, Dave and six teammates, including Doc and Marcelina Gonzalez, who would eventually set a world record with the University of Illinois mile-relay team, traveled to Indianapolis for the Indiana state track championships. Once there, Dave set a state high-jump record of six-feet four-inches that would stand for sixteen years. No sooner was that event completed, however, than Froebel's star broad jumper was sidelined with an ankle injury.

"Let Minor jump," his friends urged the coach. Even though it was an event he'd never competed in, they argued, "He'll kill himself before anybody beats him." True to their predictions, he won the state championship in the broad jump. Then one of Froebel's mile relay men got sick.

"Let Minor run the relay!" his teammates again pleaded with their coach. With Dave Minor running the third leg and Doc running anchor, the mile-relay team finished second, and the team went on to win the state track championship. It was clear, at least in

1. The Brainerd Warriors team picture, before the January 1944 game with the Bemidji Lumberjacks. Team captain Whitey Skoog with the ball. Coach Kermit Aase, back row, far right. Other players: Johnny Benson, no. 56; Chuck Warnberg, no. 55; Marv Bollig, no. 50; Jack Hoffman, no. 51; Eivind Hoff, no 54. (Courtesy of Whitey Skoog)

2. Whitey Skoog's jump shot with the Minneapolis Lakers during 1953. This picture demonstrates Skoog's patented leg kick, which young Midwest players tried to imitate. In time Whitey simply let his legs hang straight on his shot. (Courtesy of Whitey Skoog)

Gonzales guarding;
Fujita with ball

Best of luck
to a fellow
Fujita

3. Gonzales guarding Fujita. John "Mouse" Gonzales, later John Burton, played lightweight basketball as a sophomore at San Francisco's Lowell High. He was not yet five feet tall, or a hundred pounds. In this yearbook photo from the fall of 1941, he is pictured guarding Yoshio Fujita. (Courtesy of John Burton)

4. Tiny John Burton of San
Francisco State uses his
leaping ability to rise high
above San Jose State opponents for a jump shot at San
Francisco's Kezar Pavilion
early in 1948. Burton scored
twenty-two points to lead the
Gators to victory. (Courtesy of
John Burton)

5. (*Left*) John "Bud" Palmer at Princeton, 1943. Although he had a well-developed jump shot at this time, he seldom got a chance to use it in the Princeton offense. (Courtesy of Princeton University)

6. (*Above*) The day they left to go "down state" for the 1941 Indiana State Tournament finals, the Froebel Blue Devils gathered in front of the school. The iron fence behind them is the same one Davage Minor jumped over to demonstrate his leaping ability to friends. Minor is front row, second from the right in the porkpie hat. Pete Mandich is second row, far left. Simmie Isabel is front row, second from left. Coach Hank Mantz is directly above Froebel cannon. (Courtesy of the *Gary Post-Tribune*)

7. (*above left*) "Minor Got His Shot." On March 22, 1941, Gary's Froebel High School, led by Davage Minor, met the Madison Cubs in the opening round of the state tourney. Minor is pictured scoring the only basket he made in a narrow loss. (Courtesy of the *Gary Post-Tribune*)

8. (*Below left*) Surrounded by transfer controversy, Joe Fulks played his senior year in 1939–40 with the Kuttawa Lyons. In this picture, Joe Fulks is back row, center. "Carrots" McQuigg, who in 1976 was a volunteer with an emergency ambulance service, was the first to respond the night of Joe's murder. He is no. 33 to Joe's left. "Teeter" Martin is no. 11. Coach J. Holland Harvey is back row, far left. (Courtesy of the *Lyon County Ledger*)

9. (*Right*) Though Bro Erwin coached the Beebe, Arkansas, Badgers for twenty-three years and became an Arkansas legend for his coaching success, his least recognized achievement may have been that he did *not* discourage Johnny Adams's jump shot, but rather encouraged Johnny's teammates to experiment with a shot few ever learned. (Courtesy of Roy Simmons)

10. Starting five, Arkansas University, 1941. In 1941, the NCAA tournament involved just eight invited teams—four to compete for the East title, four for the West. The Arkansas Razorbacks, led by Jumpin' Johnny Adams, made it to the western finals in Kansas City. Characterized by the press as an "Eiffel tower lineup," the starting five are pictured here after defeating Wyoming in the western semifinals. Left to right are R. C. Pitts, John "Treetop" Freiberger, Coach "Gloomy" Glen Rose, Gordon Carpenter, Johnny Adams, and "Red" Hickey. (Courtesy of R. C. Pitts)

11. The brothers O'Neale (left) and Johnny Adams (right) in their Arkansas uniforms, 1941. O'Neale was the workhorse rebounder and defender, Johnny the deft shooter with the bizarre, top-spin jump shot that O'Neale could not master. (Picture collection, Special Collections Division, University of Arkansas Libraries)

12. By 1945, playing at the Naval Training Station at Norfolk, Virginia, Belus Smawley's twist-around jump shot was unstoppable. Johnny Barr is the teammate watching from the distance. It was Barr who alerted the St. Louis Bombers to Belus's unique shot. (Courtesy of Belus Smawley)

13. Belus Smawley and the 1946–47 St. Louis Bombers. Belus is no. 20. Coach Kenny Loeffler is front row, far left. Johnny Barr is no. 13 in the back row. (Courtesy of Belus Smawley)

14. University of Wyoming, 1943
NCAA Champs, with their coach Ev
Shelton. Kenny Sailors is front
row, no. 4. Milo Komenich, back
row, no. 17, was the only player
not from Wyoming. (Courtesy of
Kenny Sailors)

15. Kenny Sailors with the Boston
Celtics, 1950. After the Denver
Nuggets folded, Kenny Sailors
finished out the 1949–50 year with
the Celtics. (Courtesy of Kenny
Sailors)

16. In early January 1946, Wyoming came east and met Long Island University in front of eighteen thousand people in Madison Square Garden. On January 21, *Life Magazine* captured Kenny Sailors high in the air on a jump shot that he had discovered over a decade earlier at a windmill basket in Wyoming. (Eric Schaal, *Life Magazine*, © Time Inc.)

Gary, that Froebel was passing through one of those rare cycles when chance brings together under one school roof a group of gifted athletes. No telling what they would do the next year.

The 1940–41 school year, Dave Minor's senior year at Froebel High School, was a dream. He had athletic friends, white and black, who slept at each other's houses, grabbed quick meals before and after games from whichever house was most convenient, and Dave even stood in for the bashful Doc when it came to romance.

The object of Doc's consuming but shy affections was an attractive Froebel senior whom he was determined to marry one day. The only difficulty was *asking* her, and the problem consumed him so utterly that he let his schoolwork slide and wound up ineligible for the start of basketball. Finally, it was Dave who acted on Doc's behalf in the corridors of Froebel.

"You know Doc loves you," he began. "But he's shy."

She nodded.

"He wants to marry you, but he doesn't know how to ask you."

She knew that also, but for a moment she said nothing. In the silence Dave began to sweat, as if it were a proposal on behalf of *himself* he had just offered.

"Well," she finally spoke with only a small smile, "you can tell Doc I'll marry him."

Dave left her in the corridor and almost sprinted back to Doc. "She'll marry you," he delivered the message breathlessly.

Of all the privileges Doc and Dave enjoyed, one was *not* the guarantee of success in romance, and Doc was speechless at the news that his proposal by proxy had been accepted. He might have insisted on marrying the girl then and there in the corridors of Froebel High before she changed her mind, with Dave Minor standing in as his best man, if there hadn't been other, important business for Dave to attend to.

That business was trying to win the Indiana state high school basketball championship, perhaps the Mother of All Tournaments, with a history that went all the way back to 1911. It was a spectacle which so gripped the entire state that it seemed to develop a dramatic will of its own, producing cliff-hanging finishes and stunning upsets. Because there was no egalitarian system to separate schools by size, a team from tiny Beaver Dam might tangle with a mighty Muncie Central. Even team rosters read like the dramatis personae from a playwright's hardwood script: *Homer Stonebraker, Candy Miller, Fuzzy Vandiver, Babe Wheeler, Buster Brown, Stretch Murphy, Lester Stout*. And "wonder fives" ran "spring wheel" offenses scripted by basketball gods.

In 1919 the tournament finals moved from Bloomington to Lafayette, where the "sweet sixteen"—suvivors from the hundreds of schools that had started out with high hopes—battled it out for the crown over the course of a weekend in late March. Then in 1936 the system changed to a so-called Final Four. By 1941, when Dave Minor and his Blue Devil teammates from Froebel began their season, hundreds of schools would have their hopes dashed in sectional and regional and then semifinal tournaments before that Final Four emerged.

In their league—the Northern Indiana High School Conference—Froebel had done nothing that would have made them candidates to go "down state" for the Final Four. Behind what the *Gary Post-Tribune* called "Wheelhorse" Dave Minor, whose legs were more like a thoroughbred's than a dray horse's, Froebel jumped off to a 4–0 record, good enough to share the conference lead with neighboring Hammond Tech, reigning state champs.

They next met a mediocre team from Lew Wallace. With only ten seconds on the clock and a one-point lead, Froebel tried to stall. The ball came to junior Pete Mandich, a five-foot-ten-inch substitute guard who had made only spotty appearances throughout the season. He was five feet from the basket and unguarded when he shot with overanxious quickness, a reflection of his inexperience.

The rushed shot caromed off the backboard. A bony Lew Wallace speedster named Ted Szikora grabbed the rebound and raced down the sidelines. At his own baseline, Szikora slipped around Dave Minor and came out with a soft shot as both officials blew whistles that nobody heard and the ball dropped through the basket. One official had called traveling on Szikora, the other a foul on Minor. Despite a furious argument and a floor packed with angry Froebel fans, the foul call prevailed, the basket stood, and the Blue Devils suffered their first defeat. After the loss, Pete Mandich was inconsolable. Meanwhile, the *Post-Tribune* call Froebel's chances for the league championship "about as bright as London in a fog." To add insult to injury, on Monday morning the *Post-Tribune* ran a picture of Szikora taking his winning shot.

Then Hammond Tech, apparently on track for a repeat state championship, won its twenty-first straight game with an easy victory over Froebel. Despite Froebel's sweet revenge in February against Tech, who seemed to have been suddenly derailed, the Blue Devils finished league play in fourth place and might as well have been on a railroad siding headed nowhere.

On Thursday, February, 27, 1941, 777 Indiana high-school basketball teams in sixty-four sectional centers throughout the state began what the *Post-Tribune* called the "ruthless whittling down process" that would lead to the state championship. Because so many powerful teams came out of that sixteen-team, northern Indiana sectional that included Froebel, they called it "The Little State." Win it—as Hammond Tech had done the year before—and the regional, semifinal, and Final Four competition would be a breeze.

For Froebel, the only bright spot for the season had been the end of Doc James's academic ineligibility and his return to the team for the last two games. With him in the lineup, Froebel had won those last two games. Now, in the opening round of the sectional, in front of five thousand fans at Gary's Memorial Auditorium, Doc and the Wheelhorse of Steel City led the Blue Devils in a third quarter rally to an easy victory over Whiting. In that same round, reigning state champs Hammond Tech went down to defeat, and the surprising elimination of the powerhouse gave new hope even to the long shots.

The next afternoon, behind a sixteen-point performance from their jump-shooting Wheelhorse, the Blue Devils beat Washington of East Chicago. It meant that on Saturday they would have to win two games in one day—the first at two o'clock in the afternoon, the final one at eight o'clock—if they were to emerge as sectional champs.

Winning both ends of a basketball doubleheader? It seemed impossible, even if the team had a indefatigable Wheelhorse to pull it along. In the two o'clock game against Tolletson, also from Gary, the Blue Devils struggled for most of the game before they finally earned a six-point victory. With only a few hours' rest, what would they and their leaping Wheelhorse have left in their legs for the Horsemen of Horace Mann, the other finalist, who had trotted to a semifinal victory and looked tireless.

Not much, it turned out. Before the game, Horace Mann warned that it intended to lodge a formal protest with the Indiana State High School Athletic Commission if Froebel center Doc James played in the game. The charge was that James had illegally played "independent basketball," and Coach Mantz had no choice but to drop him from the roster immediately. Then, after a violent collision during the game, Simmie Isabel, the handsome, five-foot-ten-inch Froebel forward with the Cab Calloway pencil mustache, was rushed to the hospital to have his shoulder x-rayed for possible broken bones. Meanwhile, Dave Minor took so many "leaping, one-handed flings, . . . bordering on the supernatural" that his legs cramped repeatedly, forcing Hank Mantz to take strategic time-outs in order to massage the muscles of his Wheelhorse.

Finally, with two minutes left, Dave was exhausted and had to hobble to the bench, his "face twisted in pain." The truth was that he was as angry over the loss of Doc James as he was hurt, and his brilliant twenty-eight point performance brought a standing five-minute "howling tribute" from the overflow crowd. The next day the *Post-Tribune* headlines read "Minor Wins Sectional." The subsequent story credited him with a "heart as big as all outdoors." He was, they wrote, "the whole show, the most dazzling exhibition of individual basketball brilliance" they had witnessed covering Hoosier hardwood hysteria.

A week later, on Saturday, March 8, sixty-four sectional champions, including Froebel, met to continue the elimination process at sixteen regional centers from Gary in the north to Evansville in the south. What had been ruthlessly whittled down was everything but the hysteria of the survivors who had, the *Post-Tribune* wrote, "successfully evaded a knockout punch."

Half of the teams who had made it to competition in the other regional centers were considered surprises, and the *Post-Tribune* described the regional tournaments as "the looniest ever." Maxwell, Pittsboro, Dana, Pine Village—they listed some of the lowly survivors. Portland, Jackson Township, Gosport, Tell City. "Ever hear of those towns as producers of outstanding basketball teams?" the paper asked rhetorically.

Anything was to be expected, and most of all at the Gary regional center where all four teams were surprises. The issue of who would survive was anybody's guess, but Froebel seemed unlikely. Although x-rays revealed that Simmie Isabel had no broken bones, Dave Minor hobbled on gimp legs all that week in practice. Starting center Doc James was gone for good.

It was enough to give Edison of East Gary, Froebel's first opponent in the regional, a surge of confidence. "Edison Has No Fear of Froebel," the *Post-Tribune* reported. They were big, they were rugged, and they were determined to win the regional, "Froebel or no Froebel, Davage Minor or no Davage Minor."

It was again an exhausting double-header format, with the first contests in the afternoon and the finals Saturday night. Gary's Memorial Auditorium was packed for the Froebel-Edison afternoon matchup. Hundreds of disappointed fans were turned away and had to stand outside in the bitter cold and try to follow the game by rumor. In an effort to report what was going on, the *Post-Tribune* ran a "Bulletin" in its early afternoon edition, but the brief report that Froebel "held a 7–3 margin over Edison at the end of the first quarter" hardly told the full story of the action inside.

Halfway through the first quarter, Dave Minor suddenly went to his knees on the floor and then hobbled to the bench. It looked like temporary leg cramps again, but it was worse: a twisted ankle too sensitive even to stand on.

While Froebel's Wheelhorse hunched over in pain, Hank Mantz looked down his bench at Pete Mandich, the skinny substitute who had been the last-second goat in Froebel's first loss earlier in the year. In the sectionals he had taken just seven shots and missed them all, but he was a tenacious defender who also could handle the ball, and Mantz picked him.

It was the unlikely Mandich who was the difference that afternoon. Beyond his superb defensive play, he scored eleven points and appeared to the *Post-Tribune* to be the only Blue Devil ready to play. No sooner was he on the floor than he scored, helping Froebel earn the 7−3 margin reported by the paper's urgent bulletin.

Taped and still hobbling, Froebel's Wheelhorse returned to the game in the second quarter. It was Mandich and Minor together who gave the Blue Devils what looked like a comfortable half-time lead of eight points. By the end of the third quarter, behind Mandich and Minor still, the lead was ten points. It was a lead Mantz decided to sit on, and Froebel did not score a single field goal in the last quarter while·Edison slowly closed the gap and Froebel fans nervously watched the clock.

The final six-point sputtering victory for Froebel that afternoon was too close for comfort. It was equally unsettling when Hank Mantz announced later in the afternoon, as Froebel tried to rest, that he would start Pete Mandich that night against the Rensselaer Bombers in the second half of the double-header.

Was Froebel so uncertain of itself that it was still fishing for a starting five? The answer was yes. After all, what did they have to be confident of? They had been mediocre in their league. The one bright spot, the return of Doc James to the lineup, had been short-lived. Now Simmie Isabel was nursing a bruised shoulder. Their Wheelhorse, who was on the verge of breaking down with muscle cramps and a twisted ankle, had an improbable, leaping flat shot that not even his coach liked. Finally, it had taken the spunky play of an unheralded bench sub to lift the Blue Devils to victory. The chances of that happening again seemed remote.

A standing-room-only crowd of screaming fans, split evenly between Rensselaer and Froebel, pushed their way into Memorial Auditorium that night to watch the 8:00 P.M. finale. Continuing Froebel's theme of improbability, tiny forward Willie Martin, who often played with his lips parted to reveal his toothy grittiness, opened the game with two long, high-arching field goals that made the bank of fans in the bleachers immediately behind the backboard crane their necks like airplane spotters. Incredibly, both shots were good. With contributions from their hobbling Wheelhorse as well as Pete Mandich, who remained sublimely unaware that he wasn't supposed to be a starter or a scorer, Froebel led 12–9 at the end of the first quarter.

Unfortunately, the double-header format again proved too much for the Wheelhorse, whose leg muscles twitched and cramped, and he could not come off the bench to start the second quarter. With two regular season subs in the lineup now, the Blue Devils played as if they couldn't figure out who should have the ball, and they scored only a single free throw in the second quarter.

Trailing 14–13 at half, they repaired to the locker room, where Hank Mantz rubbed down Dave Minor's legs. Shortly into the third quarter, Froebel regained the lead when Pete Mandich hit a looping one-hander from the free-throw line. The Bombers raced back the other way and scored. Pete Mandich put the Blue Devils back on top with two free throws. Another free throw and their lead was 18–16. The Bombers answered with a pair of free throws and then a reverse lay-up that put them ahead, 20–18. Froebel tied it up, Renssalaer turned it over, and then "Wee Willie" Martin, in what the *Post-Tribune* later called an "express special," went the full length of the court with machine-gun dribbles, his teeth clenched for everybody to see, and eventually delivered a miraculous shot that banged through the basket.

22–20, Froebel.

It was fire and mayhem enough to bring the Wheelhorse back off the bench, his teeth clenched too. His two quick free throws put Froebel up by four, but the Bombers came right back with two free throws and a lay-up to tie it at 24–24. Finally, as the quarter wound down, Dave Minor took a long pass at midcourt and raced for the basket. There wasn't time to go all the way, or even stop and jump. Without breaking stride, he crossed into the key and threw a hook shot off his hip that dropped through the basket as the noise of the gun sounding to end the third quarter was swallowed in the pandemonium.

26–24, Froebel.

It was the shot that finally broke the back of the Bombers, who could not get any closer than two points throughout the fourth quarter before they went down to defeat, 36–32.

Notwithstanding the victory, the *Post-Tribune* reported the next day that Froebel's "fire just wasn't there." Still, of the 777 original competitors, the Blue Devils had made it to the "sweet sixteen," who would battle it out at four semifinal sites up and down Indiana— Hammond, Indianapolis, Muncie, and Vincennes. Some folks argued that Froebel had played sluggishly against Rensselaer because Hank Mantz, looking ahead to that semifinal competition, had rested his players. The semifinal would be another exhausting double-header format at each site, with an afternoon game and then an evening championship contest. Mantz might have had good reason to rest at least his Wheelhorse in the Rensselaer contest, to leave something in his legs for his unique leaping toss. The higher he was able to jump, the more time he had in the air to shoot with touch rather than just to fling it hastily. That much Mantz understood about the unusual shot.

Coasting against any team from the Steel City leagues flew in the face of the argument that they presented the toughest competition in the run for the state championship. So the truth was that the Blue Devils had given it their all against Rensselaer and barely escaped with a victory. High-point man for them in the two regional contests had not even been their leaping Wheelhorse but rather the unlikely Pete Mandich. It did not bode well for the Blue Devils' chances the next weekend at a neutral site in Hammond against a good team from Logansport, always dangerous in tournament play and regular contenders for the state championship.

Meanwhile, that "ruthless whittling down" of competition had eliminated all the dark horses. Six of the sweet sixteen were former state champs. What at one stage had been "looney" competition with plenty of underdogs was now a "brawny" as well as a sweet sixteen. If the Blue Devils managed to get by the Logansport Berries, whose nickname belied their strength, there would be even mightier fives to face.

On Monday and Tuesday before the semifinals, while Dave Minor soaked his injured ankle nightly in hot water, the *Post-Tribune* tried to find something that would recommend Froebel as contenders. The best it could do was to remind readers of the "Steel City basketball tradition"—six previous Gary teams had gotten to the semifinals. Beyond that, they wrote, five members of the team were "hitting the hoop from the field at better than a .230 clip."

Whatever the *Post-Tribune*'s noble intentions, it sounded like a dismal batting average in baseball. The truth was that Froebel was a long shot in the sweet-sixteen competition. And tradition or not, it had been more than a decade since Froebel had had a basketball team good enough in semifinal competition to win the right to go downstate to Butler Field House in Indianapolis for the clash of the Final Four to decide the state championship.

Having the talent to do it was one thing, but Dave's Uncle Lincoln, influenced also by the lessons of iron-willed Claudia McMorris, knew that having the *desire* was another. Lincoln McMorris did his best to create that desire in his nephew by promising him, "Look, if you guys can win in the semis and go down state, I'll get you a car."

It was a promise that inspired the Wheelhorse of Steel City to exceed himself again, and in the matinee game on March 14 against the Logansport Berries, the Blue Devils fought back from an early deficit and behind Dave Minor's sixteen points raced to an easy 43–32 victory. Then they sat as a team in the stands with five thousand other fans—including Indiana coach Branch McCracken and an assistant coach from Notre Dame named Ray Meyer—and watched the second matinee game in which a powerful South Bend Central team, with a 25–2 record, held Jefferson of Lafayette to a meager twenty-one points. It was a tactical game played in an adagio tempo that was the exact opposite of Froebel's earlier allegro game. The major architect of that sleepy pace was the Central coach, a thirty-one-year-old English teacher named Johnny Wooden.

Wooden's demeanor stood in sharp contrast to Mantz's. Mantz was intense, excitable, and beady-eyed, Wooden, wide-eyed and studious. Mantz had almost a decade of coaching experience behind him, as well as the privilege of having studied almost at the feet of Wisconsin's Walter E. Meanwell, whose little black book had been the country's basketball bible for years. Against Johnny Wooden, Mantz seemed to have the advantage. But there was something commanding in the wide, eager eyes of the Central coach, as if nothing that happened on the floor, or wasn't happening on the floor, escaped him. He could be combative and quick-tempered, but he also seemed to be drinking in everything and by virtue of that careful scrutiny, controlling it.

In the Froebel-Central matchup that night at 8:00 P.M., Wooden's remarkable control was apparent from the very first second, and in a matter of minutes Central had jumped off to a 8–0 lead before Froebel scored. A minute later the score was 12–2. Only a desperate, long basket by Wee Willie Martin as the quarter ended gave the Blue Devils any hope. Froebel's Wheelhorse had done nothing that first quarter, and the college scouts who sat watching had seen little to recommend him as a prospect.

In the huddle, Hank Mantz turned his beady eyes on the entire team. "I want you to get the ball to *Minor*. I want him to shoot." It struck Dave as an artificial, selfish limelight, and he immediately tried to object. But Mantz cut him off. "I want *the Kid* to shoot," he repeated, this time using his affectionate nickname for Froebel's Wheelhorse.

The Blue Devils responded immediately. On defense in the second quarter, they double-teamed and swarmed and repeatedly stole the ball. Slowly, they began to close on Central. Then two high jump shots by Dave Minor tied the score at half time and made it clear there was still plenty of bounce in his slim thoroughbred legs.

There was not much Hank Mantz needed to say at half time to inspire the Blue Devils. They had fought their way back into the game. *They* were the ones who were now in control, not Central or their commanding coach.

Throughout the third quarter, the lead seesawed as the teams traded baskets. Then, with less than three minutes left in the game, the Wheelhorse soared high one more time, and his sixth field goal of the night gave Froebel a one-point lead. On Central's next possession, Froebel's tenacious defense forced a turnover, and with only two minutes left the Blue Devils spread out on their half of the floor and began to stall.

It was Hank Mantz now, not John Wooden, whose control and wisdom were in the spotlight. How could he possibly keep his charges under control in the midst of the escalating frenzy? And why was he trying to sit on a narrow, one-point lead? As Central defenders swarmed and double-teamed the Blue Devils, trapped ball handlers pivoted and twisted their bodies and then finally hurled desperate passes that narrowly escaped interception. A half minute of furious action passed before Central fouled. On the floor the Wheelhorse bent over to catch his breath and glanced at his coach. It was Mantz's decision to make. Take the free throw and the chance to build a two-point lead or keep precarious control by electing to take the ball out of bounds and continue the game of keep-away?

It took only a second for Mantz to make up his mind. *Keep control!* He pointed to half court and the designated in-bounds spot. Froebel's inbound pass was a long, cross-court heave that seemed doomed to interception, but a Blue Devil player snatched it and dribbled himself free before he passed off and the chase resumed.

Another harrowing half minute passed before Central fouled again.

Once more it was up to Hank Mantz to decide whether to shoot the free throw, or continue a cat-and-mouse game that with each second grew riskier.

Keep control! He pointed to half court a second time.

This time, as four Blue Devils scrambled to get open, Dave Minor flashed to the free-throw line, *wide open.* He took the pass with his back to the basket, pivoted, and with just over a minute left stared in disbelief at the open space between him and the basket. Two steps and he could have an easy layup . . . maybe. Or just leap immediately and let go one of his jump shots.

Keep control! he decided quickly and pivoted again to pass off.

Central fouled three more times in the last minute as their hectic efforts to pick off passes led to violent collisions or near dismembering hacks. Each time, with a calm that grew icier as the crowd's frenzy rose, Hank Mantz pointed to half court.

Keep control!

There was one more test of that control. With twenty seconds left and a noise so earsplitting that even the studious Johnny Wooden was on his feet, Froebel substitute guard Steve Benko found himself alone with the ball under his own basket. Once more there was not a Central defender within fifteen feet. He glanced up and seemed to be drawing a quick bead for the shot.

But in that split second, he relived the awful nightmare defeat by Lew Wallace earlier in the year, when Pete Mandich's last-second rushed shot had missed and led to Ted Szikora's winning basket. That heartbreaking loss had been the turning-point *down* for Froebel. The instant recollection of it as well as Mandich's regret afterward were enough for Benko to make his decision.

Keep control!

He passed off quickly. A clutch of Central players chased the flight of each subsequent pass. With ten seconds left, Froebel's luck finally ran out when an errant pass came straight to a Central player. Startled by the realization that their desperate efforts had finally paid off, he paused for a second before he tore off downcourt.

At half court he shot a pass ahead to a teammate wide open along the baseline. He turned to face the basket, stepped quickly for the shot, and with five seconds on the clock, the ball sailed on a course that looked as true as all heartbreakers.

Afterward, where the Wheelhorse had come from to bat away that last shot and preserve Froebel's one-point victory, nobody could say. All that anybody knew for sure was that the final Froebel stall had been the most frenetic two minutes *ever* in Indiana basketball. For long afterward, up and down the state, it was the one game from the 1941 Indiana state tournament that sportswriters talked about. In Michigan City they wrote that Froebel had "stumbled, fumbled and mumbled" its way through the season and had gone from the "ridiculous to the sublime." In Valparaiso they said the game was one that would be talked about "for years to come." In Indianapolis they wrote that Dave Minor was Froebel's "guiding light," which was an awkward metaphor for the man who had snuffed out the light of Central's last promising shot. And forty years later, at a speech in Indianapolis, Johnny Wooden remembered that loss as the most disappointing of his coaching career.

Froebel, Washington, Kokomo, and Madison met for the final-four double-header in Butler Field House in Indianapolis on Saturday, March 22, 1941. For the Froebel Blue Devils, who lost by two points in the opening afternoon round to the Madison Cubs, it turned out to be anticlimactic. For the Wheelhorse from Steel City, it was a sudden and disappointing end to his high-school basketball career. Despite owning a brand new Plymouth four-door sedan, which he and his uncle picked out from a showroom in Gary, he scored only a single field goal in the packed Butler Field House and that in the final minutes of play. Afterward, he blamed his performance on the strange atmosphere in the field house, which had double rims for extra support on the baskets and high windows, which gave an eerie sunlight backdrop to the backboards.

That night, Washington beat Madison to capture the 1941 Indiana state high school basketball championship. But in Gary the whole story was Froebel's incredible run, and the following Monday, beneath a headline that read "Minor Got His Shot," the *Post-Tribune* ran a huge picture of the Wheelhorse in the act of shooting the only shot he had made while losing to Madison. Calling it simply his "favorite shot," and failing to identify it as the first jump shot ever pictured in historic Butler Field House, it was that very same shot that he had accidentally discovered four years earlier as a Froebel freshman. Now, however, he was higher than ever, his head silhouetted in the light from one of those lofty windows. As he hung in the air, his right leg was slightly crooked, and his left arm was stuck straight out to the side, as if he were that five-year-old again, standing for the measurements of a new suit. Otherwise, the slim body of the Wheelhorse of Steel City was arrow straight. His right arm, which had already released the shot, was lifted still, as if he were reaching to touch Butler's roof. Just off his splayed fingertips, the ball was frozen, lit up like a soft moon from the sunlight streaming in the field-house windows.

One night in December 1941, just before Dave Minor left for Western Michigan University to play basketball, an angry snowstorm hit Gary. The Wheelhorse of Steel City lay on his bed in his stocking feet in his home on Jackson Street. Nine months had passed since Froebel's incredible run for the Indiana high-school championship had come up short in the Butler Field House. Dave could not buy a basket that night. "That shot's gonna be your downfall," Hank Mantz had warned beforehand about Dave's flat jump shot. To have such a dismal night in front of nearly twenty thousand fans hadn't ruined him or even tempted him to give up the shot. But none of the disappointment of that matinee loss had disappeared.

Outside, the wind was howling off Lake Michigan and driving the snow sideways in the glow of the streetlights. Aunt Claudia was at the kitchen table doing the books for the apartment properties she had acquired. From the back of the house, Dave heard the doorbell ring. Then he heard a cheerful, confident voice ask Claudia, "Does Dave Minor live here?" Dave sat up, slipped on his shoes, and came to the door. Two men in buckle overshoes and with icy eyebrows greeted him.

The one with the cheerful voice spoke first. "I'm Abe Saperstein." He turned to a tall, husky black man beside him. "This is Inman Jackson, our player-coach. How would you like to play a game with us?" Both Jackson and Saperstein shook Dave's hand, while he struggled to think of what to say.

"We've got a game in an hour over in Michigan City," Saperstein explained, "but some of the Trotters are stuck in Chicago in the snowstorm."

"The *Globe*trotters?" Dave was incredulous.

Saperstein smiled. "We've been watching you for two years, Minor. You can cut it with *anybody*. And we need a pick-up player tonight."

"Well . . . sure," Dave managed to stammer.

Claudia raised her hand to restrain her overeager nephew. Then she turned to Saperstein. "I'm Claudia, Dave's aunt." She shook Saperstein's hand, then got right to the point. "How much does he earn for a game?"

"We'll pay him six dollars."

It was a moment before Claudia nodded and said, "That seems fair."

Fair, Dave thought. *Six bucks to play in a short basketball game was a fortune!*

Saperstein insisted there was no time to waste, and Dave quickly threw together his equipment. Then he and Saperstein and Jackson piled into a car and sped off through the furious snowstorm for Michigan City. On the way, it was Jackson who finally explained to the Wheelhorse of Steel City, "Now, you're gonna be Jack Fox."

"Jack Fox?"

"You can't use your real name."

"Why not?"

"You're plannin' to play college ball, aren't you?"

"Sure."

"Then you better play under a different name. Playin' for money will mess up your eligibility."

While he got dressed, he worried that somebody in Michigan City would recognize him. He also tried to think of how to explain to Claudia and Louella and Lincoln, who had taught him always to be proud of himself, that he had assumed an alias.

Once the game started, the Globetrotters who managed to show up in the storm showboated and clowned, but "Jack Fox" played with a solemn face and scored again and again on soaring jump shots. Somewhere halfway through the game, one of the Trotters snarled at him to "lighten up!" From then on, in each of the brilliantly choreographed comic routines, he slipped off toward the sidelines and tried to stay out of the way.

After the game, while Dave sat in the locker room unlacing his shoes, Saperstein came to pay him and thank him for filling in. But Dave almost felt the need to apologize for not being able to fall in with the comedy.

Saperstein laughed. "All we needed you to do was to shoot that jump shot of yours . . . and score," he added.

The mysterious Jack Fox had done plenty of that.

"In fact," Saperstein offered, "we'd like you to play with us *permanently.*"

"As Jack Fox?"

Saperstein laughed. "As Dave Minor."

"Well, I dunno," Dave said. "I've got college ahead of me still."

As if anticipating the arguments of Aunt Claudia, Saperstein said, "We'll pay you seventy-five dollars a month."

Seventy-five dollars a month! That was another fortune, and Dave stared at Saperstein.

"I don't know . . . ," he finally managed to stammer. "I'll . . . have to think about it."

Saperstein nodded and handed Dave his card. "Well, lookit, if you wanna play with us, here's my number. Call me."

Dave took Saperstein's card and thanked him. Then after Saperstein reminded him again to "Call me anytime," Dave sat looking at the card and the offer it represented. On the surface, it was an attractive offer with the specifics of good money and famous teammates. Despite those specifics, it did not offer anything as promising as the real future that lay ahead.

After false starts at several colleges, including Long Island University and Western Michigan, Dave Minor played his first year at Toledo University and became the only freshman All American selected that year. In December 1943 Dave married a striking college girl with long brown hair named Ollie Mae Carter, and their marriage eventually brought them four children, ten grandchildren, and two great-grandchildren. After three years of wartime service in the army, during which time he played with a rising black basketball star from the University of California Los Angeles named Don Barksdale, he ended up at UCLA and finished there as an All American. Despite those achievements, the color line in professional basketball was not broken until 1950, and Dave Minor, with teammate Don Barksdale, continued his basketball career with the Oakland Bittners in 1949, winning sixty-seven out of sixty-eight games and the national AAU title. In 1951, at thirty-one years of age, he turned pro and was among the first blacks in the NBA, playing with Baltimore and Milwaukee. Eventually, the Wheelhorse returned to his Steel City and took over the real-estate business established by his Aunt Claudia. Finally, on the strength of what scribes called his "amazing jump shot," Dave Minor became one of only a few black celebrities who could boast that a street had been named in his honor, in his case in a suburb of Orlando.

That future, however promising, Dave had only dimly sensed as he sat staring at Abe Saperstein's business card after the Trotter game. What was crystal clear was that playing basketball with the Trotters meant the sudden end to everything for which his aunts and uncle had sacrificed. For as long as he could remember, a college education had been a foregone conclusion. Not for basketball, for his mind. For that independence and pride he had learned since he was old enough to walk. When he had started to grow like a weed, they hadn't driven him to Chicago every six months for a new suit only to have him wind up playing the clown on a basketball court. They hadn't struggled to buy a house of their own and keep him in school only to have him wind up on a traveling basketball team, no matter how famous it was. They, more than anyone, were the ones who had made him into "The Wheelhorse of Steel City."

He looked at Abe Saperstein's card one more time and then dropped it in his travel bag.

I'll never call him, he told himself.

Joe and His Magic Shot

On December 9, 1936, the *Paducah Sun* reported in bold headlines that King Edward VIII had abdicated the throne. Buried deep in that same issue of the *Sun* was a small story that few people would have read, even in that part of western Kentucky: Birmingham had beaten nearby Gilbertsville in basketball. For Joe Fulks, the shy and gangling ninth grader who was singled out as high-point man for Birmingham, the story marked what would be his long, slow rise from obscurity to a fame nearly as worldwide as King Edward had enjoyed.

The only way to get to Birmingham, on the bottomland alongside the Tennessee River, was by a narrow gravel road that wound down through the thick hillside forests of oak and hickory and led to the Birmingham ferry. The ferry crossed to the "Land Between the Rivers," a long finger of remote wilderness between the Tennessee and Cumberland Rivers. In the 1800s that wilderness had been the center of an iron-mining industry so promising that Birmingham had been created as a small river port that was expected to grow larger than its English namesake. By the turn of the century, however, the ore deposits had been exhausted, and Birmingham and the Land Between the Rivers became mired in poverty. Instead of ore barges, only paddle wheelers with their calliopes echoing in the river valley stopped at Birmingham to pick up cargoes of barrel staves, wheel spokes, or railroad crossties manufactured from the hardwood forests along the river.

During the winters a haze of coal smoke and river fog hung over the town and made it difficult to see across the Tennessee to the Land Between the Rivers. Each year heavy winter and spring rains flooded the surrounding bottomland with backwaters that retreated slowly in the first humid days of summer and left behind only the smell of sodden mud and brackish water.

On the hottest summer days the boys and girls of Birmingham swam in the Tennessee River or rode the Birmingham ferry as it crossed back and forth on the cool waters. It ran day and night, carrying as many as four cars at a time to The Land Between the Rivers, where the bootleggers produced what was considered to be the best moonshine in the world. It was so good, in fact, that the Land Between the Rivers became the major supplier for the Chicago speakeasies run by Al Capone's gang. Birmingham residents learned to recognize one of Capone's black limousines coming off the ferry, its rear end raked from the load of whiskey in the false gas tank.

It was no secret that the moonshiners were desperately poor sharecroppers and backwoods folks who, in the grip of the Depression, had turned to moonshining in order to survive. One man had even stood before his church congregation to announce, "My family's hungry. I can't earn a living farming, so I'm resigning this church. I'm gonna start makin' whiskey."

Despite what everybody knew, the revenue agents who regularly rode the ferry at night on still-busting patrols into the Land Between the Rivers usually came up empty-handed. What the agents didn't know was that a ferry signal light that was pointed toward the far river bluffs alerted a sentinel parked in a car watching for the patrol; the sentinel then took off, sounding his horn as he went to warn the moonshiners to shut down. Those Birmingham families too principled to turn to moonshining tried to scrape out a living picking strawberries or fishing and musseling in the Tennessee River. The mussel shells, retrieved off the bottom with draglines dropped from john boats that drifted in the current, brought fifty cents a carton from button factories across the Ohio River in Illinois.

Meanwhile, the hard times of the 1920s shrank Birmingham to a bottomland enclave of fewer than two hundred poor citizens. Their simple frame homes with crude porches were clustered around a post office, a dry goods store, two groceries, and half-a-dozen other businesses—all connected by wood sidewalks. There was no electricity or plumbing, no telephones, and most of Birmingham saw whiskey as relief from economically as well as emotionally hard times. Even after prohibition Birmingham's two roadhouses, Woody's and Pat's, did a brisk business selling Swamp Root Bitters, Hostetter's Bitters, or Log Cabin Bitters, which were nothing but moonshine laced with a few ounces of Pepsi syrup and served to local folks and thirsty visitors as "stomach bitters" for liver, kidney, and bladder cures. One of the cafe owners walked among the tables of her establishment without betraying that between her legs and underneath her long dress, slung from a leather holster, she had a demijohn of whiskey from which she could pour shots for her customers.

The roistering and drunkenness of Birmingham's roadhouses soon gave the isolated town a reputation for being a lawless river outpost. Woody's was the place where on Saturday nights everybody carried a gun and liked to shoot out the bottles with kerosene wicks that served as dance-floor lights. After twice warning a drunk from the Land Between the Rivers not to disconnect the battery wires to the dance-floor jukebox, Woody Oliver shot the man point blank in his left eye.

There were less violent moments. Every day at noon a handful of folks would gather in Mr. Lee's Grocery, site of the only battery-run radio in town, to listen to a program that day after day featured the same nameless harmonica tune crackling through the static. In Birmingham they laughingly called the song the "Foxchase" because it set half the town's dogs to barking and howling. For two days after Shorty Provine returned from Detroit in his new Model A with a green body and a black top, townsfolk gathered in front of his house to admire the fancy car. The men of the town, many of whom had no regular work, spent so much time at the recreation of pitching washers the size of silver dollars into tiny pits that the decision was finally made to forbid this recreation on Sunday.

Kentuckians fix their place of origin by county, and Joseph Franklin Fulks was born on a farm just outside Birmingham in Marshall

County, Kentucky, on October 30, 1921, the first child of Mattie Jo and Leonard Fulks. At six feet and 230 pounds, Leonard Fulks was proud of his enormous capacities for farm labor, but that great body also proved to be a storehouse for disappointment and self-pity provoked by the hard luck and afflictions of the Great Depression. Whenever his despair overflowed, he disappeared for weeks at a time to pitch wild drunks. Nobody could say where for sure—over with the moonshiners in the desolate woods in the Land Between the Rivers, perhaps, or somewhere else remote and secret where his family didn't have to suffer. At least Mattie Jo could be grateful for that. Leonard Fulks never abused her or his two children or embarrassed them with the inconvenience of his drunken presence. Sooner or later he returned sober to find work and income wherever he could, laboring as a deckhand on the ferry or musseling and running trotlines in the Tennessee River.

In 1927 the family moved twenty-five miles north to Paducah, where Leonard found work with the railroad. Unfortunately, it was short-lived relief, and after Leonard injured his arm in a railroad accident, he was given fifteen hundred dollars to compensate him for his injury and then laid off. Complaining more than ever about his bad luck, Leonard Fulks moved the family back to Birmingham to a two-bedroom frame house. There, Leonard's fits of sadness and depression grew ever worse, and it was soon rumored that during one of his secret disappearances, in the clutches of drunken melancholy, he had tried to drown himself in a dishpan of water.

Except for sad, hazel eyes, there was little about Leonard Fulks that was reflected in his son. Leonard Fulks was stocky and muscled, Joe was wiry, with a sharp Adam's apple and a thin face. Joe wore his auburn hair cleanly parted down the left side and brushed into a huge, neat wave that hardly reflected he had the same capacity for self-destruction as his father. He spoke in a slow southern drawl that suggested a deep calm, and despite the habit of long silences in the company of his friends and a timidity around strangers, he was considered easy-going and friendly. "There's not a better boy in Birmingham," they all said.

One of his first Birmingham companions was James Defew, three years younger than Joe but just as wiry, with a deep, hard voice that delivered words in elliptical bursts. Early on nicknamed "Tiny" because he hadn't grown for years, James Defew had suddenly exploded with pent-up growth and quickly caught up to his older brother "Dub," whose classmate was gangling Joe Fulks.

The three boys became regular companions who increasingly turned to basketball as relief from musseling in john boats with their fathers or watching the men of Birmingham try to find diversion from hard times by indulging in the dull game of pitching washers. For years basketball had been the one recreation in Birmingham that wasn't an artificial distraction. Year in and year out Birmingham had good teams, some of the best in Marshall County, and on the afternoon of games the entire town gathered to watch at Birmingham School's outdoor court. On wet winter days they sprinkled the court with furnace cinders to keep the muddy surface playable. In time, they built a ten-foot-high wooden wall around the court to protect fans from the cold winds that blew from the direction of the river. The handful of boys who were good enough to play on the team enjoyed glory in the town of Birmingham.

For young boys such as Joe Fulks and the Defew brothers, who had plenty of time to daydream as they drifted the Tennessee currents in their john boats, achieving that same basketball glory became their greatest ambition. At first, however, because the impoverished Birmingham School possessed only two basketballs—one for practice and another for games—Joe and his friends had to improvise by stuffing rags, grass, toilet paper, or sawdust into a sock. Then they practiced their shooting skills with a sock ball at a hoop fashioned from an axle band and nailed to the side of Joe's house. Of course the sock would not bounce, so it meant they had to simulate dribbling by bobbing the sock ball back and forth in their hands as they moved.

In 1932 tiny Birmingham School, with only twenty-three boys in the high-school grades, scrapped and clawed its way through one victory after another on its way to what would eventually be the school's first appearance at the state basketball tournament in Louisville. Two local heroes led the Birmingham Bulldogs. One was a tall senior named Robert Goheen, the other a freshman named Sanders Watkins. Watkins's mother had died when he was twelve, but he remained a cheerful and friendly young man, affectionately nicknamed "Hook" by the boys because of his crooked nose.

One day halfway through that season, Joe Fulks and James Defew stood with their friends at courtside and watched Robert Goheen score repeatedly with an exciting, two-handed leaping shot. For boys who had not yet even mastered the skill of bouncing the ball, the mechanics of leaping to shoot might have seemed too difficult to learn just then. Yet they were determined to copy their idol, and they quickly discovered that Goheen had apparently been taught the shot by his Birmingham coach Basil Smith.

Still consigned to the ignominy of Birmingham School's lower grades, Joe Fulks and the Defew brothers considered the distinguished-looking Coach Smith an unapproachable god. Senior Robert Goheen seemed nearly as inaccessible. But Hook Watkins was not that much older, and he was also not above joining the unpolished games that the younger boys enjoyed at Joe Fulks's home court or the court at school. Then, Sanders Watkins was trying to incorporate that same leaping shot into his own game, and he assumed the role of mentor for the young boys of Birmingham.

Neither Joe nor his friends could find the strength in their young bodies to learn to leap and shoot. For Joe it meant that he dropped the ball off his shoulder so that he could hurl it from a half windup. Each shot was awkward and far short of the basket, and so instead he concentrated on mastering the other shots that Sanders showed him. Meanwhile, Sanders also helped the boys upgrade their equipment, from a sock basketball to a real one. It was a bladderless ball that had been discarded by the school, but it was now stuffed with sawdust and was bounceable if you pounded it hard enough. Before long, Joe Fulks, in his strap overalls, was using it to practice even at night beneath the basket nailed to the side of his house, or sometimes on the cinder court at school.

"That's Joe out there," Dub Defew told his sister Ruby one moonlit night after they were both in bed—they could hear the ball bouncing. "He's working on his shots."

Hour after hour he practiced a wide assortment of creative shots that went beyond what Sanders had taught him. Baby hook shots, running or standing, shooting from his chest, or off the shoulder with his body turned, or whirling and stepping or just standing—he soon had a battery of shots that was twice what anybody else could do because he could shoot them just as effortlessly with either hand.

Shortly after Birmingham's appearance in the state tournament in 1932, the school burned to the ground. During the planning for a new school, it was clear that the outdoor court, even with its wooden wall, was too crude for a town whose basketball fortunes in Marshall County looked so promising. By 1934 a brand new school and gym had been constructed, complete with a gas-powered generator for lighting the gym. At night the surrounding river bottom rumbled and echoed with the sound of the new generator, while inside the bright, warm gym the entire town watched the Birmingham Bulldogs play basketball. Even during those dark moments when the generator coughed and died, no one thought of leaving, and instead the crowd waited patiently in the pitch black until someone restarted the generator.

Tiny Defew succeeded in obtaining a key to the indoor gym so that as long as there was daylight on weekends, the young boys of Birmingham were inside shooting baskets. In the hot summer they played in the close gym until they were sweat-soaked, then sprinted down to the river for a quick, naked swim that cooled them enough to return to their basketball.

Meanwhile, no one had yet mastered that strange leaping shot of Robert Goheen. Joe Fulks was still trying to wind up and heave it off his shoulder. Then after his junior year, Sanders Watkins, the one mentor who might have finally taught them, dropped out of school to marry and work for his father. When the talented Sanders returned a year later to complete his senior year, his graduation seemed to signal the end of an era in Birmingham basketball. But there were still three promising players in the wings, players whom Sanders himself had helped develop.

The first was freshman Dub Defew, who like his younger brother Tiny had white hair and a wiry frame. The second was Tiny Defew, only a seventh grader but still on the team because he had shot up to be as big as the older boys, who were too few in the high school grades to even fill a roster. The third was the spindling freshman Joe Fulks, already more than six feet, with long arms and huge hands and every conceivable shot but one, Robert Goheen's jump shot.

It had been four years since Goheen's play on the first outdoor court had inspired Joe Fulks and his friends. Now, reporting as hopefuls for the 1936 Birmingham team, the boys were met by Robert Goheen himself, who had returned to the site of his old glories to teach and coach. Goheen's hair was beginning to thin, but he was still young enough to recall the wild influences peculiar to growing up in Birmingham, and he tried to strike a sympathetic chord with his players.

"I care about you boys," he told them in those opening days, "and I want to make good ballplayers out of you. Anything you see me do, if you do it, I'll never criticize you for it. You hear me cuss, you can cuss. You see me drinkin', smokin' . . ."—he paused to let them appreciate that he understood the rough character of Birmingham—"anything you see me do," he continued, "I'll never criticize you for doing it. But what you *don't* see me do," he added, "I'd rather you didn't do." And it was not merely his personal habits he wanted them to imitate. He suited up himself for each practice and jumped and ran and leaped and shot as much as any of his players. He would suddenly stop the scrimmage and then snatch a ball. "Look, that's not the way you're supposed to do that." Then he would demonstrate the correct shot.

It was his instructions for the execution of the jump shot that proved to be the key for young Joe Fulks to stop heaving the ball wildly off his shoulder. "You know your legs are much stronger than your arms," he said and then leaped high to demonstrate the shot with two hands. He retrieved the ball and bounced it to Joe. "So use your legs to elevate yourself. Make your legs *push* it. Guide it with your fingers and wrists." He glanced at Joe's hairpin legs. "If you can't jump, at least get up on your toes."

While Goheen watched, Joe experimented with the shot, pushing as hard as he could with his legs and then shooting with his right hand. He did not elevate himself all that much, but what push he did create, along with the strength in his long arm from repeated shooting, carried the ball to the basket for the first time. He turned to his coach for approval.

"Better learn to shoot with both hands before you try with just one," Goheen said.

Joe shrugged. Left, right, or *both* hands, it didn't matter to him, and with Goheen's encouragement and the luxury now of a ball that bounced so that he could dribble into the shot, he slowly mastered what would eventually become his trademark shot. Jumping only a few inches, and out of habit going up with the ball still slightly off his shoulder, he lifted it over his head with both hands until at the last second he dropped away one hand or the other, depending on which shoulder he had turned away from his defender.

Still, recognition came slowly that first year at Birmingham, and his name appeared in the *Paducah Sun* on only one other occasion beyond that victory over Gilbertsville. In mid-December, when the Bulldogs trounced the Kuttawa Lyons, a team from over on the Cumberland River, the paper reported briefly, "Joe Fulks scored nine points playing guard."

What other achievements might have followed went unreported after it began raining steadily in western Kentucky, and the Cumberland and Ohio Rivers began rising four inches an hour. By January 21, 1937, the Tennessee had reached fifty-four feet, well above flood stage, and half the town's houses sat abandoned in coffee-colored backwaters that pooled higher than anyone could remember. Rumors began circulating in Birmingham that the Tennessee Valley Authority (TVA) dam upriver at Chattanooga had broken and that a wall of water was descending on the town. Without telephones to confirm the rumors, bottomland farmers moved their cattle and horses to the ridge west of town, then began fleeing their homes also. School was closed and all basketball games canceled, so Joe and his sister Barbara Nell floated around the abandoned town in the family's john boat as the waters rose still higher. Finally, with his own home in two feet of water, Leonard Fulks moved his family in with Mattie Jo's parents on the high ground of Billy Estes's farm.

When the deluge finally ended, the weather turned bitterly cold, and then it snowed. By the time the waters receded, the basketball season was over, and instead of basketball, what people talked about in Birmingham was rumors that the TVA was contemplating the construction of a huge dam somewhere downriver on the Tennessee. The impounded waters would cover up Birmingham but put an end to annual flooding that left debris and deadheads in the streets of river towns from Paducah to St. Louis.

It all fed Leonard Fulks's conviction that his bad luck was so profound that it included the curse of man-made as well as natural disasters, and his bouts of drinking continued.

Then one night Joe Fulks was bitten by a black widow spider in the family's outdoor privy. He lay in bed for days, sick and feverish, and James and Dub Defew's mother took turns with Mattie Jo Fulks in sitting up with Joe through the night and applying cold packs until his fever finally broke. The episode seemed to darken Joe's already sad eyes, and his occasional long periods of moody silence continued, whether because of the behavior of his father or spider-bite misfortunes of his own—he was too shy to explain.

For months afterwards, his body erupted with purplish carbuncles that swelled and suppurated and had to be treated by the town's only doctor. Meanwhile, if his teammates kidded him about his pin legs, or a nose as prominent as the one that had earned Sanders the affectionate nickname "Hook," Joe Fulks grew silent and moody on the court. Even the kidding of his long-time friend Tiny Defew, who regularly guarded him in practice, made him fall silent.

"Joe, I'm gonna take the ball away from you," Tiny would lay down what he thought was a healthy competitive challenge. But the challenges only made Joe angry and ineffective, and even opponents began to recognize during the second year that taunting made him moody rather than competitive.

Off the court, he remained likable but quiet, and he began dating Tiny Defew's sister Ruby. Two years older than Joe, she had no trouble carrying the burden of lop-sided conversations as they walked together to games at the new gym, whose lights spilled out into the river darkness. Walking her home again, even after frenzied games, he still had little to say, and Ruby Defew told her brothers Tiny and

Dub that Joe Fulks was one of the nicest but quietest boys she'd ever met. *What* was *the key to getting him to talk?* she wondered. Her brothers didn't know either. Beyond the pithy, grunted exchanges of a basketball game, they had seldom had a conversation with him.

Despite his shyness, Joe Fulks's reputation was spreading. In Marshall County they said he had a kind of "magic shot" in which he would whirl around and then jump and release the ball with either hand and with such deftness that it floated like a soap bubble with no spin.

Meanwhile, Congress appropriated $12.5 million for construction of a dam on the Tennessee River twenty miles downriver from Birmingham, near Gilbertsville. Immediately, wild rumors about the fate of Birmingham began to circulate again. Would it be a low dam, similar to the lock and dam over in Eddyville on the Cumberland, or would it be a high dam that would sink Birmingham forever beneath its impounded waters?

That issue was resolved shortly when the TVA began buying up bottomland along the Tennessee River. Those citizens who were resigned to the submerged fate of the town and were tired of struggling to make a living picking strawberries or selling mussel shells for buttons took what they could get for their land and homes and began leaving.

A mood of watery death and burial hung over the town even as the Birmingham Bulldogs, led by Joe Fulks playing center his junior year, defeated one Marshall County opponent after another on its way to a berth in the district tournament. Still, for Leonard Fulks, the idea that Birmingham would soon be inundated by a man-made disaster was the last straw, and he began to talk of moving elsewhere.

Whether it was his father's talk of moving or a deeper demon that Joe was too close-mouthed ever to reveal, his moodiness worsened. In the final game of the district tournament, against Calvert City, he loafed and sulked and scored little through the first half, so that at half time the Bulldogs found themselves behind. It was only Coach Robert Goheen, a genius at gentle inspiration, who managed to pull Joe out of it by addressing, not him, but the entire team at half time.

"I've always been good to all you boys. Now you're lettin' me down. You're better ballplayers than this." Then he sat beside Joe but kept his gaze on all the others. "If you don't change your attitude, you're gonna get in trouble. I care enough about you that I don't want that to happen." He stood up and raised his voice. "You played for yourselves the first half. Now I want you to play for me."

It was vintage Goheen, the ability to make a player feel personal responsibility *without* singling him out, and Joe scored fifteen points the second half with his whirling magic shot, leading the Bulldogs to a come-from-behind victory. His performance prompted the *Paducah Sun* to write that he was western Kentucky's greatest basketball player in decades.

Eventually, the Bulldogs lost to Calvert City in the regional tournament and were deprived of a trip to the state tournament. Still, junior Joe Fulks's reputation had grown far beyond Marshall County, and he was selected to the Kentucky all-state high-school team by the *Courier-Journal*. With Joe Fulks and the Defew boys back the next year, and if Birmingham wasn't under water, they would be, everybody said, one of the best high-school teams in Kentucky.

Only a few people realized that the wheels were already in motion to remove Joe Fulks and his magic shot from Birmingham.

The construction of Kentucky Dam meant the impoundment of a lake that would eventually stretch south for a hundred miles, deep into Tennessee. That foreshadowed the end of dozens of small towns like Birmingham. For the overzealous city fathers of towns not immediately threatened, it took little vision to realize that students from what they joked would be the "Land *Beneath* the Lake" would have to be educated elsewhere. "Oh, if we could get that Fulks boy," one town made no secret of its basketball dreams, "we'd whip the world."

Fourteen miles to the northeast of Birmingham, after crossing the Tennessee and Cumberland by ferry into Lyon County, the picturesque little Cumberland River town of Kuttawa had always loved its basketball. Once the site of numerous hot springs whose waters were like "liquid poems" that drew invalids for restoration, the town of more than two thousand people had a divided main street that was lined with majestic oak trees. In the spring and summer the smell of blooming flowers in Kuttawa yards was as pungent as perfume.

In 1924 Kuttawa's consolidated school had been destroyed by fire, and the new facility on a hill overlooking the Cumberland River was the best gym in Lyon County. But the town did *not* have the best teams, and led by Mr. Ed Jones, one of the town's most prominent citizens, the city fathers of Kuttawa set out to improve their basketball fortunes.

By May 1939 the town of Gilbertsville had been shut down by the construction of Kentucky Dam, and Ed Jones and his friends from Kuttawa began talking to the parents of Leonard "Red" Metcalf and Bill Dexter, two of Gilbertsville's basketball stars. Dexter wanted to transfer to Kuttawa's arch rival Calvert City, but Kuttawa prevailed in the bidding war—by virtue of what promises, no one said—and Bill Dexter wound up as a Kuttawa Lyon.

What it was that finally persuaded Leonard Fulks to move his family to Kuttawa was less of a mystery. He was promised immediate and regular work. There would be no more struggling to make a meager living off strawberries or mussel shells. With a lovely "Vista Ridge" where people liked to sit and gaze out across the Cumberland, Kuttawa was a serene and peaceful town. In all likelihood there would be no more disasters, man-made or natural, that would encourage despair and whiskey.

In Birmingham they hated to see young Joe Fulks move to a town with such poor basketball prospects—Birmingham had beaten Kuttawa 65–15 that previous winter—but all the friends of Leonard and Mattie Jo Fulks realized it was too good to pass up.

Few paid much attention to what Joe felt, nor did he, as uncommunicative as ever, give any indication of what the move would mean for him. It would mean leaving behind his friends. It would mean leaving behind a basketball team that everybody predicted would be one of the best in the state. It would mean abandoning

Robert Goheen, the young coach who had helped him perfect his magic shot and could tolerate his moods and even snap him out of them. Only once did Joe betray what he felt. It was to Ruby Defew, who still thought he was as quiet and nice a boy as she'd ever met.

"I'll make them sorry they made me go," he told her.

Shortly after the Fulks family moved that summer into a small, white bungalow on Poplar Street in Kuttawa, a freak tornado back in Birmingham sliced through town and tore the roof off the school and its gym. Safe in Kuttawa, Leonard Fulks could only assume that he had finally shaken his bad luck.

Ten miles away near Gilbertsville, the Corps of Engineers' construction site on the Kentucky Dam had become a city of thousands of people, with many opportunities for employment. But the story soon circulated about one of the first Kentuckians who showed up for work and faced a single question to determine his eligibility: "What does 'hydroelectric' mean?" The man had scratched his chin before he drawled, "Well, I guess it means I don't get the job."

Leonard Fulks was unskilled, but the town fathers of Kuttawa managed to find work for him as a guard at Kentucky State Prison, two miles away in the Cumberland River town of Eddyville. With a crenellated roof line and windows as narrow as gun embrasures, the old maximum security, gray-stone prison stood like a Norman castle on a hill in the center of town. Built in 1889, it had housed the most violent murderers and felons in Kentucky. It had whipped them until 1913 and still in the 1940s would not permit inmates to use forks or to talk in the dining room. The prison also housed the state's electric chair, which on a single day in 1929 had executed seven men. From its inception there had been frequent escape attempts, during which guards had been shot or wounded. For the desperate few willing to work there as guards, there were no impossible questions to answer.

Joe's new coach at Kuttawa was J. Holland Harvey, a muscled history teacher with a booming voice who couldn't wait to start the new basketball season. He now had the talented recruit Joe Fulks, who could shoot from anywhere. Harvey also had two good veteran forwards, whom he directed to feed Joe Fulks. The first was Timer McKinney, who also had been recruited to come to Kuttawa. The second was a handsome, husky rebounder and defender named Douglas McQuigg, whose bright red hair had earned him the nickname "Carrots."

Those same city fathers who had found a job for Leonard Fulks to give Joe's recruitment the legitimacy of a family move did not bother about those niceties with guard Bill Dexter, the star recruited from the defunct Gilbertsville team. Dexter himself was given a job at the Kuttawa Drugstore and took up residence in Miss Julia Martin's big rooming house on Oak Street.

Meanwhile, Dexter's running mate at guard was Teeter Martin, only 122 pounds, the runt of the team. Except for gangling Joe Fulks, the others were muscular and square-jawed and sturdy. Whatever reluctance Joe might have felt about coming to a new school, he betrayed none of it as he posed in the center of the team picture. Taken as the season commenced, it featured every member of the proud, ten-man squad wearing thick knee pads, matching striped knee socks, and fancy satin jackets. Young Joe Fulks had come a long way from his old Birmingham days of outdoor courts and sawdust basketballs, and there was just the touch of a smile on his face in the picture, his wavy hair as neat as ever.

Other pleasures might have been behind Joe's thin smile. He had begun dating one of the Kuttawa cheerleaders, and after a double date to the movies at the Kentucky Theater in nearby Eddyville, he and teammate Teeter Martin and their dates shot pool or drank Cokes and danced in the Turnaround. The teenage hangout had a romantic rear deck that hung out over the water when the Cumberland River rose. For Joe, a night of movies and dancing—even if they had to walk a wood plank over backwaters to get into the Turnaround—was a long way from the deprivations of Birmingham.

The Turnaround sounded as if it were a club named in honor of Joe Fulks and his magic turnaround shot. With his back to the basket, Joe would flash from the low post to a spot either side of the free-throw circle. Once he got the ball, he spun quickly, faked left or right, then dropped several quick dribbles. The eventual fall-away jump shot, still more two-handed than one-handed, was impossible to guard, even if they double-teamed him. He was soon the hero of Kuttawa, whose basketball team began defeating one opponent after another in Lyon County. On game nights the Kuttawa high-school gym was packed with admiring fans who came to see his magic, turnaround, fall-away shot. A three-foot-high wooden wall, right on the edge of the court, kept fans from getting too familiar with their basketball idols; it would have seemed inconceivable that any of them had clay feet.

But the seeds of aggravation had been sewn, not just in the mysterious and personal demons that seemed to haunt Joe Fulks and bring on his moodiness, but in the circumstances of a stardom that made Kuttawa veterans have to stand in his shadow. Workhorse forwards Timer McKinney and Carrots McQuigg were expected to feed and otherwise indulge their new ambidextrous shooting machine. If they guarded him too closely in practice, however, or stopped him cold because they learned exactly how to predict which way he wanted to whirl before he jumped and shot, Joe would come out of his sullen quiet just long enough to challenge them angrily to meet him after practice.

It was anger that passed quickly, and before practice was over they were a team again, euphoric with the prospect of slamming another opponent. Only three episodes marred an otherwise near-perfect season. The first was the time they went up to the little coal-mining town of Morton's Gap and beat the town's team so badly that after chunky Kuttawa guard Philip Matlock coldcocked one of the hapless players from Morton's Gap, angry coal miners poured onto the court. The Lyons fled to their dressing room and locked the door, leaving Teeter Martin hiding under the popcorn machine in the lobby of the gym. Afterward, the rumor circulated that Kentucky's legendary coach Adolph Rupp had been there to see for himself how good this gangling phenom from Kuttawa was.

Midway through the season, after Kuttawa traveled east to the Pennyrile forest country and beat a good team from Nortonville, those same city fathers who had quietly recruited Joe Fulks had to continue on east by midnight train to Louisville, to stand nervously before a Hearing Board of the Kentucky State High School Athletic Association.

In a hearing that lasted from early Saturday afternoon until 3 A.M. Sunday, the board charged that Kuttawa officials had unduly influenced the parents of Joe Fulks. The Board also wanted to discuss the circumstances of other mysterious transfers. Offering the explanation that these were all players whose high schools would soon disappear under water, the Kuttawa representatives—"leading businessmen," the papers called them—protested that they had done nothing illegal. Joe Fulks's father was desperate for work. And his son had to go to school *somewhere!*

It was a half-truth. Yes, Leonard Fulks needed work, but despite impounded waters that were threatening to engulf Birmingham and a gym roof still missing from that freak tornado, the school had remained open. Joe Fulks could have played out his last year in Birmingham. Still, in the end, the Hearing Board decided not to suspend Kuttawa High School from the state athletic association, but they issued a statement in the papers saying that they "deplored the tendency of schools to build up winning teams through the use of imported athletes."

They couldn't have been talking about anyone but Kuttawa, which went on smashing opponents one after the other. By midseason those same city fathers who had escaped censure were so jubilant that they chartered a train to take the whole town to watch the first of what were expected to be the two most difficult games that season, against arch-rival Calvert City, whose star, Herb Hurley, was said by some to be the *second-best* high-school basketball player in Kentucky.

The night of the first game, revelers on the train joked that there weren't enough people left behind in Kuttawa to put out a match. Once the train got to Calvert City, it dropped off the Kuttawa fans and then chugged on to Paducah to turn around for the return trip. Meanwhile, it was pouring rain, and the Kuttawa fans had to wait outside the Calvert City gym. After the game started, in the packed gym with little air, their clothing stank of wet wool.

Herb Hurley played behind Joe Fulks, and another of his teammates fronted him so that he could take precious few of his magic jump shots. The strategy left Teeter Martin wide open. Using a crude variation of the same jump shot that he had watched Joe Fulks shoot again and again, Teeter scored twelve points, the most of his basketball career, and Kuttawa won by six points.

The celebration on the train back to Kuttawa was high-spirited. The team had beaten their toughest opponent on *their* court. There was every reason to expect that with the advantage of their home court and that peculiar restraining wall they would win easily at home. The wall was so close to the out-of-bounds line that players inbounding the ball had to stand with their feet sideways. For Calvert City it would be an especially alien setting, and the Lyons were confident of victory.

A standing-room-only crowd of six hundred people packed the gym in Kuttawa to see the rematch. Even the stage at the far end of the floor was filled with spectators, most of whom couldn't see a thing. It was a seesaw battle that featured Herb Hurley and Joe Fulks trading baskets for most of the night. After the regulation game ended with the two teams deadlocked, the game went into overtime. Fans and players alike were exhausted from the excitement and tension.

With only seconds left in the overtime, Kuttawa led by one point. Joe Fulks was protecting the ball in the backcourt as the last seconds ticked away. But Herb Hurley swept in from behind Joe, who had whirled off his dribble to escape a defender, and he stole the ball. Hurley dribbled for his goal and the winning basket. The single official sprinted from midcourt to follow the play.

With one second on the clock, Hurley picked up his dribble, took a long step, and was crouched to leap for the easy lay-up when Kuttawa's ace defender, Carrots McQuigg, caught up to him and slapped the ball away. The momentum of the two players sent them both sliding in a tangle up against the gym doors.

The pandemonium of the home crowd, convinced it had won, made it impossible for anyone to hear the shrill whistle of the official who had trailed the play. However clean the steal might have looked to the partisan Kuttawa fans, to that lone official, the sight of Carrots colliding with Hurley and then rolling into the wall in a violent tangle was enough to award Hurley two free throws.

It was minutes before order was restored and the floor finally cleared. Herb Hurley stepped to the free-throw line while a cacophony of boos drifted out to the walnut grove behind the school and out across the Cumberland River. Afterward, some said it was the worst noise ever heard in the otherwise peaceful town.

No matter the booing, Hurley made both free throws, and it was Kuttawa's first loss. School administrators had to escort the official through angry fans down to the coaches' locker room. When it was clear he still wasn't safe, they hustled him out the back of the gym to a waiting car.

The momentary anger and disappointment among the fans was too deep and consuming for anybody to see what disappointments lay ahead for the Kuttawa Lyons, who eventually lost in the first round of the state tournament. What was also lost on the crowd was the fact that Joe Fulks went over and sat on his bench and cried.

It should have been a warning of dire things to come for Kuttawa's star. With such a promising future, who would have noticed his crying or seen a warning? His reputation exceeded state lines, and he was already being romanced by half-a-dozen big universities. Much greater things were in store for this shy, unassuming stringbean with a magic shot.

Without Joe Fulks, who had to sit and watch while nursing a sprained ankle, Kuttawa lost to Morganfield by one point in the first round of the 1940 Kentucky state high school basketball championship. Despite aggressive efforts by big universities to recruit him, Joe enrolled at tiny Murray State College in southwestern Kentucky, where his distinguished play for three years earned him the nickname "Jumpin' Joe Fulks, the Kuttawa Clipper."

He was neither a superb jumper nor from Kuttawa. Even if by 1943 the abandoned town of Birmingham had finally disappeared under the waters of the Tennessee River, it was still the true home of Joe Fulks. As for his jumping ability, western Kentucky observers laughed and said with characteristic drawls that you could hardly slip a shingle under his feet on his jump shot.

Still, that jump shot with either hand, as well as a dozen other shots, which he could go a whole game without repeating, caught the eye of early professional scouts. Joe played with a Marine Corps all-star team in the Far East during the war. In 1946 he signed an eight-thousand-dollar contract with Eddie Gottlieb's Philadelphia Warriors in the newly formed Basketball Association of America (BAA).

Meanwhile, during college he met and married Mary Sue Gillespie, whose father had owned the old Turnaround restaurant in Eddyville. That first season with the Warriors, Joe and Mary Sue lived in a row house in North Philadelphia, and they regularly rode the trolley downtown to take in a movie and dinner. On the court, he was soon the leading scorer in the new league, and he began to shed the shyness that had seemed a part of his character in boyhood.

What he could *not* shed were those mysterious and deeper demons that had haunted him since childhood. Exactly when the heavy drinking had begun, no one in Lyon County seemed to know for sure. He told those Philadelphia sportswriters who said he was the "Babe Ruth of Basketball" that liquor had always been in his life, as far back as Birmingham bootleggers. Even drugstore Cokes in Kuttawa were laced with whiskey, he claimed. Some of his old Kuttawa teammates insisted that it had all begun in the Turnaround. Others wondered if the heavy drinking hadn't started while he was among dissolute Marines, or later, when he was with professional athletes whose intemperance and excesses were legendary.

Whenever it began, his old Birmingham friends didn't take notice until they drove to St. Louis in early 1947 to see their old teammate play with the Warriors against the St. Louis Bombers in St. Louis Arena. After the long drive, those friends were sorely disappointed because Joe did not play at all. At half time, smelling heavily of whiskey, he climbed into the bleachers so that he could sit with his friends and pester them with endless questions about how things were back in Lyon and Marshall Counties.

It was utterly out of Joe's quiet character, and the friends who had come to admire his playing basketball now sat among the fans, embarrassed for Joe. When his absence was noticed in the locker room, Eddie Gottlieb sent teammates back out to retrieve him. After a struggle, he left for the locker room but then also sat out the second half. The game over, he again bolted up to the bleachers to join his friends.

"These guys are from my home," he explained to the Warrior teammates who warned him that he was going to miss the team's plane. "I'm goin' home with 'em." After a long argument, he finally agreed to join the team. His old friends drove home wondering why he was so anxious to abandon a basketball glory they each envied.

Despite the demons that still seemed to possess him, opponents could not stop him. In New York, Knicks coach Neal Cohalen virtually conceded that Fulks couldn't be kept from scoring, and he instructed young Bud Palmer, whom he assigned to defend Fulks to "let him shoot. *Just don't let him get a rebound!*" Three minutes into the game, Palmer called time out. "Fulks hasn't gotten a rebound," he told Cohalen in the huddle and struggled to catch his breath. "But he already has ten points."

By January Joe was averaging twenty-four points a game, a full ten points better than Detroit's Stan Miasek who was in second place. In early February his season total approached one thousand points. In late February the Pittsburgh Ironmen double-teamed him the entire game, but he still scored thirty-five points. Finally, before a home crowd in Philadelphia on April 2, 1947, Eddie Gottlieb presented his franchise star with the keys to a brand new 1946 Buick sedan while eight thousand fans cheered wildly. It was a celebration that inspired Joe to exceed himself, and in the game that followed the presentation he scored his 1,406th point that season on a ten-foot jump shot. It broke the single-season professional scoring record set in 1911 by Willie Kummer, who played for a small Pennsylvania town in the long-defunct Central League.

After Joe's record-breaking jump shot, play was suspended so that Kummer himself, then a revenue agent, could come out of the stands. In a bit of irony that few of the fans would have appreciated, the revenue man whose agency specialized in busting moonshiners stood at midcourt and shook the hand of the basketball star from the moonshine capital of the world.

Behind Joe Fulks, the Warriors went on to win the first BAA championship. Philadelphia sportswriters wrote of their new hero: He "still looks like a country boy, with his bashful smile. . . . He is not a brilliant talker," they added, "but he makes a good, brief after-dinner speech."

However much they may have wanted him in Philadelphia that summer for after-dinner speeches, he explained, "I've got to get home. . . . I'm two weeks behind already in my potato planting."

It sounded pastoral and wholesome, but he spent most of the summer in the company of Lyon County drunks on a houseboat moored where Eddy Creek emptied into the Cumberland River above Eddyville. Before the summer was over, he had wrecked the Buick and managed to antagonize many of his old friends.

The worst episode was following the houseboat celebrations of July Fourth, after one of his old Lyon County friends had finally gone to rescue him. Unable to stand, and with a week's beard, he had had to be carried to the car. On the drive home, Joe insisted, "I ain't goin' home unless you stop and let me cash a check." Once the thirty-five-dollar check was cashed and Joe had been delivered safely to his doorstep, he turned to the friend. "Here," he said and held out the money. "I don't want some poor son-of-a-bitch doing somethin' for me for nothin'." It came across as arrogant contempt for their impoverished past, and afterward the friend made it clear that he had no more use for Joe Fulks.

Still, as if his basketball glories were a polar opposite to his sad drinking, there were greater things ahead for Joe Fulks. His second year as a Warrior, Joe again led the league in scoring. In January 1948 the *Saturday Evening Post* also called Joe Fulks the "Babe Ruth of Basketball." He was selected by *The Sporting News* as 1948 Athlete of the Year. Then on February 10, 1949, when it was obvious to his closest teammates that he was locked in a battle with alcoholism, his fame spread still farther. There were three games that night in the old BAA: Rochester at Baltimore promised to be a close game; and the Knicks at Minneapolis against the Lakers would be a scoring duel between towering George Mikan and Carl Braun. The third game, Philadelphia versus the hapless Indianapolis Jets, drew little attention, and while a furious blizzard raged outside the Indianapolis arena, only fifteen-hundred fans turned out to watch Joe Fulks and the Warriors.

In the beginning, the game was as dull as expected. Joe missed six of his first seven shots. Then he hit eleven straight baskets, most of them soft jump shots from every conceivable spot on the floor. By half time he had thirty points and a chance to break professional basketball's single game scoring record.

It was a record with a seesaw history. Mikan had first laid claim to it with a forty-two point night back in 1946. The next season the Knicks's Carl Braun, who shot his free throws by cocking his knee almost to his lips, reset the record at forty-seven points. On January 30, 1949, Mikan took back the record with a forty-eight-point outburst.

Forty-eight points in a single basketball game! It was, some insisted, a record likely to stand for years. Then, less than two weeks later in Indianapolis, Joe Fulks scored nineteen points in the third quarter alone, and with still a quarter to go, he had already eclipsed Mikan.

With two minutes left, Eddie Gottlieb called time out. "I want you to basket-hang," he told Fulks.

Joe shook his head.

"Joe," Gottlieb argued, sensing the chance for a truly impossible record, "you're already near 60 points."

Joe shook his head again. "I don't want points that way. I'll earn them."

The final score was 108–87. Joe Fulks hit twenty-seven field goals, most of which were jump shots, with not much more than a shingle of air beneath his feet, but there also were nine free throws. It was an amazing sixty-three-point explosion that would stand for more than a decade until broken by Elgin Baylor's seventy-six-point spree, and finally Wilt Chamberlain's one-hundred-point night, a scoring apogee that still stands.

That February night in Indianapolis in 1949 represents the high-water mark for Joe Fulks's fame. After that year it began a long, slow recessional. The next season the BAA swallowed several teams from the rival National Basketball League, then restructured itself as the NBA. The once-mighty Warriors found themselves in the new league's cellar, and Joe Fulks's scoring dropped to what for him was a paltry fourteen-point average. "Has the Babe Ruth of basketball reached his peak, and is he now rapidly traveling the toboggan toward the bottom?" the *Inquirer* asked.

Eddie Gottlieb also struggled to explain Joe's decline. *Why has he slipped?* he wondered. *Maybe he lost that split-second timing,* he answered himself, avoiding the real reason. *Maybe he lost that extra urge that sent him to stardom.*

Elsewhere, the reasons for Joe's decline were discussed with the same evasiveness. Perhaps he wasn't "keeping in condition." Perhaps he had "lost interest in the game." Finally, Gottlieb went on to add, "Maybe he has outlived his usefulness to us." Those words must have gone off like a siren in Joe's head. Immediately, he was "the Fulks of old . . . in top physical condition." "Fulks May Be Back in Stride," the Associated Press reported after he scored twenty-six points in a Warrior victory over the Washington Capitols. What had turned him around? Was it Gottlieb's patience? Or the ominous warning by Gottlieb that he may have outlived his basketball usefulness?

Meanwhile, a little noticed but even more ominous note had been sounded in a small Associated Press story. "Look Out, Fulks!" it was headlined. Then six short lines reported that a Villanova senior named Paul Arizin had set an National Collegiate Athletic Association (NCAA) record by scoring eighty-five points in a single game.

Paul Arizin was the Warriors' first-round draft pick the next season, and the team's second leading scorer behind Fulks. His second season, Arizin led not only the Warriors but the NBA in scoring, and this time it was clear that Fulks *had* outlived his usefulness, even though he played two more seasons before he quit.

Back in western Kentucky, Sanders Watkins, the old friend from Birmingham who had helped Joe learn the jump shot, found him a job in Calvert City with the GAF company. After repeated firings for drunkenness, Joe Fulks finally managed to dry out. He raised his family, scouted for the Warriors, fished occasionally with his father—who had gone on the wagon, too—and watched the towns of Kuttawa and Eddyville also disappear under water, this time from the construction of Barkley Dam on the Cumberland River.

In 1971, at the twenty-fifth anniversary celebration of the NBA in San Diego, Joe Fulks was selected to the league's ten-man Silver Anniversary all-star team, which included Bill Russell, Bob Cousy, George Mikan, and Dolph Schayes. Unfortunately—and again as if alcohol were a sad backfire of his fame—he resumed drinking during the celebration with old NBA friends and teammates, and he was soon divorced and steadily drunk in Lyon and Marshall Counties. Slowly, his basketball exploits were forgotten in a world captivated by athletes who could seemingly hang in the air or score one hundred points in a game.

Early in the evening of Saturday, March 20, 1976, Joe Fulks went out the front gate of the castlelike Kentucky State Penitentiary in Old Eddyville, where he worked as the prison recreation director. Joe's car had broken down, and without changing out of his prison-guard pants and a T-shirt, he had a friend drive him two miles to New Eddyville and Beckett's Trailer Court, where he spent occasional nights in the company of an attractive widow named Roberta Bannister.

That afternoon, Roberta Bannister's twenty-two-year-old son had arrived at the trailer court with his wife Sharon. "Greg Bannister thought the world of his daddy," friends said, and he also resented his mother's relationship with Joe Fulks. The young Bannisters, along with Roberta and Joe, visited for an hour until Joe persuaded Greg, who was handy mechanically, to help him fix his car. Despite the tension between them, the two left at 8:30 P.M. in good spirits and didn't return until 10:00 P.M., bearing two unopened half-pints of Tvarscki vodka.

For almost five hours, at a cramped kitchen table of the mobile home, the two drank their vodka and talked. They were a stark contrast. Greg was young, slight of build, and unathletic, with a hard and wild look about him. "I knew that kid would kill," a friend described that look later. "I knew that much about him. He was a daddy's man." Joe was tall and agile looking. He wore glasses now that made him look friendly and professorial. His wavy hair was graying, but he still kept it neatly parted on the left side.

Despite their different appearances and dispositions, gradually with each drink they became more alike—contentious and loud. When it was obvious to Sharon Bannister that her husband and Joe were in a deep, drunken argument, she undressed in the first bedroom off the kitchen and went to bed.

At 3:00 A.M., a weary Roberta Bannister told her son and Joe to go to bed. A .38-caliber pistol that belonged to Greg's wife Sharon lay on the kitchen table. Joe rose, grabbed the pistol, and headed down the narrow hallway to the bedroom in the back of the mobile home. Greg Bannister followed, arguing that the pistol belonged to him. For twenty-five minutes the two remained in the back bedroom, arguing over the pistol. Finally, Greg Bannister went back down the hall of the mobile home. He went out to his car where he kept a double-barreled .20 gauge shotgun in the trunk.

Meanwhile, groggy with alcohol, Joe sat down on the bed and struggled to undress. He managed to put his shoes and socks under the dresser. He stood shakily to place his billfold, a cigarette lighter, and miscellaneous change on top of the dresser. Then he sat down on the bed again, still wearing his guard pants and the T-shirt.

At 3:40 A.M. Greg Bannister returned to the back bedroom and stood holding the shotgun over Joe. "Go home!" he shouted at Joe.

"No."

With his finger on the trigger, Greg pointed the shotgun at Joe and began screaming at him to go home. In the front bedroom, awakened by the loud voices, Sharon Bannister got up and was putting her clothes back on when she heard the shotgun blast. Almost immediately, Greg Bannister bolted from the back bedroom and met his wife and mother in the narrow hallway.

"I didn't mean to do it!" he shouted. Then he grabbed hold of the two women. "Don't go back there!" he cried.

That night Joe Fulks's former Kuttawa teammate Carrots McQuigg was on duty as part of the county's volunteer emergency ambulance service. Carrots was sound asleep at 3:45 A.m. when his phone rang. He picked up the receiver and listened, still half asleep, as his partner explained that the county's dispatcher had just directed them to respond to a shooting at Beckett's Trailer Court. Minutes later, McQuigg's partner arrived with the ambulance, and unaware of who was involved, the two raced off toward Beckett's. They were the first to arrive at the scene, and Roberta Bannister rushed from her mobile home and met them at their ambulance.

"What happened?" McQuigg asked her.

"Greg shot Joe!" she cried out.

His mouth suddenly dry, McQuigg told her, "I'm goin' on in."

McQuigg and his partner went inside. In the back bedroom, they found Joe lying on his back on the bed, his head turned and his feet still touching the floor. The point-blank blast had severed the carotid artery in his neck, and a massive pool of blood had gathered on the floor beneath the head of the bed.

McQuigg stared at the body of his old teammate. It was obvious he was dead, and finding no pulse or vital signs, McQuigg and his partner went back down the hall. The .20 gauge shotgun lay on the floor outside the front bedroom. Through the closed door, they could hear Greg Bannister sobbing and shouting. "I didn't mean to do it! Somebody please help me! I didn't mean to do it!"

Two hours later, after Kentucky State Trooper Ron Anderson had arrived and questioned Greg Bannister and the two women, Joe Fulks's body was removed from the bedroom and taken to a local funeral home, where the county coroner took photographs of his fatal wound. At 5:30 Sunday morning, Lyon County Sheriff Bill White drove Greg Bannister to the Caldwell County Hospital, where he was sedated. A blood test determined that his blood-alcohol level was .2 percent, twice the legal limit in Kentucky.

Later that morning, Sheriff White executed a warrant against Greg Bannister for the murder of Joseph Franklin Fulks, and bail was set at fifty thousand dollars.

Hidden deep inside the few newspapers that carried it, the story telling that the one-time leading scorer and record-holder in the NBA had been murdered was noticed by few. No one from the Philadelphia Warriors attended his funeral services, and Joe Fulks was buried quietly in a small cemetery just outside the Marshall County town of Briensburg, Kentucky, alongside the relocated graves of the dead from Old Birmingham.

On August 31, 1976, a Lyon County jury in Eddyville delivered a verdict of "reckless homicide" against Greg Bannister. He was sentenced to four-and-a-half years in prison, and after six months in the penitentiary at LaGrange, Kentucky, he submitted a probation appeal.

"Due to the fact that drinking is an invader to the functions of the body, thereby causing carelessness, . . ." he wrote Circuit Court Judge Edward Johnstone, "I will never take another drink of vodka, whiskey, beer, or any other alcohol containing beverage." After serving less than two years of his sentence, Bannister was released on parole. Over the next twenty years, despite his vows of sobriety and his apparent remorse over the killing of Joe Fulks, he was rearrested and sentenced repeatedly for alcohol related offenses.

On some modern calendars Veterans Day is subtitled "Remembrance Day." In 1996, Remembrance Day came on a Monday, and early that morning a band of clouds drifted down from the Great Lakes and darkened the skies of western Kentucky. At noon the temperature dropped suddenly, and a light snow fell. When the clouds finally passed, the sky turned a bright blue, but a chill remained in the air. The small cemetery in Briensburg, Kentucky, where Joe Fulks was buried, went unvisited on Remembrance Day.

That weekend the NBA had celebrated its fiftieth anniversary by publishing a list of the fifty greatest players in league history. Joe Fulks was not on the list. That sixty-three-point night in Indianapolis had been the high-water mark of his fame. From that point on, his reputation had receded as slowly as those Tennessee River backwaters, whose rise and fall seemed to mark the design of his own life. On Remembrance Day 1996, his scoring and his magic shot were as forgotten as his hometown of Old Birmingham, which had long ago disappeared beneath the waters of Kentucky Lake. Even the stone that marked his grave was a poor reminder of his basketball glories.

"Joseph Franklin Fulks," the simple inscription read. "Corporal, US Marine Corps."

Jumpin' Johnny Adams

The first day of spring was still two weeks away, but Fayetteville was almost balmy that Thursday morning of March 6, 1941, when Prof. J. S. Waterman, chairman of the school's athletic board, busied himself in his office on the University of Arkansas campus. Professor Waterman was officious and highly organized, but what little paperwork he managed to complete that morning was done absentmindedly. Each time the phone rang, he answered it quickly and then fell into disappointed mumbling when it was obvious the call wasn't the one he was anxiously awaiting.

For almost a month rumors had circulated throughout the sleepy campus on a hill that the powerful Razorback basketball team would receive an invitation to the third annual NCAA basketball tournament in Kansas City. The Razorbacks had waltzed undefeated through the Southwest Conference—the first team in a decade to do so in conference play—and three opposing coaches had called them the best basketball team they had ever seen. Even Coach Glen Rose, whose pessimism was so notorious they called him "Gloomy Glen," even he conceded that his charges were the greatest team he had ever coached.

The problem with playing in the infant NCAA tournament was that it was so new, only a few understood how it worked.

The country was divided into eight regions, each with an official selection committee charged with inviting the best team in that region to enter the competition. After the invitations had been announced and accepted, four teams from the East competed in Madison, Wisconsin, on March 21–22 to determine the eastern champions. Four teams from the West met the same weekend in Kansas City to determine the western champion. The East and West winners then met a week later in Kansas City to determine the best college basketball team in the country. It was a system so misunderstood that one Arkansas sportswriter made the impossible prediction that Stanford and mighty Arkansas—*both* from the West—would meet in the finals.

Whatever the confusion about the new tournament, one thing was certain: the Razorbacks were a juggernaut, the tallest collection of stringbeans and Goliaths anybody had ever seen on one basketball court. They were agile and swift to boot. "We're not exactly slow," was as optimistically as Glen Rose would put it. Speed and height were behind the team's record-breaking 646 points for the season. On rainy game nights, when the long trip through the Ozarks up to Fayetteville was too perilous to make, Little Rock sportswriters stayed at their desks and used clichés to try to give life to ticker tape statistics: the "towering Porkers" were a "scoring machine" of "dashing dribblers," whose "sizzling scoring" broke every record in the books.

Their strength also lay in their coach, Gloomy Glen, who had played his basketball at Arkansas a decade earlier. As a playmaker, he had a sweeping court vision that produced such tricky passes, they joked, that he was cross-eyed and left-handed. As a coach he had the same gift of a sweeping court vision, and he insisted that his towering team run full-court, fast-break patterns that demanded the agility and clockwork precision of little men.

The Razorbacks relied on just five extraordinary players, what the *Arkansas Gazette* called an "Eiffel tower" lineup. First, they had the tallest center in the history of Arkansas basketball, a six-foot-eight-inch giant named John "Treetop" Freiberger, whose long face and high head of hair made him seem even taller than he was. Forward "Shorty" Carpenter was only an inch shorter. He had a sad mouth and an awkward, farm-boy knobbiness about him, but his sudden, graceful moves often caught opponents by surprise. Treetop and Shorty towered over opponents, and together they were as conspicuous on a basketball court as the twin clock towers of Old Main, the landmark, red brick building on the hill of the Arkansas campus.

Next, they had two ferocious defenders in R. C. Pitts, a six-foot-four-inch guard with an incredible reach, and Howard "Red" Hickey, who brought to a basketball court the same knockabout ideas of defense he practiced as an end in Razorback football.

Finally, their leading scorer and handsome star had a shambling and easy gait that prompted comparisons with Gary Cooper. But it was really the handsome young baseball player Ted Williams he most resembled, with the same wide eyes and boyish face. They wrote that he had an "unguardable leaping shot" that helped make him the greatest college basketball player in the country. Those same writers who used florid prose to give body to their statistics liked to call him "stork-legged" or "spindle-legged," or simply "Kangaroo," because of that leaping shot. But the two nicknames that stuck the most were "Long John" and "Jumpin' Johnny," which gave him the mystique of a pirate or a trapeze artist, while the truth was that his simple name, John Adams, and his real farmboy past were too prosaic for someone with such an amazing shot.

In high school in El Paso, Arkansas, his little sister had been a carefree tomboy, as cheerful as her name, "Gladene," suggested. Hardly big enough to walk, she struggled to keep up with her older brothers as they went about their chores or played their rough-and-tumble games on the family farm outside El Paso.

At night at the supper table, her brothers teased her by telling her, "Sis, if you can jump over the house, you'll become a boy." Each time they teased her, she would run outside and measure the house for a leap, only to realize again the impossibility of it. Meanwhile, she continued to try to join their games, and as she grew, she developed a strong throwing arm in baseball. Still, her brothers included her only when they were shorthanded, and then they put her far out in right field.

By the time she was twelve years old, Gladene Adams spent

much of her time on the farm, helping her mother with the daily kitchen chores. The one chore she loved best was using her strong throwing arm to ring the backyard dinner bell, which she did with such authority that even the farm mules "Jim" and "Bess" would prick their ears and come running.

After lunch one hot June afternoon in 1935, her older brothers Johnny and O'Neale had gone back out to the fields to finish chopping cotton. They worked their way side-by-side down adjacent rows, using chop hoes on cotton that had been planted thick but now needed thinning to get a good stand. They were grimy and silent from what had been a long morning of hard work, but neither complained as they sweated through the fields. They stopped suddenly when they heard Gladene ringing the dinner bell. They had already eaten lunch, but there was an urgency in the ringing that called them to something important, and they both dropped their hoes and jogged off toward the farmhouse, eager to have a break from the hard work.

Gladene met them at the hedge along the dirt road in front of their farmhouse. "Coach Erwin's here," she said and pointed to his black Chevrolet sedan parked beyond the hedge. "He wants to talk to both of you."

They glanced at the car. Everybody knew Ambrose "Bro" Erwin, and he would have made the fifteen-mile drive up from the little town of Beebe for only one reason. That winter, both boys had played for the El Paso school basketball team. O'Neale had been a green freshman, Johnny a lanky sophomore. Though O'Neale was eighteen months younger, he was huskier and stronger than Johnny, and that superior strength had been his main line of defense against the normal taunting of an older brother. What few quarrels they had as boys had seldom gone to scuffling. O'Neale would have won, and on a basketball court, even as a young freshman, he could be fierce and unyielding. There was no denying, however, that when it came to touch and finesse, Johnny was the better of the two players. Meanwhile, they played for the El Paso school basketball team, which didn't even have a gym; the team practiced outdoors. The two boys had gone down to the old national guard armory in Beebe, which had a concrete floor and low ceiling rafters, and they had led the El Paso team, with fewer than a hundred kids in the school, to victory over Bro Erwin's Beebe Badgers. Now the Badgers' coach had come calling on the two stars of the El Paso team that had beaten him.

It was nothing new. Bro Erwin often made excursions into the Arkansas countryside to find talented farm boys whom he had spotted in the county tournaments or playing against his own teams. The excursions weren't even controversial. Bro Erwin brought *opportunity*, everyone said, especially for boys from small rural schools that didn't go beyond the middle grades. The recruits would often be brothers or just friends, at work threshing or sawing logs or making hay or milking when Bro Erwin came by. He was a country boy himself, an avid fisherman and hunter, who hardly ever wore a tie. He usually just shambled up, dressed in a clean work shirt and trousers, to explain in an easy drawl that belied his education, "I just came by to see you boys . . . see how you're gettin' along."

Gladene followed Johnny and O'Neale inside the house. In the living room, around the library table that sat in front of the fireplace which served as a family gathering spot on winter evenings, the entire family—Howard, Ethel, their three other children, as well as Ethel's aging parents, Afton and Sally Neal—had already gathered in chairs.

Bro Erwin sat on the edge of one of the family's two rockers. "So, how you gettin' along?" he greeted Johnny and O'Neale when they entered.

"Oh, just fine," Johnny answered.

The two boys leaned against the dresser in the corner. Bro then talked briefly with Howard Adams about his cotton crop, the continued dry weather, and how much longer the hard times could possibly last for farmers. For Howard Adams, that couldn't be much longer. He'd bought the eighty-acre farm in 1927 for fifty-six hundred dollars; he made payments from the profits of the yearly harvest of thirty bales of cotton. Then, with the drought of 1930, they had managed to harvest only seven bales and been forced to give up the mortgage. They had stayed on the farm as renters then, but the

Dry Thirties had lingered, and dust devils the size of twisters had swept across the fields and sucked up precious topsoil from the Dakotas to Texas, leaving abandoned hay rakes buried to their axles in dusty graves. Meanwhile, Ethel's parents, Afton and Sally Neal, who had made good money in the cotton-gin business, had lost it all when Sally had had a paralyzing stroke. So in the midst of the Dry Thirties, they had moved in with the Adamses.

After supper Howard Adams lifted his mother-in-law from her chair at the dinner table and carried her to a chair on the front porch, where the entire family retired to watch the sunset.

"Oh, I'm such a chore," Sally Neal always sighed.

"No . . . no," Howard protested and lowered her into a rocker. Then for himself, he placed a chair upside-down on the porch floor and lay down against the chairback for support.

It was, Howard Adams knew as he spoke now with Bro Erwin, harder and harder to hang on. "It's a hard life," he told Bro, and then glanced at his two sturdy sons leaning against the dresser, "but it's made us all tougher."

Bro nodded. It was the perfect lead to why he had come. "OK, here's what I'd like to talk to you about." It was a speech he had nearly memorized: These were hard times, and, yes, they made *everyone* tougher and stronger. There was nothing wrong with rural life or El Paso or the Adams farm, which had no electricity or plumbing or telephones. There was nothing wrong either with the outdoor dirt court, which was the "home floor" where the El Paso team practiced. In fact, Bro Erwin felt, it was where *everybody* should start out, right at the simple root of things, without fanciness or luxuries.

He stopped and glanced at Johnny and O'Neale. "But I heard that the boys here would like to come down to Beebe and play." They both nodded. What country boy, consigned to chopping cotton or struggling to follow a horse and plow through the fields in that part of Arkansas, didn't want that kind of a chance?

"Down in Beebe," Bro continued, "our school's bigger. You'll get a chance to take more courses."

Howard Adams nodded. With only five teachers in the entire El

Paso school, there weren't any advanced courses, courses they would need if they were ever going to go to college. The only time O'Neale had ever been fired up to learn had been after a schoolwide assembly in which one of its five teachers had recited Poe's poem "Annabelle Lee." The rest of that day O'Neale had walked around the El Paso school in a daze, the lines of the poem swirling in his head. Still, the experience served mainly to remind him what little else there was to inspire him at El Paso, and Bro Erwin's talk of opportunity and inspiration in Beebe hit home.

"There'll be many more opportunities for you," Bro went on. "You'll get yourselves ready for college study."

Johnny nodded. "Well, we'd sure like to go down there."

"Seems like it'll be a better deal," O'Neale added.

Then Bro turned to the subject of basketball. "We have big crowds for our games." He didn't need to explain that when it was cold and a light snow fell in El Paso, only a shivering ring of spectators stood around the outdoor court. Meanwhile, the armory gym in Beebe may have had a concrete floor and low rafters, but it held hundreds of fans, who at times cheered and whooped so loud for the Beebe Badgers that you could have sworn those low rafters were shaking.

"We'll play bigger and better teams than you'll see up here in El Paso. There'll be college coaches who'll come to watch. They'll want you to look at their schools."

Howard did not need to hear any more, and he looked at Ethel. "Well, we hate to see the boys leave home, but there's no doubt it'll be a better deal." Howard paused and turned back to Bro Erwin. "So where'll the boys stay down in Beebe?"

"I've got other fellas comin' in," Bro explained. "I've got folks in Beebe lined up to room and board the boys." Bro also glanced at Ethel Adams. "They'll be plenty well taken care of. They'll study hard. They'll have good beds to sleep in. Their clothes will get washed. They'll get free haircuts." Bro nodded at the two brothers, still leaning against the dresser. Johnny was lean but well-muscled. O'Neale was broad and burly. "They'll get plenty to eat," Bro smiled, "though it doesn't exactly look like they're starvin' now."

That was especially true. While other farm families harvested their "truck patches" for roadside sale, the Adamses kept their tomatoes and peas and potatoes and sweet corn to feed themselves. Meanwhile, the entire family pitched in to harvest the cane from their sorghum patch, eventually taking the molasses to Conway to sell by the gallon bucket. It was the best cooking molasses in Arkansas, everybody said. Sure, these were hard times, but everybody was in the same fix, and nobody complained or talked about leaving.

The issue of who would *pay* for Johnny and O'Neale's keep in Beebe was never raised. Bro Erwin seemed to understand that however well-fed and husky the Adams boys looked, the family had no savings or extra money to support the boys away from home. Haircuts and plenty of food and good beds—they all would be taken care of. From Beebe largesse, if nothing else.

Finally, Bro got up to leave and pointed through the window out to the backyard. "Well, I see you got a nice basket ring up on the smokehouse. That's what I like to see. A handy place to get in plenty of practice."

They all laughed at the sight of the primitive but much-used court. Howard Adams explained that it was he who had come up with the idea of nailing the metal band from a wagon wheel to the side of the smokehouse, so his sons could shoot at it with a rubber ball half the size of a basketball. Shortly after he had put it up, neighbor boys were dropping by regularly for vigorous games that raised clouds of dust. Meanwhile, Howard laughed and explained that they never smoked anything in the smokehouse but instead stored their canned goods there and hung sugar-cured quarters of pork from ceiling wires.

Bro Erwin stared at the smokehouse basket and nodded. "Well, it looks to me like a good place for your boys to work out and keep in shape."

Bro Erwin left with the promise that he'd stay in touch. By the fall of 1935, sixteen-year-old Johnny Adams and his fifteen-year-old brother, O'Neale, began their junior and sophomore years, respectively, in Beebe, Arkansas. They lived with three other rural Arkansas boys in one-half of a duplex owned by an elderly couple who lived in the other half. Johnny and O'Neale shared a small bedroom and did their schoolwork with the other boys in a common sitting area. Exactly as Bro Erwin had promised, they ate bountiful meals, cooked by their landlady.

On weekends they hitchhiked home to help with farm chores and occasionally to attend an all-day singing and dinner on the grounds of the Mt. Sidon Baptist Church.

Back in their boarding house in Beebe, they spent weeknights studying hard. Johnny was a better student than his brother, especially in English and history, which he read late into the night. He was also better in basketball, and by the time the season started in November, he had grown to six-feet-three-inches and filled out his lanky frame. The high-school team practiced daily in the Beebe National Guard Armory, where soldiers in puttees and heavy boots regularly assembled and performed close-order drills on the concrete floor.

For two boys who had learned to shoot basketballs with only the sky overhead, those low armory rafters crossing the ceiling took some adjustment. O'Neale learned to use his weight and brawn to work mainly inside and close to the basket. It proved more difficult for Johnny, whose soft, outside, two-handed shot was deadly. He noticed that some of his veteran teammates, experienced at coping with the annoying rafters, had learned to change their outside shots by actually shooting up and through the rafters from certain spots on the floor. To Johnny, however, that seemed foolish. It would have forced him to introduce a wild variation in the steady mechanics of his shot. Instead, he learned that by flattening his shot, he could avoid the rafters and shoot the same way from anywhere, without any loss of accuracy.

Bro Erwin began every practice the same way: fifteen minutes of random warm-up shooting, with dozens of basketballs bouncing and colliding as he stood at center court watching his players. With his height and quickness, Johnny Adams liked to score from inside and out, and he prided himself on having a complete battery of shots with which to do so—sweeping bank shots, running shots off a swift dribble through the key, long two-hand set shots, whirling one-handers, fadeaways, all shot with a flat trajectory that meant no matter where he was, the rafters didn't bother him.

During a warm-up period one day in December, Johnny Adams noticed that a familiar figure had come into the gym. He had been immediately surrounded by Bro Erwin and veteran Beebe players at center court. His name was Gaylon Smith, and he had played basketball only one year at Beebe, in 1934. Johnny remembered him as the very same player with an unusual leaping shot who had been the mainstay of the Beebe team that El Paso had defeated a year earlier. At a stocky five-feet-eleven-inches, with fire-plug legs, he had also played football for Bro Erwin at Beebe and then gone on to greater glory as a star running back at Southwestern College in Memphis. Now, with the season over, he had returned to his hometown to visit with his old coach and bask in the glory of his football fame.

In a matter of minutes he had picked up a basketball and was shooting at a corner basket. Several of the Beebe players stopped their own warm-ups to watch this superb athlete shoot lazy baskets from every spot on the floor. At one point, almost as if he couldn't decide which of the many shots in his repertoire to try next, he stood stock still just in front of the basket for a moment before he suddenly jumped up and shot.

Watching from across the gym, Johnny Adams recognized the same strange shot he had seen when El Paso had beaten Beebe a year earlier. It was one he surely didn't have in his own varied repertoire, and it occurred to him that the shot might be a way to snag offensive rebounds. Then, while still high in the air, he could control the ball and put it back in the basket before dropping to the floor again.

Immediately, Johnny turned away from watching and experimented with it himself. At first, he put the ball straight off the backboard, then jumped to retrieve it with two hands and guide it back to the basket.

That's easy, he thought.

Then it dawned on him. *As an outside shot, it'll be hard if not impossible to guard.* So he stepped back to ten feet, jumped straight up, and shot the ball with two hands from over his head. The leap put him even closer to those annoying rafters. So to keep the shot low, like all his others, the new attempt was more of a flat throw than a soft fingertip shot.

That just doesn't feel right, he told himself. But he was determined to master the shot. For the rest of that warm-up period, he experimented with the shot from long range. After a dozen more attempts, he found that by holding the ball with his elbows cocked out and his fingertips splayed, then putting a topspin on the ball, he could still keep it soft and flat and out of the rafters. It also gave him the impression that, like a sinker pitch in baseball, the topspin would help make the ball bend off its flat plane and down through the basket.

When O'Neale noticed Johnny working on the shot, he asked, "What's that shot you're tryin' to do?"

"If I can learn it, it'll be impossible to guard."

"Where'd you get the idea?"

"Well, I watched Gaylon the other day, shootin' in close. That gave me the idea."

At first O'Neale watched skeptically. He also remembered Gaylon Smith's basketball exploits from the previous year. He had had a variety of bizarre shots all right, but were they sensible enough to bother copying? O'Neale remembered the time a year earlier at the county tournament up in Searcy, when the game had begun with the Beebe center tipping the ball back to Gaylon Smith. He had turned immediately and let go of a two-handed underhanded shot. Incredibly, the foolish shot had gone in. While the gallery roared, O'Neale dismissed it as "the luckiest shot I've ever seen."

Yet watching Johnny work on the unusual jumping toss, O'Neale could see how useful the shot might be. When he finally began trying it himself, using the same fingertip touch with the forward flick of his wrists for topspin, it felt even stranger than it had looked. Obviously, it wasn't a shot for him, mainly because he didn't have the same soft touch that Johnny had. If Bro Erwin needed brute rebounding strength from O'Neale, he could provide it. Or workhorse, smothering defense. Or close-in, burly muscle shots that left bodies scattered on the floor. But this new, deft shot was beyond him.

When Bro Erwin noticed Johnny Adams working on the shot by himself during subsequent warm-up periods, he watched carefully but said nothing. It defied most of the fundamentals of the game of basketball: a leap into the air was an act of desperation that closed out every other opportunity for maneuvering; managing a shot from that elevation would be an act of complicated gymnastics; and *topspinning* the ball instead of backspinning it was in violation of one of the cardinal rules of shooting.

So it came as somewhat of a surprise to the other players when, after days of quietly watching Johnny Adams work on the shot, their coach began to encourage the other members of his squad to experiment with it.

"I want you to get the ball, jump up, and shoot," he told his players one day. Beyond that, he gave no specific directions on execution. They were simply left to their own devices, which meant that some tried to imitate the same flat topspin version of Johnny Adams, while others struggled to find their own comfortable adaptation of the difficult shot.

Meanwhile, the Dry Thirties became drier. Weeks of one-hundred-degree weather and months without rain created a dark scud that turned midday into dusk. The Adams's well went down so low that they had only enough water for the house, and they had to drive their livestock to another farm for watering. Johnny and O'Neale hitchhiked home faithfully each weekend that first year in Beebe to help with the farm chores. On Sundays the entire family rode the farm buck wagon to services at the Mt. Sidon Baptist Church. The horse hoofs clopping on the dry road raised puffs of dust like powder explosions. Once in church, the pastor led the entire congregation in long prayers for rain, which went unanswered, and in March their parents finally gave up the farm and rented a small home in Beebe on the street directly across from the high school.

By Johnny's senior year in 1937, the whole of the lower Midwest had been turned into an arid dust bowl, and the Beebe Badgers behind Johnny Adams and his uncanny jump shot began a string of basketball victories as unrelenting as the succession of dry days.

"The team that beats Beebe will win the state tournament," the *Arkansas Gazette* predicted before the eight finalists met on March 12 in Pine Bluff to begin the competition.

The night before the team left for the tournament, Johnny and O'Neale came down with the flu; both sat motionless and sweaty in living room chairs in front of the fireplace.

"You're too weak to play," their mother worried. "You both need to go to bed."

"We'll have plenty of time to rest after the tournament," Johnny insisted.

Neither one, however, had the energy to leap or spring on a basketball court, and the Badgers were upset by Little Rock in the tournament. After they had returned home, a doctor had to be called, and he pronounced both boys sick with pneumonia. They were confined to their beds with fevers for nearly a week, and they drifted in and out of sleep as they struggled to breathe. Then one day the wind blew the stove smoke back down the stovepipe, and Johnny fell into a coughing fit as Gladene and her mother threw open the windows and doors in an effort to bring fresh air into the house. But the coughing jag went on and on, as if Johnny were trying to hack up the phlegm of defeat in the tournament. He had been so sick he had hardly been able to lope up and down the floor. Nor had he been able to find the energy in his spindly legs to leap high enough to experience that familiar moment when he seemed to have all the time in the world to cock his elbows and execute the wrist flick that gave the ball the topspin he wanted. He lay in bed, peaked and exhausted, hardly the dark-haired leaper with the ruddy good looks of an actor and the promise of a basketball future. It was as if the Great Depression itself were dragging him down into the same sinkhole of failure that was ruining half the country. Against the backdrop of such epic ruin, the joy of basketball was almost perverse, and the exultation of a jump shot was doomed to be short-lived.

Five years later, resurrected slowly from the nadir of the depression and pneumonia, "Jumpin' Johnny Adams" and his special shot were what Razorback fans pointed to when they considered their chances for an invitation to the fledgling NCAA tournament. Carpetbagging stars and transfer aliens were beginning to appear on university rosters, particularly in the East, but Arkansas could boast that their star and his jump shot were homegrown. He had come straight from Beebe to the university. A year later O'Neale had followed in his footsteps. The Razorback roster now featured players from places such as Des Arc, Ash Flat, and Little Rock. If the organizers of the fledgling NCAA tournament valued a team that was mainly homebred, then they *had* to invite Arkansas.

When the phone finally rang again in Professor Waterman's office, he jumped for it. This time it was what he had been waiting for: Prof. J. W. St. Clair, head of the Southern Methodist University athletic department and chairman of the district six NCAA selection committee.

The two men exchanged friendly greetings. Just a week earlier the Razorbacks had thumped SMU on successive nights to wind up their conference play; St. Clair had made no secret that he would nominate the Razorbacks to represent district six. But there were other considerations, he had cautioned. His was a single vote on the committee, and there were other teams to consider. Texas Tech, as an independent school, had backers. The University of Arizona had won the Border Conference. They would have their advocates on the committee. Then there was the whole business of the rival National Invitational Tournament. As struggling upstarts in the postseason tournament business, NCAA officials did not want to announce an invitation to Arkansas, then be rejected in favor of the NIT tournament.

How was Arkansas leaning? St. Clair wanted to know.

Professor Waterman explained that initially some Arkansas fans and sportswriters had been torn between the two tournaments. A few had even wondered if the Razorbacks couldn't play in both. Then "Gloomy Glen" Rose made it clear what his preference was. He conceded that the NIT had the excitement of Madison Square

Garden, for years the hotbed of American basketball, but it was designed, Rose said, only to fatten the pocketbooks of the private promoters behind it. Meanwhile, the NCAA, in only its third year of coast-to-coast competition, had neither New York basketball tradition nor a glamorous site to boast of. But to Arkansans like Glen Rose, the NCAA was free of the promoters whose major concern was not necessarily finding the best teams in the country but finding the ones most folks would pay to see.

Reassured, St. Clair went straight to the point: Arkansas was the committee's unanimous choice to represent district six in the NCAA tournament. Would they accept?

Waterman explained that it was an invitation he would carry immediately to the school's athletic board, but he was certain they would accept eagerly. Late that afternoon, as the shadows of Old Main's bell towers stretched across the hill, Waterman chaired a hasty meeting of the board, then sent a telegram of acceptance to St. Clair. The next day, the NCAA announced its pairings in the East and the West for their third annual tournament:

> At the East finals in Madison, Dartmouth would face Wisconsin, and Pittsburgh would clash with North Carolina.

> At Kansas City in the West, Creighton would face Washington State, and Arkansas would battle the University of Wyoming.

Neither Oregon, winners of the first tourney in 1939, nor Indiana, winners of the second, would be back. From the eight teams in the tournament, a new national champion would be crowned.

Ironically, Gloomy Glen Rose began his preparations for his game against Wyoming by giving his players four days off. His center, Treetop Freiberger, headed south for remote Booneville, to complete three weeks of student-teaching requirements. Meanwhile, Rose studied the roster of his opponents, winners of the Big Seven conference. They were small, with only two men taller than six feet, and without a Jumpin' Johnny Adams on their roster. They could all score, and their coach, Ev Shelton, ran an intricate pattern of fluid, moving screens and blocks that his opponents claimed again and again were illegal.

"We're a good small team," Shelton told reporters. "But Arkansas has too much height. You can't score if you can't get the ball."

Not to be outdone in gloom, Glen Rose countered, "I'm afraid Wyoming is too fast for us."

Despite Rose's cynicism, Arkansas was the early favorite to be the 1941 NCAA basketball champion. On Wednesday, March 19, Rose held his team's last workout in Fayetteville, then in the evening he presented Jumpin' Johnny Adams and the Razorbacks at a huge rally sponsored by the "Rootin' Rubes" in the Union Ballroom of the campus. In his send-off speech, Prof. Harrison Hale, head of the Arkansas chemistry department, called the Razorbacks the best team in the nation, with the best coach.

Then someone brought out a movie of the first half of the Razorback's victory over Rice back in February. It was the same game in which Long John Adams had scored nineteen points with that odd flat shot that "looked like it was fired by a crack rifleman." Odd shot or not, he could hit center bull's-eye with it, and when hats were passed around the rally so that folks could make "free-will" contributions for the team's spending money in Kansas City, the hats were filled.

The next afternoon the team left by car caravan to Bartlesville, where they boarded a train for the three-hour ride to Kansas City. They rolled north across the Oklahoma border into Kansas, through small towns whose clusters of white grain elevators in the distance looked like desolate biblical outposts. Those small towns made the eventual sight of the brand new thirteen-thousand-seat Kansas City Municipal Auditorium all the more spectacular. Built at a cost of $6.5 million, it was equipped with a theater, banquet rooms, track-and-field facilities, and a dance hall. The basketball arena had glass backboards, blue leather seats, and a new lighting system so powerful it illuminated the floor like a stage. It was as glorious an arena as any in the country, but when Glen Rose took his team onto the floor Thursday night for a late practice before facing the

Wyoming Cowboys, he had only one dour reaction: "I don't like the glass backboards."

The first NCAA tournament finals had been staged in 1939 in Patton Gym on the campus of Northwestern University in Evanston, Illinois. The expectation was that the heartland setting would separate it favorably from the crass commercialism behind New York's rival NIT. Oregon's eventual victory over Ohio State had the purity of wilderness Ducks versus agrarian Buckeyes, but only five thousand fans had turned out to see those first finals, and the tournament committee wound up $2,531 in the hole. The second year the site was moved to Kansas City, whose new prairie basketball palace with its plush leather seats invited wonder and the possibility of standing-room-only crowds. With Kansas in the finals, nine thousand local fans had turned out to see their beloved Jayhawks lose to Indiana, but the crowd was still far short of a sellout, and tournament organizers, who awarded each finalist $750 as its share of the gate, had to remind themselves they were still getting started. The annual tournament in Kansas City would gather basketball momentum, much as the first doubleheaders in Madison Square Garden had done.

By the third year, that momentum still hadn't developed, and despite the notables in attendance—Wyoming governor Nels Smith sat on his university's bench as honorary cocaptain, while Arkansas countered with university president J. William Fulbright on theirs—less than half of Kansas City's municipal auditorium was filled for the opening game of the Western tournament.

Fortunately, none of the Razorbacks—least of all Jumpin' Johnny Adams—shared their coach's cross-eyed, left-handed observations about the auditorium's glass backboards, and the first time Arkansas got the ball, guard Red Hickey walked his dribble the length of the floor and straight toward Johnny Adams to begin a play the two had used repeatedly throughout the season. Once Hickey reached Johnny at his left forward spot, Red stopped to set a screen on Johnny's defender. Then, like a quarterback he handed off to Adams who was cutting toward the free-throw line. It was the start of a classic pick-and-roll, and two dribbles off Red, Johnny braked and then leaped while Hickey rolled toward the basket. Both Wyoming defenders wound up hanging onto Johnny's arms as he went up, and his efforts to pass off to a wide-open Red on the roll—the back-up plan all season if Johnny wasn't open for his jump shot—looked as much like a futile shot attempt as a pass.

Both officials' whistles sounded like a wake-up call for the sleepy fans in the half-empty auditorium. Johnny made both free throws to tie the score at 2–2. Wyoming missed its next two shots, and each time back down the floor, the Razorbacks worked the ball at an hyp-notic snail's pace that brought a few catcalls. Despite the booing, Arkansas stayed with its game plan, and one minute later their "Treetop" center, rusty from his three-week layoff but half a foot taller than his Wyoming opponent, scored easily after almost a dozen passes that served to establish that Arkansas would never be so foolish as to try to run with the Cowboys.

Four minutes into the game R. C. Pitts dropped a long, high set shot through the Arkansas nets to make the score 6–2. Ev Shelton called a Cowboy time out; but no sooner had they returned to the floor than they turned over the ball, and Johnny Adams again took the hand-off from Red Hickey and went straight up. This time a sin-gle defender, slapping at the ball, caught one of Johnny's cocked el-bows. The blow momentarily corkscrewed his body so that he had to twist himself back to take dead aim for his bullet shot.

The shot was odd enough to begin with—a herky-jerk jumble of elbows and wrists and fingertips. Now, the corkscrew of his trunk made it almost antic. When the impossible shot slammed through the basket, O'Neale Adams expressed what every player on the bench knew: "Johnny's hot!" A second passed before both officials, mesmerized by the incredible shot, realized he also had been fouled.

Johnny converted the free throw to give the Razorbacks a 9–2 lead. Baskets by R. C. Pitts and Shorty Carpenter lengthened the Arkansas lead to 17–6 with ten minutes gone in the half. Ev Shel-ton quickly began making substitutions to find the right combina-tion of Cowboys to get back in the game. But not even the presence of a pint-sized, whirling-dervish Wyoming guard named Kenny

Sailors, with a jump shot of his own, could close the gap. Whatever Wyoming or Sailors did, Johnny Adams countered with another uncanny jump shot. As the end of the first half approached, Arkansas opened up a 29–12 lead.

The two teams traded baskets through the first minutes of the second half, and for a moment the character of the game changed. Lofty Arkansas's methodical attack made each basket seem labored, while tiny Wyoming blitzed down the floor and scored quickly with apparent ease.

A crowd initially sympathetic to Wyoming as underdogs found something else to cheer for now: maybe the Cowboys were the better team. Forward Curt Gowdy scored to close the gap to six points. When another Cowboy basket brought them to within four points, the lethargy of a mismatch suddenly became the hysteria of a toss-up. It was short-lived cheering. Johnny Adams dumped off to Red Hickey on their patented pick-and-roll.

37–31 Arkansas.

Then on successive possessions, Johnny Adams drilled two flat jump shots that opened up a ten-point lead and silenced the crowd. The eventual Arkansas victory was by fourteen points, behind eleven baskets by Johnny Adams, all but two of them jump shots.

The next morning, the Associated Press correspondent covering the game wrote that "spindle-legged Johnny Adams [had] unfurled a kangaroo shot" against Wyoming. Describing the shot as "heaves that seldom travel more than a foot above the goal," the correspondent went on to write that "Adams jumped over the Cowboy defense. . . . There is no stopping him, because his favorite shot can't be deflected."

Saturday was the first day of spring, and the Arkansas Razorbacks, full of the promise of springtime and of a shot that was described as unstoppable, were installed as slight favorites in the West finals against Washington State. But the Cougars won in a romp that required only a minimum of effort. Still, Jumpin' Johnny Adams scored twenty-two points, again mainly on his jump shot, and he was undoubtedly "the number one cager of the nation," the sportswriters wrote. His jump shots both nights of the tournament had left the fans "gasping for air."

One week after Washington State captured the Western crown in the 1941 NCAA tournament, they were defeated by Eastern champion Wisconsin, winners of the third NCAA national championship. Attendance was again disappointing, and the tournament momentum that NCAA officials had hoped for in Kansas City did not develop even the next year, when Stanford routed Kentucky. The organizers finally took their tournament to Madison Square Garden in hopes of cashing in on basketball's popularity in New York. There, as the format changed and more teams were invited to compete, the tournament began to grow in popularity, from 13,300 fans in 1943 to more than 18,000 in 1950.

The gambling scandals of the fifties prompted NCAA officials to begin moving the tournament from city to city. Standing the paradigm of the floating crap game on its head, the "Final Four" became floating *honesty* that tried to stay one step ahead of the crooks. Eventually, the steady expansion of the format to include more and more teams meant that the *journey* of all the contenders was as important as their final destination. Every March, half of the country sat down to follow the fate on TV of their favorite team on the "Road to the Final Four."

Meanwhile, Johnny Adams graduated from Arkansas as an English major and then went to work with Phillips Petroleum, starring for years with the Oilers in AAU basketball. He married, raised a family of his own, and yearly followed the basketball fortunes of the University of Arkansas, as well as the little town of Beebe.

In March 1979, gravely ill with inoperable cancer, he was inducted into the Arkansas Hall of Fame. Bald from chemotherapy treatments and weak from months of battling the cancer, he stood before the audience and mustered a strong voice to credit Gaylon Smith, who had preceded him at Beebe High School, with giving him the idea for the jump shot. He spoke of Bro Erwin's coaching genius and of the love and support he had enjoyed from his mother and father, and his own family.

Three months later, at the age of sixty-two, Johnny died. With his death the legacy of his jump shot contributions to the game of basketball seemed fated to recede into oblivion. Yet in 1996, seventeen years after Johnny's death, Curt Gowdy still remembered the bizarre shot that had bedeviled the Wyoming Cowboys.

"That shot changed the game of basketball," Gowdy claimed. "Who was the first jump shooter?" he wondered. "Coaches, broadcasters—every year at the Final Four, we stand around and argue about it. I say it was Johnny Adams."

Belus and the Sunshine Basketball Boys

At first, no one, not even Belus himself, could say for sure where his name had come from. Was he named after the mythical Assyrian king? After the Belus who was father of the tragic Queen Dido and the sculptor Pygmalion? Was his namesake the father of Poseidon, King of the Sea?

It was his mother who finally set the record straight. "One day your dad went to a Southern Baptist Convention," she explained, "and he heard a fine preacher named Belus. So when you were born, that's the name we gave you."

Many years later, when a little girl ran up to ask for his autograph after a basketball game, she said, "My dad says you're his sympathy."

Belus had no idea what she meant.

"My dad says you got the same name," the girl explained.

Belus laughed. "Well, that's only the second person I heard of who does."

Belus Van Smawley. He was born in a log home in Golden Valley, North Carolina, on March 20, 1918, the fourth of seven children of Dettie Smawley and her husband Abraham, a blacksmith and sharecropper. Golden Valley lay in the foothills of the Blue Ridge and Appalachian Mountains. Located in historic Rutherford County in the western part of the state, the valley was only three miles wide, and its place-name was too localized even to appear on state or Rutherford County maps.

The valley was more teacup-shaped than elongated. A ridge of mountains formed the lip of the teacup: Huckleberry Mountain, West, Lisenberry, Carson, Weast, Morlin, and Lone Mountains. An azure haze hung year-round over the ridges. The haze could have been mistaken for smoke, but it was really a veil-like mist. The First Broad River, more correctly a creek, drained the valley to the east.

In the early 1800s the valley was the chief site of gold for nearby Bechtler's Mint, the first private mint in the United States.

In his *Pictorial Field Book of the Revolution*, published in 1860, B. J. Lossing described the foothills as "covered with oaks, chestnuts, pines, beaches, gums, and tulip poplars . . . post oaks, laurel and sourwood." Lossing noted that the large trees stood far apart, and the smaller ones were not very thick, so that the "march of an army over those gentle elevations was comparatively easy." The marching soldiers to which Lossing was specifically referring were the Tory forces under the direction of a Scotsman named Maj. Patrick Ferguson, who had been directed by Gen. Charles Cornwallis to crush the rebellion of "Mountain Men" and Whig patriots harassing British troops east of the Broad River. In pursuit of the patriots, Ferguson and his forces eventually made what they thought was a secure encampment at the top of King's Mountain, forty miles west of Charlotte.

At eight o'clock on the evening of October 7, 1780, nine hundred patriots surrounded Ferguson's troops. The furious battle lasted only an hour and five minutes. When it was over, 1,105 men, including Major Ferguson, were lost at King's Mountain. The morning after the battle, at a place called Biggerstaff's Field, just south of Golden Valley in Rutherford County, victorious patriots returning from King's Mountain court-martialed ten Tory prisoners found guilty of murder and other high crimes, and then hanged them from a tulip tree.

The tree was still there, gnarled testimony to stern Revolutionary justice, when Abraham Smawley was born in Golden Valley 113 years later, in 1893. In 1912 Abraham met and courted Dettie McCurry, whose family also had been in Rutherford County for several generations. They were eventually married by a mountain preacher while they sat side-by-side holding hands in a buggy.

On a 125-acre bottomland tenant farm in Golden Valley, Abraham and Dettie Smawley began their family. First came Vosco, then Dolores, Cyrus, Belus, Fred, Virgil, and finally Lorene. The entire family slept upstairs in a loft bedroom accessible only by a ladder. As the family grew, Abraham made additions to the log house and then covered the exterior by splitting red oak shingles. While the boys did the farm work, Abraham set up a crude blacksmith's shop beneath a brush arbor made of lodgepoles. Not tall, but squat and lean even at two hundred plus pounds, Abraham Smawley became a Golden Valley legend for his strength and his habit of silence. He could throw a stubborn mule to the ground and shoe it by himself. Each of his sons learned to endure his embarrassing silences while sitting alone with him in a room. No one in Golden Valley thought of calling him anything but "Abraham," and from his children he expected the same unquestioning obedience that the Old Testament Abraham had given God.

Farmers for miles around Golden Valley brought Abraham mules and horses no one else was strong enough to shoe. He neither smoked nor drank, and his worst profanities were an occasional "dang" that rang like the strike of his hammer as he went about his blacksmith's work.

The closest neighbors to the Smawleys ran the nearby Church of the Brethren, whom everybody in the valley called "Dunkerds." The Smawleys were devout Baptists, but despite their differences, the farm folks in the seclusion of Golden Valley lived in harmony. After their yearly footwashing ceremony, the Dunkerds sat down to a bountiful outdoor supper. The Smawley children were invited to come and eat whatever leftovers there were.

The Smawleys never went hungry, but tenant farming was subsistence living. There was no money for clothes, and Dettie Smawley sewed for all her children. Because the overalls the boys wore had button galluses, they were teased and made fun of until the brothers learned to strike back as one force to protect their mother's honor as well as their own.

Each spring Dettie Smawley made all the children small aprons. Then, with the guidance of Abraham and to earn extra money, they spread out over the surrounding hills to dig up colonies of lady slipper, ginseng, and star root. After drying the medicinal herbs in the sun, Abraham sold them to agents who came through the valley.

In 1922, in search of better prospects, Abraham moved the family seven miles southeast over the Cherry Mountain Range to the little community of Hollis, where he continued his blacksmithing. Belus Smawley began school in Hollis when he was six. It was a one-room schoolhouse filled with kids from first grade to twelfth. The first day of school, no one could correctly pronounce his name.

"It's *Bee*-lus!" he had to correct schoolmates who stumbled over his name. But they kept calling him either *Bay-lus* or *Bell-us*, and he finally stopped bothering to correct them.

At the first opportunity, when the teacher turned her head, he was out the schoolhouse door. His mother met him at the steps of their farmhouse. "What are you doing home?"

Belus's first words as a child had been spoken with an odd hoarseness that often made them disappear into a thin whisper. Now, he struggled to put force into his whispery voice. "School's not for me!" he told his mother.

"You stay here," she told him and went to get Abraham from the blacksmith shop. He came quickly and stood over his reluctant son. "Boy, you're goin' back to school." Then he took up the hickory switch that all the boys had learned to suffer. "Now you better not leave again," Abraham warned his son when he was done.

After two years in Hollis, Dettie Smawley missed her relatives in Golden Valley, and the family moved back there. Shortly after, eldest son Vosco Smawley died of walking pneumonia, and he was buried in the Golden Valley cemetery beside the Baptist church.

Abraham Smawley had only had a third-grade education, but they said of him, "There's nothin' he can't learn to do." By the 1920s the Model-T was beginning to be popular in the Carolina foothills, and Abraham Smawley decided to learn automobile repair. After a brief schooling in Nashville, and still in search of better fortunes, in 1927 he moved the family five miles south to Sunshine.

On a treeless and flat knoll with a commanding view of the Cherry Mountains to the east, Sunshine was only a stopping point on dirt crossroads and consisted of a wood schoolhouse and church, a scatter of simple frame houses, and a cemetery. Still, compared to the isolation and hardships of Golden Valley, Sunshine offered the promise of commerce and prosperity. At the crossroads Abraham eventually opened a service station, a combination garage-black-smith's shop, a corn mill, and a grocery store, all of which his children helped run while they also sharecropped a fifteen-acre cotton field and ten acres of corn.

Shortly after the Smawleys arrived in Sunshine, the community built a new brick school beside the cemetery, and all the Smawley children, including Belus, continued their education in the new comprehensive school. Meanwhile, in a shed with a dirt floor, Abraham operated his garage and blacksmith shop, which had a huge forge and crank bellows that Belus often turned to get the iron so white hot that Abraham could lay the pieces on his anvil, sprinkle them with Borax powder, then use his powerful arms to hammer-weld them together.

Abraham also did repair work on the new T-model cars, removing the gaskets, grinding the valves, and greasing and oiling axles and bearings. When it rained in the wintertime, Abraham worked in bibbed overalls and a felt hat while neighboring farmers came to the service station to watch, loaf, or just talk.

It was the one time that Abraham, a stout Republican, grew voluble, and what would begin as rational political discussion would rise to shouting matches that could be heard all through the Sunshine village. Fearing fisticuffs, any Smawley children in the blacksmith shop cleared out, only to return hours later to find the quarrelers laughing and joking with one another.

With prohibition, the righteous and powerful Abraham Smawley was deputized as a rural policeman by Rutherford County authorities. He wore a badge, often carried a sidearm, and because of his familiarity with the hilly backwoods country of Golden Valley, he accompanied federal and county officials on expeditions to cut down stills. Afterward, the men gathered in Abraham's shop, cleared of children too young to hear about such things as bootleggers and crime, and they relived their adventures.

The children, meanwhile, were enjoying adventures of their own. Back up in Golden Valley, Abraham had found a perfectly round piece of dead wood and sawed four wheels out of it. Fixed to board axles and then stove-bolted to a riding plank, it made a perfect wagon, which all of the Smawley boys piled onto at once, one of them steering crudely with his feet as they shot down hillsides into the valley bottomland. Later, they modernized the wagon by outfitting it with the steel spring axles cannibalized from an old horse buggy. There had also been Hit The Pig, where the "pig" was a six-inch wooden football they placed on a wooden tee and then hit as far as they could with a stick. Or they cut loose a green grape vine from one of the trees overhanging a cliff in the hills, then made a run and swung out into space.

Because Abraham was so good with his hands, he also learned carpentry. Before long, poor mountain families who had lost loved ones came down out of the woods to order simple but carefully crafted wooden caskets. It was meticulous but grim work, and none of the Smawley children wanted to be around when he went to work constructing a made-to-order casket. The Sunshine graveyard next to the school, with its tombstones, crosses, clipped grass, and occasional bunches of sad flowers laid on the graves was enough of a reminder of funerals and death. The Smawley children became engrossed in their new friendships and in the vitality of the brand new Sunshine school, with nearly one hundred eager students from the surrounding foothills. None of them could have foreseen how soon death would strike their family.

Lorene, the last of the Smawley children, had been born in Sunshine, not long after their arrival there. At eighteen months, she was bright-eyed and pretty, and her older brothers especially liked to play with her in a sandpile near the house. In 1928 a diphtheria epidemic spread through the foothills like a firestorm, and the very society of the Sunshine school that provided joy and friendships also proved a public breeding ground for the disease. With Lorene already ill, Abraham and Dettie loaded the family in their new T-model touring sedan and headed for the county medical clinic in Rutherfordton.

All six children received shots. Then, with the five older children jammed in the backseat, and Abraham driving while Dettie held Lorene, they began the twenty-mile drive back up to Sunshine. It was as they moved through the city streets of Spindale that Lorene began a coughing spasm. When she turned beet red from the coughing, Abraham began searching for a sign that would indicate a family doctor. When he finally found one, he stopped the car and left the door open as he sprinted for the house and pounded on the door. An elderly doctor finally opened the door.

"I don't doctor on the road," the man said slowly.

Abraham could hear his daughter coughing still in the car. "*You don't doctor on the road?*"

"I don't doctor *people* on the road," was what he meant.

Abraham sprinted back to the car, his face twisted with anger, and he began a frantic search of the Spindale streets for another doctor's sign. Meanwhile, Lorene had stopped coughing. Her color turned from red to pale gray. In the backseat, the children fell silent. Their mother, who had been rocking desperately forward and back with the baby in her arms, suddenly stopped. "She's gone," she announced.

They buried her back in Golden Valley, in the backwoods cemetery beside her oldest brother Vosco, hardly remembered by the other children. But Belus could not bring himself to go to the funeral. It was not disobedience that could have been cured with a hickory switch, and Abraham and Dettie talked and talked with him, begging him to come, but he steadfastly refused. His voice was more whisper than usual. "I just don't want to see her dead!" he insisted.

None of the brothers remembered which of them began playing basketball first or exactly why. In some ways it seemed a natural progression from the simple and carefree recreational spirit of Hit the

Pig or swinging like Tarzan on a grapevine. Those things had been diversions from the sweat and monotony of farm work. When he was nine, Belus and his oldest brother, Cyrus, broke the ground for cotton planting with a horse-drawn turning plow. Then their father did the finer work of mulling the soil, using the single slip plow to lay out straight planting rows, which Belus and Cyrus followed with the horse-drawn planter.

When Hit the Pig became too simple a diversion from these chores, the older boys began playing basketball at a crude outdoor court beside the school up in Golden Valley. By the time they got down to Sunshine, they all played on an outdoor court in the small field between the new brick school and the cemetery. While the surface was less pockmarked than the Golden Valley court, the hoops at Sunshine were nailed to plank backboards, bolted without any overhang to huge square posts that threatened to flatten anybody who, in the heat of play, forgot where they were.

Soon, the Smawley brothers, joined by the Freeman and Philbeck boys and Willard Devaney and Willie Norville, were the "Sunshine Basketball Boys." None of them were in high school yet, but they were as good a team as anybody had ever seen. All of the Smawley boys had natural spring, inherited from the squat power of Abraham. But it was Belus who could jump the highest and snatch the ball out of the air, enveloping it with huge but soft hands that made the ball look like a tiny grapefruit when he shot it. He became the best shooter on the team, and the leading scorer.

At first, Abraham Smawley watched the new recreation of his sons with benign skepticism. "That old ball playin' won't ever get you nothin'," he told Belus. When it became more than idle recreation, with a Sunshine School uniform and games against surrounding country schools, all of whom they beat, the patriarchal Abraham put his foot down and insisted that the boys could only play on Saturday when the chores were done.

Some games were scheduled on weekday afternoons, and without Belus the Sunshine Basketball Boys had no chance of victory. But with his brothers covering for him, Belus sneaked off to those games, his uniform concealed underneath the first pair of Levis he had ever owned, bought with money earned digging herb roots up in Golden Valley. Once at courtside, he took off the Levis but kept them carefully folded and nearby in the event his father appeared from his blacksmith shop or he got called home and had to jump quickly back into his work clothes.

One day Belus and the school bully, Fay Robinson, got into a scuffle during recess in the woods west of Sunshine School, where the boys gathered to talk and smoke. In a matter of minutes Belus was mauling Fay. Mercifully, Belus suddenly let up and then began to get the worst of it himself, while Cyrus ran home to tell Abraham. By the time Abraham arrived in the clearing, everybody but E. G. Freeman and Belus had run back to school.

"What happened?" Abraham demanded to know. Belus explained that he could have beaten Fay but had let up out of mercy. "Then Fay beat the tar out of me," Belus admitted.

It had taken a long time for Abraham to accept the idea that recreation had any place in the lives of his sons. But the men of Sunshine who gathered in his blacksmith shop to argue politics and talk had told him over and over, "Everybody's braggin' on your boys, Abraham. About how good they are in basketball. They're the talk of Sunshine." And the likable E. G. was telling everybody that his friend Belus was "the most perfect boy I ever seen." Perfect or not, the talk of all Sunshine or not, Belus still needed to learn a few things, and in the woods Abraham took Belus's arm. "Come on!" he barked, and the two marched off toward the school, E. G. trailing behind.

Abraham Smawley found Fay Robinson sitting alone by a window in the school library. Abraham jerked Fay to his feet and delivered one mighty punch with the same force with which he wielded his blacksmith's hammer. Without a word to amplify his lesson, he went straight back to his shop.

Eventually, Abraham was brought before a magistrate in Rutherfordton and fined one hundred dollars for striking a pupil. If that was all it cost, it was well worth it to teach Belus that no matter whether it was the simple recreation of basketball or a fist fight against a bully or *anything*, just holding on in hard times and not being weakened by mercy or your own faint heart—*no matter what, you never, ever let up.*

Neither he nor Belus talked about the incident afterward, and it was left to E. G. to try to describe the depth of Abraham's anger. "That was the maddest man I ever seen in my life," he told his friends. "He knocked Fay clear to hell-and-gone."

Tired of the hard work and meager returns of sharecropping, Abraham called the family together one night in January 1932. For weeks he had been going back and forth between Sunshine and the village of Ellenboro, fourteen miles southwest, in the lower foothills. "There's eighty-five acres of good cropland for sale down in Ellenboro, just outside town. I'm done lookin' at it," he said, "and I'm discussin' buyin' it." He searched the circle of his healthy, strapping sons. "Will you all stay with me if I buy it? Until it's paid for," he added. "If you're not gonna stay with me, I'm not gonna try to buy it," Abraham finished. "Because I can't work it and pay for it myself."

It was the first time that Abraham had acknowledged that his own extraordinary strength and handiness were not enough to run a farm. The idea that this powerful man might be vulnerable in any way came as a shock to his sons, who studied each other nervously and waited to see who would speak first. None of them, not even Cyrus, was old enough to be thinking of going anywhere in the foreseeable future. They were farm boys who knew nothing of the larger world. The county seat of Rutherfordton was as far as any of them had ever traveled. What could they do *but* stay with Abraham?

Belus's hoarse voice was the first to break the silence. "I'll do my part to help," he said.

"It'll mean no more of this ball playin'," Abraham said. Did he mean, without the Smawley brothers, it would be an end to the promise of the Sunshine Basketball Boys? Or did he mean that moving to Ellenboro and becoming landowners would be an end to *all* recreation?

Belus spoke again, straining to get conviction into his hoarse, thin voice. "Well, we can play basketball anywhere." One by one, the others agreed, pledging themselves to stay with Abraham on the new farm until the thirty-two-hundred-dollar mortgage was paid. Before the summer was over, the family moved to Ellenboro. Dettie and Dolores rode down in a Chevrolet truck driven by Abraham and loaded with the family furniture. Fred and Virgil walked down, leading the animals beside a horse-drawn wagon that Cyrus and Belus handled.

The town of Ellenboro sat on the highest point of the highway between Charlotte and the Carolina mountains. Compared to the village of Sunshine, it was a metropolis, with stores, service stations, cafes, a volunteer fire department, a post office, two-story brick buildings with vaulted windows, and on the main street, a pedestal bird-bath fountain that spilled a sheer circle of water into a pool.

First settled as a nameless village in the mid-1800s, it was nothing but a store, a few houses, and a log school. When the rare mineral monazite was discovered in the nearby foothills, the village became an important shipping center. In 1874 the Old Seaboard Railway came through, a depot was built, and the once nameless village acquired the name of Ellenboro, after the terminally ill daughter of the engineer of the first train. From the Central Depot, where people came to watch the passage of freight and passenger trains, the village grew and was incorporated in 1889.

A second railway, called the Old Southern Line, was established a mile south of town as a freight and passenger line between Charlotte and Asheville. Its small depot was hardly the attraction of the Central Depot, but by the early 1900s, monazite production had begun to decline, and both depots gradually gave way to the town's nineteen churches and its new brick high school as the centers of activity. When the Smawleys arrived in the summer of 1932, it was a town whose heyday had come and gone. Its streets were quiet, and the steam whistles of the trains that came through on both lines had the sound of loneliness more than commerce. It now seemed an unlikely place for the making of basketball history by Belus Smawley, the transplanted Sunshine Basketball Boy who had natural spirit and spring.

The eighty-five acre Smawley farm was two miles straight south of town on the Ellenboro-Caroleen road. The Smawleys lived in a white frame house with six rooms and a front and back porch. Out the back of the house and down a hill the boys discovered a small creek everybody called "the branch," and the brothers laid plans to dam it with rocks for a swimming hole when the hot Carolina summer came. The farmhouse also had a huge dining room where the family ate ceremonial meals, including breakfasts of fried chicken and corn-on-the-cob. All the children talked at once from the excitement of new schools and the promise of being landowners. Just as Belus had predicted, the boys could play basketball anywhere, and at the dinner table he and Cyrus were the most animated, both of them having been installed immediately as regular members of the Ellenboro High School basketball team by Coach C. P. Misenhemer, who was grateful for the unexpected blessing of two new players.

That winter the family hauled rocks, filled in ditches, and cleared fields for crops. By spring Abraham had set up a new blacksmith shop on the Ellenboro-Caroleen road. Meanwhile, he stuck to his conditions of work-before-play for his sons, who pulled together to get their cotton crops worked over by Saturday so that they could play baseball for an Ellenboro farm team that wore uniforms sewn out of old fertilizer bags.

Basketball was still the first love of the brothers from Sunshine, however, and especially of Belus. He was the youngest boy in his class in his freshman year, but he was almost six-two and at thirteen was able to jump higher than any other boy or man in town. That summer somebody got together a pick-up team for a game against the "big city" boys on an indoor court down in Spindale. To his deep disappointment, Belus was considered too young to go, but Cyrus went with the team and came back to report with wonder in his voice, "They got nets on the baskets!" Belus kept his disappointment to himself but secretly vowed, "This is never gonna happen to me again."

His first efforts were directed at improving his already amazing leaping ability. An oak grove acted as a windbreak for the Smawley farmhouse and barn, and Belus committed himself to increasing his vertical leap by jumping to touch high tree limbs as he went back and forth on his chores. Once he could touch a specific limb, he picked an even higher one and began the process all over again. Daily, his strength and leaping ability developed until it was clear to him that in basketball he was better than any of his brothers and as good as any boy in the high school, even though he wasn't yet a sophomore.

From the Smawley farm, the Old Southern Depot was only a minute's jog down the Ellenboro-Caroleen road into town. It was a square white building with a pitched roof, lap siding, and an old freight dock that was beginning to collapse from neglect. When the Smawleys had first arrived in Ellenboro, the passenger train was still in service. Belus and his new friend Paul Padgett, who was nearly as big and strong as Belus, often rode the train to Shelby for a quarter to visit Paul's mother on weekends. Now that the passenger service had been discontinued and the depot abandoned, the building sat empty but with its doors open, the perfect nearby retreat for the Smawley brothers and their friends.

One day Belus and his brothers, along with Paul Padgett and half-a-dozen others, were idling away a Sunday afternoon in the shade of the loading dock. Challenges to feats of strength or agility were regularly laid down, especially to the Smawleys, whose father's strength was fading but still legendary. Which of his sons would continue the tradition? Cyrus was strong for his size. Belus needed no help to heave a two-hundred-pound bag of fertilizer to his shoulder before carrying it out to the field. Young Fred was already bigger than any of his brothers. And Virgil "ate like a plug horse," they said, "and was already as strong as a mule."

Lazing now on the Southern Depot dock, somebody spotted a twenty-foot section of steel rail left beside the dock by a track crew. At the least, it weighed four hundred pounds.

"I bet you can't pick that up," the challenge was laid.

In a second, Belus and Paul Padgett jumped off the dock. Belus squatted at one end of the rail, Paul at the other. On the count of three they both heaved and strained and then lifted the rail over their heads like weight lifters. It proved that as far as Smawley strength went, the legacy of Abraham seemed to be passing mainly to Belus.

Every fall in Ellenboro, school adjourned temporarily so that farm families could pick cotton. The Smawley boys dragged their burlap bags down one cotton row after another. At dawn Abraham took the bags bulging with cotton bolls into the Ellenboro gin, sometimes waiting all day for his turn beneath the suction chute. It was often dark by the time he returned to the farm for another load, which was taken for ginning the next day.

In the fall of 1934, after the hard work of cotton harvesting was finished, Abraham reckoned the income: twenty-five bales delivered to the gin, at twelve hundred pounds a bale, eight cents a pound. Even after fertilizer and seed expenses, it would make a tidy profit. Elsewhere, times were hard, but Abraham and his sons were confident that it would not be long before the farm was paid for. It gave him the confidence to relax his restrictions of work before play for his boys, and they began to look for opportunities to spend more time practicing basketball.

The problem was that the rain and drizzle darkened the skies frequently in the winter and made the outdoor high-school court unplayable. One rainy, overcast Sunday afternoon in late October a dozen boys of Ellenboro, including the Smawley brothers, were hanging out with long faces in the Old Southern Depot, staring out through the sliding door at the rain. Then one of them had an idea. "Why can't we play ball in here?"

Immediately, all of them began sizing up the old passenger waiting room. At most, it was only forty feet long, and perhaps twenty feet wide. Though half the size of a regulation court, it was all they needed. The rafters of the passenger waiting room were high enough, and enough light filtered in through the sliding door for them to see to play. The old floor planks were rough and uneven, but it would be better than the gravel court at the high school, where you had to pound the ball to keep your dribble. The only thing missing was baskets. They solved that problem when Fred Smawley remembered that the wicker baskets they used for cabbage picking on the farm were just the right size. "After all," Fred joked, "don't they call it *basket*ball?"

Fred sprinted through the rain down the Ellenboro-Caroleen road to get a hammer and nails. Someone else ran to get a ball. When Fred got back, they knocked the bottoms out of the tapered baskets and nailed them at a ten foot mark on opposite walls. Then the other boy returned with a rubber ball, smaller than a basketball and slick to the touch, but another acceptable improvisation on the real thing.

They played all that afternoon, their shouts and whoops echoing in a room that had for years heard only the flat voices of train passengers headed for Charlotte or Shelby or Asheville or other points along the Southern Line. Eventually the young boys of Ellenboro gathered regularly in the depot to choose up sides and play basketball. Belus Smawley and Eugene Padgett, who were proving to be the two best players in town, did the choosing of sides. They played for hours on end, stopping only to go as a pack across the dirt road from the depot to a farmhouse that had a deep well with a bucket on a windlass, which they cranked up for water.

Sometimes young girls from Ellenboro came and sat in the sliding doorway and watched silently. The boys hardly paid attention to them, dismissing their presence with the observation, "Well, wherever there's boys, there's gonna be girls." What mattered was who was scoring and how to stop him. What mattered was how long everybody could play before one or two or three had to go home for supper or chores, which, of course, broke up the teams. For most of the boys, it was idle recreation, leading nowhere except to the end of the day. It was a prelude to nothing, a self-contained event whose connections to the future, if indeed there were any, were less important than the excitement and play-by-play uncertainties of a rip-roaring game that provided relief from the tedium of another long Ellenboro afternoon.

The exception was Belus, whose father had once declared that ball playing was a dead-end, which would get him nothing. But the pounding of Belus's footsteps on the plank floor of the Southern Depot was so heavy, and the action so furious, that at times Belus could feel the little building shaking. It was action that *had* to lead somewhere, Belus dimly sensed, even if he could never have articulated exactly where. He was now the best player in Ellenboro. He had been one of the high-school team's leading scorers as a sophomore. No telling what scoring feats he would achieve as a junior. Beyond that, even greater things seemed to be in store.

That he was headed for greatness became even clearer one rainy Sunday afternoon during furious, depot-shaking action. Along with the honor of choosing sides, Belus and Eugene Padgett, by virtue of their jumping ability, faced off for the center jump after each basket. Belus controlled the tip back to one of his teammates. Then he cut for the basket and called for the ball.

He was just across midcourt of the shortened depot floor when he received the pass. Still, he was within easy range of one of the cabbage baskets. He put down several dribbles but found the congestion of the cramped depot court too tight to work his way through. Then he stopped and went into the same deep crouch he had used to explode off both feet when he jumped to touch higher and higher oak limbs. It had been jumping done for no specific purpose other than to earn the praise of those who said he was a "born leaper." And up until that moment when he crouched in the depot, holding the ball off one hip, it had seemed a vain power with no real purpose.

He exploded upward with a leap that shook the old floor. As he rose, the habit of reaching to touch an oak limb was too powerful to ignore, and he extended the ball in his two stiff arms, as if he were reaching again for a limb. For a split second at the top of his leap he experienced the sharp feeling of hovering over everybody else. How long he hung there, he felt, was not a matter of chance or gravity, but of his own strong willpower.

Finally, he cocked his arms and let the ball go with one hand. Still in the air, he watched it travel in a high arc to the goal. His landing shook the depot floor as he watched the ball swirl and settle into the cabbage basket.

Much later that afternoon, after he had tried the shot half-a-dozen times, he walked home with his brothers Cyrus and Fred.

"You can't do that," Fred told him.

"Can't do what?"

"That business where you jump up and shoot."

"Why not?" Belus wondered if there were some new rule he hadn't heard about.

"We can't guard you," Fred admitted.

Before long, the other boys were trying the shot in the dim light of the depot. None could master it, and one day one of them finally pressed Belus to explain his secret.

He remembered that feeling he had had the first time, of being able to stop himself in midair, and his voice seemed hoarser than usual as he struggled to explain it. "Well, I can hesitate . . . I can *hold in the air*," he said. "You have to *practice* it," he added.

Beyond that simple advice, he could not explain to anyone's satisfaction how he had learned to "hold in the air," or for that matter what had inspired him to come up with such an unusual shot. If anything, it came from years and years of watching his father be so willful and ingenious. But then why couldn't his brothers master it?

That winter, practice at Ellenboro High School began every evening at seven o'clock to accommodate the farm boys who had chores to do. Belus and Cyrus walked together along the Ellenboro-Caroleen road into town. They stuffed their pockets with peanuts and spit the shells into the grass shoulders of the road as they walked. Belus wore new black tennis shoes he had bought with money earned selling peaches in Forest City.

Using his new shot regularly now, Belus became the leading scorer for Ellenboro High School in his junior year. Few spectators attended the games on the outdoor gravel court behind the school, and there was no newspaper account of the many victories of the team behind the scoring of Belus Smawley.

His peculiar leaping shot became a trademark around Ellenboro, as unique as his odd voice. "The way he shoots," teammates and opponents agreed, "you can't guard him." Driving to his left, he would stop suddenly and leap with his body sideways to the basket, twisting only his head and arms for the shot. Going right, he stopped just as suddenly with his back to the basket, then leaped and corkscrewed himself around in the air so that he could draw a bead on the basket.

That season he scored almost at will. One night at the mill town of Caroleen both teams used the same dressing room, and the Caroleen school superintendent came into the locker room before the game to announce, "When we beat Ellenboro tonight, I'm gonna get me a new hat."

Belus's throaty voice answered for Ellenboro. "If you never get a new hat 'til you beat us, you better cut your tail outta here."

That night Belus scored twenty-nine points for the win, and by the end of the year his reputation as a star basketball player was widespread in Rutherford County. He was one of the Sunshine Basketball Boys, the son of Abraham Smawley, had come down from the foothills, and now had a shot nobody could stop. His old friend E. G. Freeman from Sunshine had come down to watch Belus play and then bragged, "He's the best there is."

So it appeared as if his promising basketball career would be cut short when he told Cyrus the following summer, "I'm not goin' back to school this fall."

Cyrus showed no surprise. Several years of good cotton crops had relieved them of their pledges to stay with Abraham until the farm was paid for. Soon enough, they would all be leaving.

"Well, what are you gonna do?" Cyrus asked.

"I already got a job at the Burlington Mill in Caroleen."

"Doin' what?"

"Workin' in the spinning room, oiling and banding. I'll be makin' twelve dollars a week."

"Well, if you can make a dollar, why not?"

However good he was, basketball led nowhere. "That old ball playin' will never get you nothin'," Abraham had proclaimed. Nor would school, for that matter. Mathematical formulas and fancy stories and ancient history—they were all self-contained activities, too, whose connections to anything productive seemed remote. Nowhere in the experience of school had Belus ever felt the buoyant power of a will strong enough to hold himself in the air. If anything, in school it was exactly the opposite, as if his willpower was being frustrated.

Few in Rutherford County ever saw school through to the end. Meanwhile, there was a future in work for money, and no one—not Abraham or Dettie Smawley, not even his Ellenboro coach—challenged him or tried to talk him out of leaving school.

So it was left to his old friend E. G. Freeman to fashion an epitaph for Belus Smawley's apparently brief basketball career. "He was the best I ever seen." E. G.'s eyes went distant with recollections of Belus's play as one of the Sunshine Basketball Boys. "He'd go up like a kangaroo and whirl in midair! I believe you might say he invented that shot. I never heard tell of another one like it."

Only Belus knew somehow that his basketball days weren't over. Even as he worked in the noisy spinning room of the big Burlington Mill in Caroleen, surrounded by men for whom the future held nothing but millwork, even as he worked he knew it was only a stage, like going off to school. His mother made him sandwiches every morning to take to work. A friend named Dutch Allen picked him up at dawn and drove him to work.

Then one day sponsors of an AAU basketball team called the "Spindale Firemen" approached him. "We'd like you to play with us," they offered. For a moment Belus was reluctant. Only one of the Spindale Firemen was in fact a fireman, or from Spindale. The rest were experienced college players from Duke and Wake Forest and the Carolinas. It was the best team he had ever heard of, making a name for itself since 1932 in AAU competition against teams from as far away as Georgia. There had even been exhibition games in front of huge crowds against the original New York Celtics and a team of bearded stars called the "House of David."

"I'm only eighteen," Belus hesitated.

But they had seen him play with Ellenboro. "You're good enough," they assured him, "*no doubt.*"

For two years he played with the Spindale Firemen, three games a week, forty and fifty games a year. They played in front of rabid basketball fans who had crowded into the balcony of the Spindale House, a red brick community center with elegant white colonnades that made it look like a temple. It was a long way from basketball with the Sunshine Basketball Boys, or the gravel outdoor court in Ellenboro, and especially the old Southern Depot.

He became the youngest of the Spindale Firemen, the least experienced player, but by virtue of his jumping ability and that peculiar shot of his, he was soon the leading scorer. Guarded by much taller men now, and often double-teamed, he learned to fall backward on his spinning jump shot, using *both* hands on the shot because he felt that he could guide the ball better, and that he needed more power.

They nicknamed him "Turnip," because he was the hillbilly with the rubbery, hoarse voice who had learned his basketball in Golden Valley and Sunshine, and they kidded him about his "blind shot."

"You can't even see the basket," they told him. "Who showed you how to do that?"

"Nobody!" he insisted.

One night, two former Sunshine Basketball Boys, E. G. Freeman and Willie Norville, came down to the Spindale House to see Belus play. Warming up, Belus was decked out in a magnificent blue satin uniform, and the crowds were already hanging out over the balcony.

From courtside, E. G. and Willie got Belus's attention. "Where you from?" they joked, as if to remind him of his past.

"Golden Valley," he answered without smiling.

Once the game started Belus began scoring his fall-away jump shot from everywhere, and the crowd roared its approval.

"Belus, where'd you say you're from?" Willie shouted it again.

"Golden Valley, by God!" Belus managed to shout back in his thin voice. He let them know he still hadn't forgotten Golden Valley and Sunshine and his humble beginnings.

Despite the razzing, despite mocking Belus's "blind shot," other team members were soon trying to copy it. The only successful imitator was L. C. Davis, a small Spindale forward who needed some advantage to get his shot off over much taller men. After studying Belus carefully, Davis developed a blind shot of his own. His version began with a fake one way before whirling back the other direction and twisting in the air.

Izzy, his teammates began calling him. *Is he gonna fake, or is he gonna shoot?*

"There he goes with that blind shot again," they mocked him, too.

In 1937 Belus Smawley and the Spindale Firemen were invited to Atlanta to play in an AAU tournament. Trailing by one point with only seconds left in a game against the eventual tournament winner, Belus was fouled while shooting one of his fall-away blind shots. He stepped to the free-throw line for two free throws that could win the game. Swinging the free throws in an old-fashioned underhand style, he missed them both and the Spindale Firemen lost. On the long drive back to Rutherford County, Belus swore over and over, "That's never gonna happen again either."

Back in Spindale he began practicing a two-hand free throw from up over his head. It was the same motion as with his "blind shot," and the new technique instantly improved the accuracy of his free throws. It also gave him greater range and control on his jump shot. Before the season was over, college recruiters from half-a-dozen colleges, big and small, were after him.

The catch was that he still had no high-school diploma, and they all told him the same thing: "You're gonna have to go back to high school." So early in the spring of 1937 he went to see the principal of Ellenboro High School.

"I'd like to come back to school," he told the principal.

"Are you kidding?"

"No, sir. I've got invitations to go to college. There's two months of summer school comin' up. If you'll let me come back, I'll be a model student."

He was almost twenty, an improbable candidate for a model student, especially in light of his indifference to study his junior year, when he had flunked English. But Belus was determined, and the principal called in Mr. Crow, the English teacher who had flunked him. With cold eyes that Belus felt looked right straight through him, Mr. Crow greeted his former student and shook his hand.

"Belus wants to come back to summer school," the principal told Mr. Crow. "What do you think?"

Mr. Crow only nodded.

"But we've got a problem," the principal explained. "He lacks a unit in junior English. How are we gonna get him *two* units of English?"

Mr. Crow turned his cold eyes on Belus. "Do you really want to come back to school?"

"More than anything else."

Mr. Crow looked at the principal. "I'll tell you what. If Belus can pass my senior English this summer, we'll give him two units for English."

Possessed by that same feeling that he was headed somewhere other than merely the end of the day, or the end of the summer, he passed the course with an A and that fall accepted an athletic scholarship to attend Appalachian State, a small school up in Boone, North Carolina, only miles from the Tennessee border.

Coach Flucie Stewart, who had been at Appalachian State for years, worried that Belus would repeat the shaky academic performance of high school. "Now one thing, Belus," he warned him. "I don't wanna have to come and get on you about your studies at the end of each quarter."

"Coach Stewart," Belus said, his eyes as cold as Mr. Crow's, "I'm comin' to Appalachian for two reasons. Number one is to graduate." He stopped, his mind clearer than it had ever been about where his life was headed. "Number two is to play the best basketball I can for you."

In September he said good-bye to his parents in front of their farm home in Ellenboro. Then he climbed in a truck with four other new students and began the drive up to Appalachian State.

They were just out of Ellenboro when two assistant coaches from the University of North Carolina intercepted the truck. For weeks they had been trying to talk Belus into playing for the Tarheels in Chapel Hill, so now they were making one last effort to convince him. "North Carolina is a big university," they reminded him. "Known all around the world." The implication was: Who the hell had even *heard* of Appalachian State? "At North Carolina you'll be able to get the finest education."

It flattered him to think that they wanted him so badly they had chased him down on the road. Deep down, the University of North Carolina had been where he really wanted to go all along, he had convinced himself, and he did not put up much of a fight.

"I already sent a suitcase full of my clothes on up to Appalachian."

"Get in," they said and ushered him into their car. "We'll go get your clothes."

They drove to Appalachian, picked up his clothes, and the ecstatic North Carolina coaches put two cigars under Coach Flucie Stewart's door. They also left him a note saying, "Thanks for letting us have a good player."

In Chapel Hill, as part of his athletic scholarship, Belus went to work in the cafeteria to earn his meals. But one night in the second week, as he stood in front of the food cashier with his tray, she told him, "You're gonna have to pay for that."

"I haven't got any money. I can't pay for it."

"Well," she said, "go ahead and eat tonight. But tomorrow, you pay."

It made him angrier than he had ever seen his father. In the room provided for him under the baseball stadium, he shouted and swore and stomped. In a matter of minutes, the two coaches who had lured him away from Appalachian showed up. They put him in their car again and drove him around Chapel Hill, repeating their arguments about the university's worldwide reputation. And, no, he would not have to pay for his meals, they reassured him.

Calmer now, Belus nodded as they spoke, but he knew what he was going to do. It had been a whirlwind two weeks of first here, then there. Where was that flow, that direction? Where was that sense of purpose he had always felt so keenly in the old Southern Depot in Ellenboro? Twice now, it had appeared to come to a stop for him. The first time was after dropping out of Ellenboro High School, the second, with the circular turmoil of the last two weeks.

He listened without argument to all their reassurances, his

mind set as strongly as his father Abraham had ever set his. *I am Belus Van Smawley*, he told himself, *originally from Golden Valley, by God! And after that, simply one of the Sunshine Basketball Boys. I know where I belong.* They let him out of the car back at the baseball stadium. From his room he immediately called Coach Stewart at Appalachian State.

"He's not here right now," Stewart's wife answered. "Give me your number. He'll sure want to call you."

Belus paced nervously for thirty minutes before the phone rang. It was Coach Stewart. "Belus," he asked, "what's up?" His voice was cautious, reflecting the irritation he still felt at having lost such a promising prospect, whose strange name and odd voice were complemented by an absolutely unique shot.

Belus wasted no time. "Coach, would that scholarship still be good?"

"You're damn right! Now you get on the first bus comin' up here."

Belus Smawley majored in history and physical education and played four years of intercollegiate basketball at Appalachian State College in Boone, North Carolina.

Unable to pronounce his odd name correctly, teammates soon settled on "Bee" as a nickname. Their new star, at six-feet-two-inches and more than two hundred pounds, had the size and strength of his father. He even had to have special trunks made to accommodate the muscular thighs he had developed while jumping to touch tree limbs in Ellenboro; even so, in the team picture of the Appalachian Mountaineers his pants were still as tight to his legs as bike shorts.

In 1943, after the Appalachian coach was drafted for the war effort, the athletic director offered Belus the job as player-coach for the Mountaineers. "I'll coach," Belus agreed, "if you'll give me the authority I need," he added.

"The authority to do *what?*" the athletic director wanted to know.

Belus's explanation was a reflection of the absolute obedience he had given Abraham Smawley. "If a player doesn't do what I tell him," he said, "he's no longer on the team."

That afternoon the athletic director explained to the team Belus's new role as player-coach. "If you don't do what Bee tells you," he added his own authority to Belus's, "you lose your scholarship."

Behind Belus Smawley's scoring, Appalachian State went all the way to the semifinals of the National Association of Intercollegiate Athletics (NAIA) tournament in Kansas City in 1943. Even though they lost, the sportswriters selected Belus Smawley, whose jump shot had changed little since the Ellenboro Depot days, as most valuable player of the tournament.

After graduation in 1943 Belus joined the navy and played basketball for two years with the Naval Air Station in Norfolk, Virginia. "It was as good a team as I ever played on," he would later recall and then recite the names of his teammates: "Ray Lucas. Ben Cunningham. Don Lockard. Charlie Ward. Bob Carpenter. Johnny Barr. Bubba Hart—I was gonna play at one guard. At the other guard was gonna be the greatest player there ever was, Hank Luisetti. Then he got spinal meningitis and we lost him. Or we'd have *really* had a ball club."

It was with the naval team that Belus made the last refinements of his unique jump shot. He found that whether he drove left or right, if he stopped suddenly and then pivoted back in the direction he had come, he could leave his defender standing helplessly on the floor as he rose and twisted in the air to draw a bead on the basket.

In January 1945 Belus and his Naval Air Station teammates were in the base recreation office, poring through the team's scrapbook. They had it opened to a picture of Belus, suspended in the air, twisted around in the act of his strange shot, when a statuesque brunette came into the office looking for a job. Belus was the first to spot her, and he quickly approached her with the scrapbook. "You put your trust in that man," he told the startled beauty as he pointed to the picture of himself, "and he'll take care of you the rest of your life." From then on Joyce Seymour called him "Smawley," and not long after their first meeting, Smawley went to meet her family in Norfolk.

After Joyce's mother spent the weekend listening to Belus talk in a high, hoarse voice that made him sound like Rochester from the popular Jack Benny radio program, she had only one reaction: "He seems like a nice enough person," she told her daughter, "but I don't know why in the world anybody would wanna talk like that."

Within a year, Belus and Joyce were married in a small church in Forest City, North Carolina, where Belus taught high-school history and coached basketball. One day in the fall of 1946, he was helping out during football practice when he was approached by two men.

"How would you feel about playing some basketball over in Asheville," they offered. "We're starting a semipro team. We're gonna travel around the Carolinas, playing teams."

Belus hesitated. "Well . . . I dunno."

"We'll pay you $250 a month." On top of his teaching and coaching salary, it meant he'd be making more than $500 a month; his first thought was, *Lord, I'm rich!*

That fall he played throughout the Carolinas with the semipro team from Asheville. Meanwhile, his reputation continued to spread. In St. Louis one afternoon, officials of the St. Louis Bombers met after practice in the team's locker room in St. Louis Arena. Among those present were Paul Buck, the team's general manager, and Coach Kenny Loeffler, who had starred at Yale and then taught in Yale's law school before switching to coaching. It was only a few weeks until the first games in the newly organized Basketball Association of America, and the Bombers were still trying to strengthen their roster.

After Buck and Loeffler traded the names of possible new players, they were joined by forward Johnny Barr, who listened a moment before he suddenly broke into their conversation. "I know a guy . . . ," he began excitedly. "I played with him in the Navy in Virginia. He'd stand with his back to the bucket and jump up and turn around and shoot. When he's on, you can't stop him."

That night, during a March of Dimes charity game in Spartanburg, South Carolina, Belus was scoring from everywhere with his corkscrew shot when his coach abruptly took him out of the game. "Go to the office," the coach explained before an obviously angry Belus could object to his removal. "You got an urgent phone call."

In the office, dripping sweat onto the telephone, Belus listened as a strange voice began, "This is Kenny Loeffler with the St. Louis Bombers." Belus had never heard of either Loeffler or the Bombers.

"How would you like to come to St. Louis and play basketball for us?"

"I have not followed pro basketball or ever heard of your Bombers," Belus admitted in a high, rubbery voice that for a moment made Loeffler doubt his own offer. How could such a rube be good enough to play professional basketball?

Yet, Johnny Barr had insisted that the "rube" had an unstoppable shot. "What would it take to get you to come to St. Louis?" Loeffler persisted.

"I haven't thought anything about it. I'm playin' pretty well here. I'm makin' good money. I bought a home. I'm pretty well satisfied."

"Let me ask you something," Loeffler continued. "Would you consider it if we gave you a thousand dollars to sign, and five thousand dollars a year?"

Belus began to waffle. "Well, let me think a little on that. Call me back in two days."

"You're crazy if you don't go," his old Spindale Firemen friend Izzy Davis told him. "That's more money than you'll make in two years teachin' school."

"Bay-lis," Loeffler began two days later when he called back, "have you made up your mind?"

"I've decided I'll come."

His first game with St. Louis in Philadelphia was a nightmare. Loeffler did not put the new player, whose name nobody could pronounce correctly, into the game until the last five minutes in the first half. Belus failed to score a single point. In the locker room at halftime, he sat seething with anger, comforted only by the thought that at least the man he had defended—the Warriors' sparkplug guard George Senesky—hadn't scored either.

With his team badly behind, Loeffler looked at all his players and then began tearing into Belus. Belus jumped up. "I haven't played!" His normally foggy voice broke into a shout. "Get on these guys that played!" But Loeffler continued haranguing Belus, who interrupted his coach a second time. "I didn't score! But my man didn't either. It'd still be nothin' to nothin' if everybody had done that."

Loeffler was momentarily stopped by Belus's defiance. Then he resumed his tirade.

"Give me a ticket back to St. Louis," Belus interrupted his coach a third time. "I'm goin' home."

Loeffler stuck out his chin. "What are you, a man or a mouse?"

With only a bench between them, Belus snarled back, "You step across that bench, I'll show you what I am."

The rest of the team froze. For a moment, both men seemed on the verge of leaping the bench to attack each other. But then Loeffler stepped back and managed to turn the discussion to *team* errors, while Belus stood glaring at him with his fists still clenched.

Back on the floor, Johnny Barr told Belus as they were warming up for the second half, "You just have to overlook what he says. He loses his cool. He'll calm down in a bit."

After the game Loeffler took Barr aside. "What kind of a man did you bring me?"

"Coach," Barr answered, "I brought you a man that'll give you one hundred and ten percent. But he won't take any bullshit."

Not long after, Loeffler called Belus up to his hotel room and asked him to sit down. "Bell-us," he began, "I want to talk to you. I just want you to remember. From the time the game starts 'til it's over, you don't pay attention to what I say. I lose my cool, and you just get out there and play like I know you can." From then on, Belus played regularly, and by the end of that first year the rookie with the shot as strange as his first name was leading the Bombers in scoring.

"He hangs in the air like a balloon," one of his teammates complained after trying to guard him in practice. "I timed myself against the guy. When he stopped and twisted up into the air, I counted two before I jumped. I was up and down again before he released his shot, and the damn thing was good."

At the end of that first season, C. D. P. Hamilton, the owner of the Bombers, personally drove Belus to the train station for the ride home. On the way Hamilton raved about all of Belus's rookie accomplishments. "Next season," Hamilton gushed, "Bell-us Smawley could be one of the best in the league."

"Well, then, Mister Hamilton," Belus drawled, "you'll have to give me a raise."

They both laughed, but over the summer Belus drafted a letter to Mr. Hamilton asking for a thousand dollar a year raise and a two-year contract. Weeks passed with no response from the Bombers, and that fall Belus returned to teaching and coaching in Forest City, convinced his professional basketball days were over.

In October, however, Coach Loeffler finally called from St. Louis. "We need you, Bay-lus," he begged. "You can help the ball club. We'd like for you to come back."

"Well, coach, I don't know. Only thing I'll consider is a two-year contract and a thousand dollar raise each year." Loeffler promised to pursue the issue with the St. Louis ownership, but a week later he called Belus again and pleaded with him to join the team. Belus reminded him of his terms.

"I haven't made any progress on that," Loeffler apologized and hung up.

The next day the principal used the school's intercom to interrupt Belus in the middle of a history lesson. "You've got a visitor." It was Loeffler, who met Belus on the steps of the brick school. "How in the world you doin'?" Loeffler greeted Belus and shook his hand.

"Well, just fine, I guess."

Loeffler then went straight to the point. "We really need you."

"Coach, I already told you. If you want me to come back, send me a two-year contract with a thousand dollar raise. And give me a thousand before we start," he added a new condition.

Loeffler went back to St. Louis with the news that the longer they negotiated with Belus, the more he demanded. Two days later Loeffler called a final time. "Bay-lus," he said, "get on the train. It's all arranged."

Belus Smawley played four years with the St. Louis Bombers and soon drew the nickname "Waddlefoot" because of his habit of tossing his shoulders and duck-walking in anger when he missed a shot or failed to stop his man. His play was so unique that the *St.*

Louis Globe-Democrat claimed that even if the lights went out in the St. Louis arena, "few fans wouldn't be able to recognize [Belus] by his walk or his shot." He was among the top scorers during the short history of the BAA, but no matter how prolifically he scored with his twisting jump shot, it seemed as ungainly as his odd name and his hoarse drawl. Belus Smawley remained the most underrated player in the BAA.

In 1950 Belus was traded to the Syracuse Nationals, who relied upon their agile "scoring forward" Dolph Schayes for offense. There were few provisions for a guard to leap up with a spiral shot from outside. One night, after only a month with the Nats, Belus came down from one of his corkscrew jump shots, twisted his ankle, and staggered into the lap of Baltimore coach Buddy Jeannette.

"Take it easy on that ankle," Jeannette said and helped Belus regain his balance. It was concern that seemed strangely inappropriate from an opponent, but it wasn't until the next day that Belus understood the reason for it. Called from the floor to the Nats' front office during practice, Belus was greeted by Baltimore's Jeannette.

"You belong to *me* now," Jeannette smiled.

"Well, thank God," Belus said. "I'm the happiest man in the world to get outta here." Nats' owner Danny Biasone seemed offended and wanted Belus to explain. Belus grinned with the recollection of thousands of shots, from as far back as his first games with the Sunshine Basketball Boys. "I've never played before when I felt like every time I took a shot, I should apologize to somebody."

Freed of the shooting guilt that plagued him in Syracuse, the first time the Nats came to Baltimore Belus scored thirty points on his two-hand spiral jump shot. It was a wonderful object lesson, nearly as dramatic as the time his father had coldcocked the school bully in Sunshine. Yet, throughout the rest of his NBA career, which ended in 1952 after two years with Baltimore, he would remain as unassuming as if he were still one of the Sunshine Basketball Boys, just a quiet, unheralded guard whose first name nobody could pronounce.

He and Joyce moved back to North Carolina where they began a family, and Belus resumed a teaching career that eventually led him into administration. For years he was the principal of a junior high in Mooresville, North Carolina, and on field trips to Raleigh students from his school visiting the North Carolina Sports Hall of Fame were stopped dead in their tracks by the huge picture of the husky player with the powerful legs, frozen high in the air on a jump shot.

"That's our principal," they shouted and pointed. "That's Mr. Smawley!"

But if anybody asked him to see his scrapbook, his explanation was as artless as his hoarse country drawl. "You know, I don't have a scrapbook. I've never been one to do that type thing. You were supposed to be quiet individuals back then."

"But, Mr. Smawley," the young admirers protested, "you're in the Hall of Fame!"

His droll answer came as if Abraham Smawley were speaking through him. "Yeah, that and a quarter will get me a cup of coffee."

Kenny and Bud

At six-five, Bud Sailors was the tallest human being most of the folks on the High Plains around tiny Hillsdale, Wyoming, had ever seen. Since his sophomore year in the Hillsdale Consolidated District, with only forty students in the entire school, Bud had been a basketball-court Gulliver. Following Coach Floyd Domine's directions to "hold the ball up high and just shoot," teammates and opponents scrapped and struggled at his feet.

His occasional habit of lowering the ball to his hips where opponents could swat it away from him needed correction, and Coach Domine encouraged Bud to work on the flaw on his own time, over the spring and summer before his senior year.

So it was in May 1934 that Bud approached Domine in the Hillsdale gym. "I would sure like to have a basketball to practice with," he told his coach.

Domine picked up one of the loose basketballs. "Where?"

"We got a hoop we're gonna put up on the windmill."

The wooden windmill of the Sailors 320-acre farm, four miles south of Hillsdale, was visible for miles around. All winter long, Bud had been planning to nail together a backboard and then hang it off the windmill.

"If we can have a ball," Bud explained, "we'll practice there."

"We?"

"Me and Kenny."

Domine nodded. He knew Bud's little brother Kenny well. He was the best of the pack of half-a-dozen sixth and seventh graders who were waiting every morning when he opened the gym before school. They played a game called "keep-away," the object of which was to be a dribbling jackrabbit while the pack of hounds chased you in circles all over the court until you lost the ball. Little Kenny Sailors, who was a foot shorter than his big brother, was a masterful dribbler and quick, too. Once he got the ball, none of the pack could take it away from him. But Domine balked now at the idea of Kenny Sailors dribbling the leather ball on the farmyard gravel until it was shredded.

"Well, I'm not really supposed to." Bud let his lanky frame sag with disappointment. Domine held the ball off his chest. It had hand-sewn seams, a canvas bladder, and a stem that you blew into and then laced back up after the ball was fully inflated. "These aren't expendable, you know."

"Well, we'd be durn happy to have one for a while."

Domine began turning the ball in his hands.

"We can't just go out and buy one," Bud added.

Domine stared at his star, whose dedication to basketball was so complete that for two years, before the family had scraped together enough money for an old Chevy, he had been riding bareback into Hillsdale every evening so that he could attend basketball practice. Bud's long, powerful legs almost dragged in the snow. Then he rode back home in the early winter dark. There wasn't much in Hillsdale—Curry's General Store with groceries and clothing, a post office, the Methodist church, the Union Pacific Depot, the Hillsdale Consolidated School, and half-a-dozen houses scattered here and there. To those few folks who watched Bud Sailors come and go nightly, bundled against the cold, riding bareback on his pony, it seemed an extraordinary hardship. But as long as they could remember, both the Sailors boys had been riding bareback, in obedience to their mother, who had seen enough runaways and farm accidents in her time. "I don't want either of you ridin' saddle," she had laid down the law when they had first begged to have riding ponies. "If that pony falls, you could get your feet tangled up in the stirrups and you'll get hurt. You'll ride bareback."

There had been no point in arguing with her. It wasn't stubbornness. It was conviction so deep it would have been just as pointless to talk her out of having brown eyes.

The effect on the Sailors brothers was to instill in both of them determination and grit, particularly on the basketball floor. That previous winter, against Burns, Wyoming, Bud's thirty-nine individual points were more than the opponent's total score. His basketball talent wasn't the miracle, however; the miracle was that he and his little brother Kenny even found time to play basketball in between helping their mother keep the farm going, avoiding the perils of drought, foreclosure, and cash crops it hardly paid to plant. In the spring, when Bud and Kenny left for school in the early morning, they saw their mother out working in the fields. In the evening, when they came home, she was still out there, caked with dust and bone tired. Sometimes all three of them spent days hand hoeing a forty-acre field of potatoes. Meanwhile, they sold yellow bantam sweet corn in Cheyenne for fifteen cents a dozen, or traded the potatoes and eggs and butter at Curry's for flour and Post Toasties. They surely didn't have the money for the luxury of a basketball.

"Well, I think I could let you have one," Domine finally agreed. "But give it back to me before we start practice next fall."

Bud Sailors's height came straight from his granddad, a tough, towering disciplinarian who had left teachers college in New York and come out to the Great Plains to teach school. D. D. Houtz's first teaching job was at the turn of the century in the mining country of Cripple Creek, Colorado. Hired to straighten out the ragtag students from age six to twenty-five, who had already run off several teachers, Houtz lined everybody up outside the first day of school and told them, "I understand several of you older boys have had a lot of fun runnin' off teachers." The older boys smirked. "Well," Houtz said, "we might as well get this thing straightened out." He paused. "Do any of you think you can run me off?" It was the oldest student who stepped out, a bearded and muscled lout who smiled confidently. "Yeah, I think we can," he volunteered. Houtz smiled back and then delivered one quick punch that knocked the volunteer flat on his back. "Now," Houtz invited, "is there anybody else?"

Eventually, Houtz became state superintendent of schools in Nebraska, serving from 1905 to 1920 before he retired to the northwest corner of Nebraska to run a small country grocery store in the town of Fall City. While his married daughter, Cora Belle Sailors, helped run the store and began having children of her own—first a daughter named Gladys, then after a pause of ten years, sons Barton and Kenneth—Granddaddy Houtz sat in his cracker-barrel rocker philosophizing about the ruination of the country. "They can talk all they want," he told whoever would listen, "about these new fandangled ideas for rehabilitation, but there's only one thing that will ever deter crime where we honest people can live with it, and that's the certainty and severity of punishment."

D. D. Houtz died of a heart attack in his rocker, but not without passing along the legacy of toughness and stoicism to his daughter Cora. Divorced from her husband before her two young boys were old enough to remember him, Cora sold Granddaddy Houtz's store and bought a 320-acre farm just across the state line in Wyoming.

The farm lay four miles south of the little town of Hillsdale. The high country was desolate and utterly flat, but there was a cozy security in the way the buildings had been laid out. Across the grass yard from the farmhouse, which was a pitched-roof structure with shiplap siding and a screen porch, had been built a sturdy barn, a wooden windmill, and a granary, all far enough apart so that the happenstance of a prairie twister touching down with its furious needlepoint wouldn't suck up all the buildings. Just to the north, a windbreak grove of elms and Russian olives closed the horseshoe and provided protection against the harsh north winds.

Daughter Gladys had married and left home, and Cora settled in on the Hillsdale farm to raise her two sons, steeling them against the severe winters and the cataclysms of the depression by investing them with a curious combination of fatalism and determination. "Lord," she would end the family prayers at the supper table, "not my will, but Yours." Then she would lecture her sons. "It doesn't make any difference if you get knocked down seven times. *You get back up again.*"

It was exactly what the two boys needed, because the High

Plains kept wanting to knock them down. "Boys," their mother would direct them during snow-whipped winters, "go out and get some fuel." That meant either cow chips gathered off the prairie or roadside pieces of rubber tire that would burn with a fierce heat in the big stove in the front room of their farmhouse. To keep warm at night, the two brothers slept together upstairs in a bed with straw ticking. During the summer, violent prairie hail and rainstorms appeared suddenly. At the first sight of a black stalactite of clouds forming up in the distance, Cora Sailors would cry out "storm cellar" and then push both boys ahead of her down into the dark cellar where she would recite a prayer just loud enough to be heard over the howl of the passing twister. Inside the farmhouse, the illumination was by carbide light, produced by pouring water into a container of carbide pellets. The lamps made enough soft yellow light for the boys to read, and young Kenny was particularly fond of the outdoor adventure stories of Zane Grey.

Life was already hard enough, the boys knew, so it was foolish to stir up trouble on your own. "Kenneth," his mother began formally one day, which was a sure sign he was in trouble, "your hound dog's been sneakin' into the hen house and eatin' the eggs." She handed him an egg she had just finished soft boiling. "He's out there right now. Go out there real quiet and put this egg in the nest." Minutes later, the dog's howl from the hot egg could be heard all over the farm. While Kenny felt sorry for the animal, his mother only nodded. "He'll never go in there again." It was a lesson that didn't need repeating, and the Sailors brothers learned quickly not to repeat their own mistakes. If they did, it was only because of the zeal with which they applied their mother's lessons of enterprise and resourcefulness.

One year, after their success selling sweet corn door-to-door in Cheyenne, Bud and Kenny raised hogs with the hope of earning hard cash. In the spring, they butchered them into half-hogs, wrapped them in white sheets, and loaded them into the two-wheeled trailer that they pulled with the old Chevy they'd managed to buy. "We'll sell you half a hog for fifteen dollars," the two boys said as they went door-to-door again in Cheyenne.

It was better than they even dared hope, and they had a pocket full of cash and were down to their last half-hog when they were stopped by a Cheyenne police officer with a huge star badge. "Well, now, what are you two boys doin'?"

Bud did the explaining. "We're sellin' some pork we had."

"Do you have a license?"

"Sir?"

"Do you have a license? If you don't, you're breakin' the Green River Law."

The Green River Law? Neither boy knew what it was, but the simple ordinance against peddling sounded as if it were a holy commandment with the same biblical authority they heard from the pulpit at the Hillsdale Methodist Church.

"Sir, we don't know about the Green River Law," Bud explained. "And we don't have a license. We just have one piece of hog left. We're tryin' to sell it." Bud looked down at Kenny. "We'd take anything to get rid of it, wouldn't we?" Kenny nodded enthusiastically. Bud looked back at the officer. "We'd even take ten bucks." The officer nodded slowly and then smiled at Bud. "Follow me." It was six blocks to the policeman's house, but when they arrived, the officer purchased the last half-hog. But the brush with the law sobered the Sailors brothers for months, and they said nothing about it to their mother.

Meanwhile, Cora Belle Sailors had dreams of her own. Since childhood, when Granddad Houtz had taken her to hear a black violinist, she had loved the instrument. Now, on the hardscrabble prairie with nothing but the whistle of the wind and the metallic shrieks that came from the windmill pump house, she longed to hear again those sweet violin sounds; she scraped together the cash to buy a violin so that Kenny could take lessons in Hillsdale.

Kenny went along willingly and began struggling just to learn to play the scale. Day after day, the slow *squeeeeek squaaaaawwk* of the bow across the strings pierced the farmhouse quiet.

Finally, Bud confronted his little brother. "*Squeeeek-squaaaawk, squeeeeeek-squaaaaawk!*" he delivered a high screeching sound from his throat at the same time he drew an imaginary bow across his forearm. "Go practice in the barn!"

It was no better in the barn, and while Kenny sawed away with flagging interest, Bud decided after two months that he could stand it no longer. He also knew that despite Kenny's faithful daily practices, his little brother's heart wasn't in it.

"Kenny's no violinist," Bud told his mother. She had to agree, and the violin was sold in order to buy Kenny a single-shot, bolt-action .22, which he used to hunt jackrabbits and ground squirrels. His reputation as a deadly shot quickly spread to other farms, and by the spring of 1934, when Bud Sailors was dickering with his coach for a basketball, Kenny Sailors was earning a nickel apiece from farmers for every ground squirrel he picked off foraging along the edges of cornfields.

Once Bud got the basketball from his coach, he and Kenny sawed and then nailed flat boards to two-by-fours laid out on the ground. They fixed a netless hoop to the makeshift backboard, then marked the exact ten-foot height on the wooden windmill columns. Because the old windmill had a slight pyramid shape topped by the mill blades, they had to hang the backboard out using two-by-sixes to get it perpendicular to the ground.

Their first one-on-one games occurred in May 1934 in the fading afternoon light. They were lopsided affairs during which Kenny dribbled with the same keep-away skill he had developed in Hillsdale. The dribble permitted him to control the ball at will until the other pursuing hound dogs jumped him out of frustration in order to get the ball. Still a foot taller than his brother, Bud's strategy was merely to sit back and wait until Kenny's spins and turns had taken him to within range of the basket, when he had to stop and collect himself to shoot.

Actually shooting was part of the game that seemed to Kenny secondary to the performance of dazzling dribble escapes and jackrabbit dodges. Shooting wasn't something he had concentrated on, and each time he got within range he heaved the ball at the basket with a crude lunge. But each time, Bud was standing there with his arms outstretched, to slap the ball back in Kenny's face.

"That's a foul, that's a foul!" Kenny would holler.

Bud laughed. "There's no blood, there's no foul."

On offense, Bud was too tall and slow to execute clever fakes or drives around his quick smaller brother, so he backed his way into the basket, pushing Kenny across the dirt, even if he set his feet and tried to hold his ground. Because of the soft surface of pea gravel and sand, Bud had to hammer the ball onto the ground to keep his dribble. When he finally turned to face the basket, he practiced holding the ball high, exactly as his coach had insisted, while Kenny jumped and swiped the air and Bud easily pushed the shot into the basket.

On hot days they would pause for drinks, putting their dry lips to the mouth of the water pipe running ice cold well water into the stock tank just to the east side of the windmill.

"Well," Bud teased while Kenny drank, "it looks like you're not big enough to shoot over me."

When it was Bud's turn to drink, Kenny studied his big brother, who had to scrunch himself down to get his lips to the pipe.

How could these two be brothers? Side by side they looked unrelated, the one tall and deliberate in each of his movements, the other darting and spontaneous. Now and again Bud would call Kenny "little runt." But it was only good-natured teasing that could never undo the kinship of trying to make things easier for their mother. They had that in common, and at least one other similarity. They could both jump. For as long as Bud could remember, his long, wiry legs seemed to have the bounce of leaf springs. But he had had it pounded into his head by his coach Floyd Domine that you never left the floor in basketball, *you never jumped*. Except to snatch a rebound, you kept your feet on the floor and counted on both arms and your shoulders to propel the shot. If that hadn't been a basketball commandment as rigid as what he heard in church, Bud Sailors could have leaped up effortlessly and merely dropped the ball into the basket like a piece of fruit.

Bud never challenged his coach, largely because he could get his shot off *without* jumping. Then, too, if the pure joy of leaping was the issue, there had always been the sport of track and field where he could exercise his talent. As a junior, he was the best high-school high jumper in Wyoming, and it was a good bet that as a senior he would break the state record.

When Bud finished his drink that warm day in May, he invited Kenny to resume the one-on-one with the challenge, "Let's see if you can get a shot up over me."

Kenny's mother's homily about perseverance was still fresh in his mind. Meanwhile, he had already suffered too many losses, already been knocked down too many times not to get up again, *way up*—exactly the way his brother could high jump. The pause for the drink had given Kenny time to set it in his mind: *I can shoot over him if I can get up in the air.*

Minutes later, Kenney tried the first shot. It came at the end of a long and apparently aimless course of dribbling and circling. Bud stepped back and watched with awe, because his little brother's talent was spectacular. The ball seemed fixed to the rapid flutter of his hand by an invisible rubber band. But Bud also couldn't help but watch with amusement, because it was all useless dazzle. When Kenny finally decided to shoot, Bud was confident he could slap the ball away easily, just as he had always done.

Then Kenny stopped suddenly and jumped. For a moment, Bud stood watching as if he were transfixed by the surprising sight of his brother rising high in the air. Then Bud realized it was not a pointless, acrobatic leap. It was the prelude to a shot! But before he could close and bat the shot away, the ball was sailing over his long arms.

Much later, Bud would laugh deeply and insist that his little brother's first awkward jump shot hadn't reached the backboard, or even hit the windmill. But the minute he shot it, Kenny Sailors watched it sail away, for once free of the leather *swack* of Bud slapping it aside, and his only thought was: *This is a shot I can do something with!*

That summer, Bud heard about a job working for forty cents an hour on the railroad. It sounded like a chance to earn cash for the farm, and he met with railroad officials in Cheyenne. "We need a couple of men on the spike maul," they told him. Convinced he was being offered a cushy job as a machine operator, Bud answered confidently, "Well, I can run one of them." He learned quickly that spike mauling meant one man driving in railroad spikes in the blistering prairie sun with a heavy maul, while the other held the spike with tongs. If you didn't hit the spike squarely, it would *ping* like crystal and then fly off across the field.

It was exhausting work, but despite his fatigue, Bud and Kenny played one-on-one whenever they could. Bud learned to hold the ball high above the clawing reach of his scrappy little brother. Gradually, Kenny learned that the higher he managed to jump, the more time it gave him to cock his arms properly in order to get power into the shot. But there were still things about the shot that didn't seem right. After he stopped dribbling, he had too little time before he jumped, to get a proper grip on the ball. Once he was in the air, it was hard to know exactly when to drop away his guiding left hand and let the right hand alone do the work of shooting. And then he often found himself in the air sideways or oblique to the basket, and that meant trying to twist and turn his body in order to draw a bead on the hoop.

By fall, when Bud returned the basketball to Floyd Domine at the Hillsdale school, it was scuffed and frayed by a summer of hard dribbling on the windmill court. In spots, the seam stitching was split open so that you could see the canvas bladder. Domine took the ruined ball back without comment. If his star had practiced that much, it could only mean the hope of a more powerful team at the tiny school.

That hope proved a reality, and the Hillsdale Pioneers, led by Bud Sailors, handily defeated one opponent after another. The only hitch along the way to the hopes of a chance to go to the state championship was a brief episode that threatened two of the team's players.

The way Bob Todd had explained his plan to teammate Bud Sailors, it seemed a simple way to raise quick money. "Sailors, I've got some hound dogs. We'll put the hounds in a cage on the back of my Model A. We can get five bucks a head bounty on ki-yoots. We'll chase those suckers with my car until their tongues are hanging out. Then we'll let my hounds out, and they'll nail 'em."

At first it was simple, and they drove right through what few prairie fences they came to in hot pursuit of the coyotes. The first time, they ran down two animals and sold them to the county agent for the bounty. But the second time they cut school right after lunch, one of the ranch owners spotted their car raising a funnel of dust on his property. Superintendent Revelle, who ran the Hillsdale Consolidated District, called both boys into his office once they had sneaked back to school.

"So, where you boys been?"

"We had some work to do," Bud answered.

"Both of you?"

"Yes, sir."

"Doing what?"

Bud could not bring himself to lie. "I dunno . . . just stuff."

"I got a call from a rancher that you were chasing coyotes on his property."

Neither boy spoke.

"Were you?"

"Yes, sir," they admitted.

"Well, they'll be no more of it," the superintendent warned, and they were dismissed without punishment. It was their honesty that saved them, as well as the unlikelihood that Hillsdale would make it to the state basketball tournament without them.

Tiny Hillsdale defeated the Wheatland Bulldogs to earn the title of District Champions, with the right to go to the 1935 Wyoming State Tournament in Casper. With only seven boys on the team, and hardly forty students in the entire school, their matchup against Rock Springs in the semifinals was billed as a David versus Goliath encounter, although with tall Bud Sailors leading Hillsdale, it muddied the issue of exactly who the Goliath was.

Bud Sailors controlled the mandatory center jump after every basket, and the entire Hillsdale offense was built around him. With superior shooters and a deeper bench, however, Rock Springs defeated Hillsdale and eventually won the state championship. Still, the loss in no way diminished the reputation in Hillsdale of Bud Sailors, who assumed heroic proportions in the eyes of his little brother. At night, along with his boyish dreams of riding his pony and hunting squirrels with his rifle and his own hound dog named Blackie, Kenny Sailors imagined himself enjoying the same prairie fame as his brother, playing for the Hillsdale Pioneers. That was glory enough, and what might come *after* it, he never bothered to dream. He was only dimly aware that there was a university in Laramie. And if somebody had told him that one day his picture would be in *Life Magazine*, hanging high in the air above the floor of a place called Madison Square Garden, it would have seemed inconceivable and pointless. Whatever world there was outside Hillsdale, Wyoming, he hardly cared.

Early in the spring of 1935, Kenny returned home from school and met his mother on the porch. "Kenneth," she began, and he braced himself for news that he was in trouble, "I had men here today, and they offered me forty-five dollars for that pony of yours." She paused to make sure he appreciated how much that was. "I sold him," she finally said.

Kenny bit his lip but knew it was pointless to argue. For weeks, there'd been talk that he'd hardly listened to of selling the farm and moving to Laramie so that Bud could enroll at the university. He'd already been offered a basketball scholarship. Beyond that, for years his mother had talked with such certainty of a college education for both of her sons that it had the same inevitability as winter or hard times. Yet, the instructions to sell his favorite pony gave an awful immediacy to what had been only a distant presumption.

"You're gonna have to get up tomorrow morning early," she went on, "and ride your pony into Hillsdale. Take him to the stockyard corral. They'll put him on the train."

"For where?"

"They'll take him to folks in Pine Bluff. That's who bought him."

The next morning before school, Kenny rode his pony bareback to the small stockyard beside the Hillsdale Depot. "Here's my pony," he told the station agent. He hugged the animal once, then walked slowly to school. That night when he got home and Bud saw his long face, Kenny would only admit, "I might have cried a tear or two." Then he told Bud, "Blaine Reed wants me to stay here and play with Hillsdale next year."

Blaine Reed was manager of the Stockgrowers National Bank in Cheyenne. When he had heard that the Sailors were moving to Laramie, his first thought was to find a way to keep Kenny in Hillsdale. It was clear he would never have the height of Bud, but he could dribble and dart and shoot—occasionally in leaping ways that seemed bizarre. Nobody he played against on the Hillsdale eighth-grade team knew quite how to stop him, and by a different route, he promised to continue the high-school basketball fame that towering Bud Sailors had brought to tiny Hillsdale.

The next day Kenny's mother told him, "Blaine Reed was out to visit today." Kenny nodded to indicate he knew what Reed was trying to orchestrate. "Kenneth, Blaine Reed wants me to take his daughter along with us to the university. In turn, he's offered to keep and board you so you can stay here and play basketball in Hillsdale."

Again, something that had seemed remote now had a frightening immediacy, and Kenny stiffened at the thought of being separated from his mother and Bud.

His mother shook her head. "Kenneth, you are *not* staying here. You are going where your brother and I go. Wherever we go, you are going. Now you get that straight."

Cora Belle Sailors's characteristic single-mindedness was a relief, and without objection, Kenny pitched in to help his mother and Bud prepare to move to Laramie. Earlier that spring, they had made an arrangement with a neighbor for a sack of seed potatoes in return for every sack of harvest potatoes. The eventual crop, yielding a bountiful two hundred bushels of potatoes an acre, was the best anybody around Hillsdale could remember. The cash from the sale of potatoes, as well as the sale of the farm, gave enterprising Cora Sailors the money to buy a spacious rooming house in Laramie for university students. The house had dormers and gables, half-a-dozen rooms that she sublet to students, and a concrete driveway where Bud Sailors immediately hung a basket for his little brother.

For both boys, it was almost a new world. There were still the adventures of hunting jackrabbits and antelope, and fishing the Laramie River or Lake Hattie or the "Snowy Range" west of Laramie; but the experience of indoor plumbing and the urbanities of a university town, even if it was in the middle of the High Plains, were a far cry from the drudgery and wind-whistling loneliness of farm life outside Hillsdale.

Bud got a job working at the university's agricultural experimental station outside of Laramie. He also found a job driving in the evening with the Laramie Yellow Cab Company. Showing a touch of his mother's enterprise, Bud had cards made up that he distributed to university co-eds. "Call Bud for a Cab," the cards said, but after he missed several freshman basketball practices because of his driving duties and his work at the agricultural station, his coach Dutch Witte confronted him.

"What's goin' on here?" Dutch wanted to know.

"I'm working," Bud explained, "making a little extra money to help out with family expenses."

"This can't happen," Dutch insisted. "We can get better jobs for our players."

Bud agreed not to miss any more practices. Still, despite his coach's offers to help, Bud wasn't confident he could even make the freshman team. He had been Hillsdale's hero, but at the university he was just another tall basketball player. What if he quit his job and then got cut? He'd be out of basketball *and* work.

He determined to keep the job with the experimental station. Meanwhile, Kenny Sailors was already making a fair name for himself at Laramie High. More and more, against older and taller players who presented the same daunting defense as Bud, he found himself stopping suddenly on the dead run and then leaping into the air, sometimes floating into his defensive man or twisting still because he hadn't perfected the shot entirely. But he was developing an uncanny accuracy that made him a high-school starter, even as a sophomore.

His Laramie coach was Floyd Forman. The first time Forman saw Kenny's strange, leaping shot, he asked, "Where'd you get that queer shot?"

Kenny knew perfectly well where he'd gotten it: it was the only way he could shoot over his lofty brother. Yet he had acquired the habit of respectful silence around inquiring adults, and he only shrugged.

"Well, why you shootin' that way?" Forman continued to press him.

"What way?"

"The one-handed part of it."

Kenny tried not to smile. If anything was odd, it was his high leap into the air, in defiance of gravity, and the holy basketball commandment to *stay on the floor, stay on the floor.* But the shot was also in defiance of an even older commandment, which Forman tried to make his players obey: whether swinging the ball toward the basket from deep between your legs or stepping and then letting the shot go with wrist roll or pushing it from your chest, *you shot with two hands.*

Despite Forman's reservations, Kenny practiced driving down the right side of the floor, stopping his dribble on a dime, then leaping to release his new shot. And by Kenny's junior year in high school, Forman found himself conceding in the huddle, "Kenny, if we're gonna win this game, you're gonna have to get goin'. *You* bring the ball up court!"

It was tacit approval of Kenny's unusual shot, and he slowly learned to bring the ball up off his hip while jumping, to keep opponents from stripping him of the ball. When Forman saw Kenny using his deft dribbling skill to maneuver defensive players into screens, the coach turned improvisation into deliberate strategy, and he instructed Kenny's teammates to position themselves as standing screens.

His junior and senior years at Laramie High, Kenny Sailors led the Laramie Plainsmen to the state championship in Casper. They lost both times in the finals, however, first to powerful Rock Springs, then to Casper. Like his big brother before him, Kenny Sailors was selected to the Wyoming All State Team. Also like his brother, Kenny was given a basketball scholarship to attend the University of Wyoming. In other ways, their worlds were separating.

In Hillsdale they hadn't even had an opportunity to read a newspaper. Troubling events in Europe threatened to reach all the way to Laramie, and Kenny listened to Bud and his friends talk about what they were going to do. He and his friend Ditch Day, who had played freshman basketball with him at Wyoming, got out maps and studied Europe. War seemed inevitable, and Bud told Ditch, "Tall as we are, if we get an army commission, we'll be the first ones shot." Ditch agreed. "The Army Air Force sounds like good, clean work. We'll travel a lot."

Bud passed the physical exam but was judged too tall for enlistment. It took string-pulling by a general from the airfield outside Laramie to secure a height waiver. Once that was done, Bud's enlistment was immediately approved.

Cora Sailors was now as well off as she had ever been, from running her Laramie boarding house. Yet for Bud, after all the hardship he had watched her endure, leaving her for the first time was painful. Nonetheless, the family habit of stoicism and restraint was too deep for any of them to indulge in sentimental farewells at the Laramie train depot in January 1941.

After he was sworn in, Bud went to Oxnard, California, to begin cadet training. "All right," a flight instructor quizzed the raw recruits on their aviation experience, "how much time have you got?" Bud Sailors, who had never even been in an airplane, smiled confidently. "Oh, I got *all day*."

"All right, smart ass," the instructor snarled at him, convinced he was a wiseacre, "you're first!"

With Bud up front in the Stearman, the instructor took off and promptly put the plane through a grueling series of snap rolls, spins, chandelles, and lazy eights.

"ok, Ace, you got it," the instructor said finally, encouraging Bud to show what *he* could do. It was an awkward, sickening beginning for his military duties, but before long—his mother's prairie examples of hard work and perseverance almost habit with him now—he was training as a cadet at Randolph Field in Texas.

Meanwhile, Kenny's world was expanding, too, and it wasn't just the urgency of the news of the Japanese attack on Pearl Harbor or letters from his brother somewhere in the South Pacific that began to make him worldly. "If we're ever gonna make the big time," Coach Ev Shelton reminded his University of Wyoming players again and again, "we gotta play big-time teams. We gotta go to New York. It's where the publicity is."

Shelton had learned his basketball in California, and he was in only his second year at Wyoming. Yet, it was already clear to him that small schools such as Wyoming would have to go east if they wanted to destroy the myth that they were nothing but bow-legged, clumsy cowboys. It meant that during Christmas vacation of Kenny's sophomore year, the country Cowboys traveled east to play Georgetown, Canisius, Long Island, St. John's, and CCNY, slowly putting the University of Wyoming on the basketball map.

By March the Cowboys had worked their way to the huge Municipal Auditorium in Kansas City for the Western Semifinals of the Third Annual NCAA tournament. In their first game the Cowboys were soundly beaten by heavily favored Arkansas, whose six-foot-three-inch Jumpin' Johnny Adams was one of the shortest men on the Arkansas roster.

Despite twenty-six points from Adams, whose strange shot "seldom traveled a foot or more above the goal," the newspapers reported the next day that "a spindly-legged sophomore who was on the [Wyoming] bench at the start of the contest won the crowd. Although he led a losing cause, there's no doubt that Ken Sailors was the hero of the day." The papers described Kenny intercepting passes and then whipping the ball in the basket after full court, slashing drives that utilized his quickness.

It was Ev Shelton who taught him how to use that slashing quickness to drive to the basket. "If you want to drive to the hoop,

Sailors, don't pussy-foot around that guy," Shelton told him. "Take his arm off, right here." Shelton demonstrated by pounding a fist against one arm. "Think about taking that arm off when you drive. That'll knock him off balance. If he's got that arm out there, aim for it. Right here!" Shelton continued to pound his arm. "Hit him."

But it was Kenny's jump shot that was drawing attention, refined now so that he could square up and shoot it from either side of the floor, and with range. In writing about it sportswriters struggled to describe it and kept repeating phrases such as "leaping one-hander" and "unorthodox" and "shot-put throw."

To Kenny, it was simply "my shot." What they named it wasn't important. What mattered was that he had a shot he believed in and could call his own, a shot that was not in obedience to the game and its rigid history, but a shot derived from his *own* history. It was as much a part of him as farm life and his brother and the windmill starkness of the High Plains. Not that he believed his shot was unique, or even original. Again and again, even after they began referring to it regularly as a "jump shot," sportswriters pestered him to explain, "Were you the first man to ever shoot a jump shot?"

"Good heavens," he always declined to take credit. "How would I know?"

Back in Wyoming, Kenny's buddies at the university told him one day, "There's a cute cheerleader from Casper you oughta get to know." She was dark-haired and spritely and told everybody just to call her "Boky." She boasted with just a touch of mockery in her voice that she was from Casper, *the hub of Wyoming.*" If anybody asked what she was studying, her quick answer was always the same: "Boys!"

Their first dates were fly-fishing expeditions along the Laramie River outside of Laramie. Boky packed the lunch, then she went upstream to fish while Kenny worked his way downstream. It might have looked like the organized tactics of experienced fly-casters working an entire stream, but Boky's explanation was simpler. "It's to make sure there's no hanky panky," she insisted.

In early January 1943, Ev Shelton took Kenny Sailors and his Wyoming Cowboys to the NCAA finals for the second time, and on this trip Shelton told his players he didn't intend to lose. After come-from-behind wins against Oklahoma and Texas in the Western regionals, on March 30, 1943, the Cowboys easily defeated Georgetown in the NCAA finals in Madison Square Garden. In recognition of his spectacular play, Kenny Sailors was selected Most Valuable Player of the tournament, the smallest man from an NCAA championship team ever given the honor.

Despite the award, Kenny spent most of the tournament thinking about his brother Bud, who was a squadron flight commander piloting B-25s in the South Pacific and making long, harrowing bomb runs from Guadalcanal to the Japanese stronghold on Rabaul.

"There's a war goin' on in the Pacific," Kenny reminded himself, "and I'm headin' out of here."

Kenny enlisted even before they had stopped celebrating the Cowboy's NCAA championship back in Wyoming. He served nearly three years in the Marine Corps, first in San Diego, then the South Pacific. Discharged from the Marines in late 1945, Kenny still had a year of athletic eligibility remaining, and within days of his discharge he found himself in Madison Square Garden again. This time Ev Shelton had taken his undefeated Cowboys on an eastern road trip during the holidays, and in front of partisan New York fans who cheered wildly for their local team, the Cowboys defeated Long Island University.

One shot by Kenny Sailors in the first half remains historic. The Cowboys were leading nineteen to sixteen. He had stolen a pass and then raced down the left side of the floor with low, quick dribbles that blurred his hand like the beat of bird wings. At the top of the key, he cut to his right and then stopped suddenly and jumped. Courtside spectators in folding chairs watched as he seemed to rise up into the scoreboard.

It had been more than a decade since Kenny had executed his first crude and desperate jump shot, which his big brother continued to insist, with a twinkle in his eye, "hadn't even hit the windmill." Now, at the peak of his jump and hanging-in-the-air in Madison Square Garden, he drew a bead on the basket with the same concentration he had once used on the farm to pick off squirrels or to shoot a basketball over his brother.

Just before he dropped his left hand away to release the shot, a photographer's flashbulb exploded silently. To the 18,056 fans who were watching, the flashbulb explosion seemed to freeze Kenny Sailors in the air, while beneath him men as floor-bound as statuary looked up in awe. Two weeks later *Life Magazine* ran a photo story of the game. Among the pictures accompanying the story was the shot captured by the flashbulb explosion in the first half. "*Kenny Sailors jumps and shoots*," the caption for the picture read.

It would be another six years before professional athletic journals even recognized, much less analyzed, the unique shot. Still, millions of young players saw that picture of Kenny's jump shot in *Life*, and that flashbulb explosion in Madison Square Garden began a chain reaction in basketball. A shot whose origins could be traced to isolated pockets across the country—from the North Woods to the Ozarks, from the Appalachian Mountains to the Pacific—was suddenly by virtue of one picture as widespread as the game itself. Everywhere young players on basketball courts began jumping to shoot.

After Kenny Sailors finished his last half-year of eligibility at Wyoming in the spring of 1946, scouts from the National Basketball League's Rochester Royals, who had seen Kenny in the East-West game, paid his way to come to Rochester to discuss a contract for professional basketball.

Professional basketball! It was a world he had hardly even heard of, something strange and cosmopolitan out of the East. Not sure it was for him, he traveled to Rochester and listened carefully to their offers. Meanwhile, the Cleveland Rebels of the Basketball Association of America topped Rochester's offer by several thousand dollars. The additional money and the advice of the football All American Otto Graham helped Kenny decide eventually to sign with Cleveland. Graham had also been an All American in basketball. Now, after playing professional basketball for a season in Rochester, he was giving up basketball to concentrate on professional football in

Cleveland. "You should go over to Cleveland," Graham told Kenny. "They're gonna have a good basketball franchise. You should talk to them."

Late that fall Kenny reported for the first practices in the Cleveland arena. Cleveland's coach was Dutch Dehnert, a teammate of Joe Lapchick and Nat Holman on the original New York Celtics team. Cleveland's front office had signed Kenny without Dutch's ever having seen him play. Dutch, who spoke with a streetwise Eastern accent that separated him from drawling cowboys, watched skeptically as his All American from the tumbleweed prairie worked out off-season kinks in a one-on-one game with teammate Frankie Baumholtz.

Kenny was about to step into the shower after that first practice when Dutch approached him. "Say-*lors*," Dutch pronounced Kenny's name. "Where'd you get that leapin' one-hander?"

"I been shootin' it ever since I was a kid."

Whether that satisfied Dutch or not, his face gave no hint. "And that dribblin' of yours," he continued. "You don't dribble in this league. You pass the ball."

Kenny shrugged. "I have to dribble to shoot my jumper, Dutch."

"I'm gonna give you some advice, Say-*lors*. If you're gonna go in this league, you gotta forget about that dribblin'."

Kenny turned to enter the shower.

"And you gotta get yourself a good two-hand set shot," Dutch shouted after him.

If that's true, Kenny thought as he disappeared into the steam, *I'm a dead duck.* Kenny ignored his coach's advice, and for the first half of the season he played very little. It wasn't just Dutch Dehnert's skepticism about his leaping shot that kept him on the sidelines. Circumstances in the Cleveland arena also worked against him. The arena was home ice for Cleveland's hockey team. For basketball games, the floor was simply laid over the ice, and when crowd warmth created condensation on the floor, the slick surface made it difficult for players to drive. It was impossible for Kenny to put on the brakes and then leap for his shot.

"We can't stand up," several players complained to Dutch during a time-out in their first home game. "We can't drive!" The rest of the players nodded. But Dutch waved off their complaint. "If you guys would forget about the pretty *goils* in the crowd and the *earl* on the floor, we'd win this game."

"It's not oil, Dutch," one of them explained, "it's condensation!"

"It's *earl*," Dutch insisted, "and they'll wipe it off at half time."

Unable to convince Dutch there was a place in professional basketball for his shot, or a circumstance that permitted it, Kenny remained on the bench. Finally, his teammate Big Ed Sadowski took him aside. At six-feet-five-inches and 240 pounds, Sadowski's muscu'ar, ferocious play stood in sharp contrast to Kenny's speed and deftness. "If you don't get to playin' before this season's over," Sadowski told Kenny, "your career as a pro is gonna be over with."

Already twenty-six years of age, Kenny realized that Sadowski was right. He had to start playing soon or it would be too late. But he was not about to change over to a two-hand set shot to do it. So he went straight to Cleveland's front office. "Look," he told Cleveland's general manager, "I don't fit in with Dutch's system of play. Trade me to a ball club where I can start playin'." The general manager dropped his voice to a conspiratorial whisper. "Kenny, you just hang in there a few more games. Some things are gonna happen in a week or so." A week later, Dutch Dehnert was quietly removed from his coaching spot and sent on the road as a scout. The general manager took over the coaching duties.

"I have no obj :ction to the way you shoot," he immediately told Kenny. "Or you · dribbling. You're gonna get plenty of playing time." So Kenny began playing regularly and scoring frequently on the jump shot he had refused to give up. He also found that he could use his quickness to slip inside the big men to steal rebounds they were too slow to go after.

But one night, against the Chicago Stags, he had stolen a rebound from a clutch of big men and then jumped in their midst to put it back up when Big Ed Sadowski's elbow came down on his skull like a sledge. Kenny's arms suddenly went limp, the ball slid from his hands, and he staggered in a circle. Sadowski approached and put his hand on Kenny's shoulder. "Shake it off, Kenny," he shouted. "You're in the big leagues now!" Blood began pouring from Kenny's head. Trainers hustled onto the floor to soak up the blood with towels. Now Sadowski looked down on the rookie. "I guess you better go sit down, son."

The incident served to remind Kenny that it was no longer Bud Sailors he was trying to leap over. These men were mountains. Still, he remained convinced that there was a place in professional basketball for his jump shot, but only if he picked his spots more carefully.

By the end of his rookie season in 1947, Kenny Sailors had made second team All Pro in the BAA. At the end of the year, however, the Rebels folded, and Kenny's contract was picked up by the Providence Steamrollers. Over the next four years he played with several different teams—including Providence, the Denver Nuggets in the first year of the NBA, and then the Boston Celtics. Each year, on the strength of his unique jump shot, he was among the league's leading scorers.

By 1951, at almost thirty years of age, Kenny found himself playing for the Baltimore Bullets with a former St. Louis Bomber named Belus Smawley. Neither man drank, smoked, or swore, and they were friends immediately. They rented new homes across the street from each other on Annellen Street in Baltimore, and between games and road trips, they and their wives played the card game hearts in one house or the other. In these regular games they were joined by Cora Hershiser, Boky's aunt, who helped with the Sailors' two young children. There was little talk of basketball among the five of them. Kenny was still nearly as quick as anybody in the league but dwarfed by the new young giants. He could only have boasted of a few records here and there. His thirty-seven-point outburst one night in Baltimore stood as an arena record for several years. With the Denver Nuggets he had finished fifth in the league in scoring. Otherwise, there wasn't much to brag about, except— with tongue in cheek—endorsements for prune juice. For Belus, the impact of his unstoppable turnaround, corkscrew shot was overshadowed by followers whose graceful imitations seemed more in keeping with the new artistry of basketball.

Their basketball competitiveness was now focused on the game of hearts, and all five of them kibitzed on how the cards were "running." They laughed wildly at the sudden reversals of fortune that struck whoever got stuck with the Queen. Belus's high hoarse laughter rode on top of Kenny's explosive guffaws. Meanwhile, neither could yet appreciate the deeper significance of their friendship. Separated by half a continent, but in the same wink of basketball history—the one in May 1934, the other in October of the same year—the two men had helped break ground for an historic and revolutionary shot. Kenny had made his discovery at a hoop nailed to a windmill by his brother; Belus had made his more than a thousand miles away in an abandoned railroad depot. Now, almost two decades later, after dozens of different teams and a thousand games between them, they had wound up at the end of their careers on the same team, living on the same street in Baltimore, enjoying friendly games of hearts at the same card table. It was a coincidence that seemed inspired by the basketball Fates.

In the off-season during his professional career, Kenny and Boky lived in Jackson Hole, where he and Boky managed the Jackson Hole Lodge and ran the lodge's recreation programs. Just before he retired from basketball, he and Boky bought the *Heart Six* dude ranch near Moran in Jackson Hole, where Kenny turned his lifelong love for hunting and fishing into an occupation as a guide and outfitter for expeditions into the Teton wilderness area.

The trouble was, in Kenny's eyes that wilderness and the independent spirit it inspired were disappearing. Despite serving a term in the Wyoming State Legislature in the fifties and having an active political career, he seemed unable to stop the encroachment of civilization that threatened the spirit of rugged individualism he had learned as a boy. He was defeated twice in Wyoming elections for the House of Representatives, and in 1964 he again had to swallow political defeat, this time in the election for the U.S. Senate.

"I could see that there would be big changes coming," he later explained, "and rather than wait to see how it all turned out, I decided it would be exciting to start over in a place that was like Wyoming had been forty or fifty years ago." That place was Alaska, and in 1965, after he sold the *Heart Six* ranch to his brother Bud and his wife Betty, Kenny and Boky headed north, pulling an Airstream trailer behind their pick-up, in search of the new wilderness.

They arrived in Alaska on Independence Day, 1965. That same year he and Boky acquired a homesite near Gakona on a ridge overlooking the Copper River. It was rugged country with a view of the Wrangell Mountains. Together they built a log cabin with a view to the east of sixteen-thousand-foot Mt. Sanford. To hold the heat during sixty-below winters, the cabin had a low ceiling and a five-foot door jamb that Bud Sailors cracked his head on the first time he came to visit his little brother.

Off and on for the next fifteen years, Kenny Sailors coached and taught in the high school in nearby Glennallen. Wearing a Marine-style haircut, an old cowboy hat, and a wiry beard, he also led hunting and fishing expeditions into the Wrangell Mountains. Meanwhile, Boky took care of their home and never hung out the wash without a shotgun beside her for protection against the bears. "Oh, sure," Kenny joked to friends. "If the federal government insists, we'll give up our guns."

While Kenny was in Alaska, his mother, Cora, died at a convalescent home in Cheyenne. At her funeral ceremonies in Wyoming, Kenny remembered keenly the spiritual influence she had had on his life. It wasn't just a religious spirit, acquired through regular church attendance and praying before mealtime. It was the spirit of toughness and resolution that he had witnessed in her as she endured the hard life of the prairie. He knew that the same toughness of spirit was in everything he did, from playing basketball to loving a day's hard work to deliberately seeking out the frontiers of Alaska.

In 1987, at sixty-eight years of age, Kenny and Boky moved to Angoon, a small village of Tlingit Indians on Admiralty Island, accessible only by airplane or boat. There, Kenny taught school and coached girls basketball, compiling a record of fifty-three wins and only fifteen losses. But there were more bears than people on the remote island, and Kenny and Boky had shotguns laid across their laps as they drove along beside the girls during road work.

Despite Kenny's withdrawal from the civilized world, sports-writers from New York to Anchorage kept seeking him out and re-membering his basketball past. "Hank Luisetti and Kenny Sailors have to be the two who most influenced the game," Joe Lapchick re-called in a *New York Times* article. DePaul's venerable coach Ray Meyer wrote him, "You were the first I saw with the true jump shot." Others wrote that he was the "father" of the jump shot, and he did his best at least to *look* like a patriarch as he aged and his face be-came leathery and his Alaskan beard turned salt and pepper. Still, when they pressed him to answer if he was in fact the inventor of the jump shot, he gave a stock answer: "How would I know if I was the first one? Maybe Naismith himself jumped and shot a time or two."

In March 1990, the Final Four met in Denver to determine the NCAA collegiate champions. On Thursday night, March 29, before the four teams clashed, Kenny Sailors was one of the guests of honor at the pretournament banquet attended by more than a thousand people, including the Final Four players, sportswriters, coaches, and tournament officials.

Kenny was sixty-nine-years old. He had eight grandchildren and five great-grandchildren. It had been almost half a century since he had played in Denver with the original Nuggets, whose franchise folded shortly before its first season ended. Seated now at one of the banquet tables in the Colorado ballroom of Denver's Marriott City Center, he remembered those tedious road trips by car from Denver to Rochester and then even farther back, those fierce one-on-one games with Bud at the windmill basket.

After dinner, the master-of-ceremonies introduced former presi-dent Gerald Ford, who gave a short speech to the huge crowd. Then the Final Four coaches spoke, each walking a fine line between false modesty and irritating smugness. Finally, the master-of-ceremo-nies took the microphone again. "We have a another special guest tonight," he told the crowd. *"The man who developed the jump shot."*

Tournament officials had taken that old jump shot photo from *Life*—the one that had electrified the basketball world—and they had blown it up as a life-size action shot, which had been on display with other basketball memorabilia at a downtown Denver bank. Those in the crowd who had visited the bank's display began to crane their necks. Who was the man high in the air in that old picture? In real life, did he look anything like them, or was he some freak from an alien world of ancient sneakers and underhanded shots?

"We've asked him to say a few words about the origins of the jump shot," the master-of-ceremonies continued. "Ladies and gentlemen, please welcome *Kenny Sailors*."

The sight of Kenny Sailors, perhaps the smallest and oldest man at the banquet, rising to speak stunned half the crowd, and there was only scattered applause as Kenny made his way to the microphone.

"I'm nearly seventy years old," he began in a strong voice that belied both his size and age. "And it's a treat for an old man like me to come here and be invited to talk to such a distinguished group." He could have been speaking for Whitey and Mouse, for Bud and the Wheelhorse of Steel City. He could have been speaking for the late Joe Fulks and Jumpin' Johnny Adams. He could have been speaking for his old friend and teammate Belus. Wher*ever* they each were, in the spirit world or this one, they would be settling in to watch the Final Four battle it out on TV. Like true fathers, they would all smile with patriarchal benevolence at all the young players who carried their jump shot genes.

Kenny turned and pointed to the Final Four coaches. "These coaches, I know they're great and their records prove it. But they're not the only coaches in the country. I'm a coach, too. I coach a group of Tlingit Indian girls up in Angoon, Alaska." There was scattered applause. "And you surely know where *that* is," he added. He had to stop to wait for the laughter to subside. "So when an old man like me comes down to a big shindig like this," he continued, "it's a chance to get to talkin' about basketball." He paused again, this time in a nervous, banquet-hall silence that said: *What the hell is this old coot working up to? Some melancholy recollection of the past? Some aimless longing for the good old days?*

"You know something?" he continued, his voice rising. "I can remember every jump shot I ever took. *And every single free throw,*" he said slowly. Then a broad smile broke across his leathery face as he delivered the joke that caught everyone by surprise. "But you know something else. When this is over tonight, and I go out to the parkin' lot, I probably won't be able to find my car."

Acknowledgments and Sources

Few of us ever get to meet the idols of our childhood, and I am grateful to Bob Erdman for introducing me to Whitey Skoog, whose exploits at Williams Arena sent me out into the icy night wearing overshoes and gloves to work on a jump shot. I am grateful to Whitey for the detailed recollections of his childhood and his playing days at Brainerd, the University of Minnesota, and the Minneapolis Lakers. Coach Mike Zauhar of Brainerd directed me to Coach Kermit Aase, who provided additional information on Whitey's high school playing days. Angela Magnan gathered copies of the *Brainerd Dispatch* that covered Whitey's high-school basketball career. Jennifer Koenen of the Bemidji State University Library found relevant copies of the *Bemidji Daily Pioneer*. In my reconstruction of the game in 1944 in which Whitey shot his first jumper, I relied entirely on accounts from the *Dispatch* and the *Pioneer*. Sue Kringen, director of the Bemidji State University Alumni Association, provided me with material from Dr. Arthur O. Lee's *College in the Pines* (Bemidji State University, 1994) for historical details on Bemidji's Memorial Hall. Whitey's Minnesota teammate Wally Salovich, and Coach Ozzie Cowles—two more of my childhood heroes—provided me with anecdotes about the development of Whitey's jump shot as a Golden Gopher.

Gus Hassapakis, from the Golden Age of San Francisco basketball, led me to former University of California coach Rene Herrerias, who had vivid but frustrating recollections of trying to stop the jump shot of Mouse Gonzales. The search for Mouse, eventually known as "Jumpin' John Burton," took four months. With help from Gus, Dallas Brock, Sam Goldman, California state senator John Burton (a basketball star himself but not the John Burton I was after), and Eamon Ryan, I finally found the right John Burton. His recollections at his kitchen table in Aptos, California, proved spellbinding. I hope I have done credit to his stories of both basketball and combat. Fred Hoshiyama, Mits Saito, and the late Yori Wada contributed background material on the history of the Buchanan YMCA. Sheila Jackson provided me with a copy of Clifford Drury's *San Francisco YMCA* (Arthur H. Clark Company, 1963). Mike Bower's recollections helped me know the legendary Benny Neff better. Bill Calhoun reminisced at length about basketball at Lowell and pick-up games at Grattan playground. John Burton's Gator teammate Dick Franks recalled their playing days at San Francisco State. Finally, the *San Francisco Chronicle* and San Francisco State's *Gator* provided additional highlights.

Twice Bud Palmer braved the high perils of the Rocky Mountains to drive down for interviews at the Brooklyn restaurant in Denver, where not even the mayhem of Stanley Cup happy Avalanche hockey fans could compete with Bud's fascinating tales. Lindbergh Hollingsworth found rare information on Lefty Flynn in an article entitled "Rarely Remembered," by George Kotchner, in the December 1982 issue of *Classic Images*. My Gator teammate Billy Aires, the best passer the game will ever see, gave me his recollections of Bud Palmer at Princeton and in the Garden. A photographic essay from the Phillips-Exeter alumni magazine entitled "A Separate Peace: Moods and Setting," edited by Thomas Hinkle and with excerpts from John Knowles's novel *A Separate Peace* (MacMillan, 1959), helped me visualize the setting for Bud's Phillips-Exeter days. Selected stories from the *New York Times* supplied details on the nameless but powerful East Coast hurricane of September 1936. Additional *Times* stories between 1946 and 1950 were the source of background information on the early Knicks.

Les McCreery's card file may be the country's best source for the whereabouts of BAA and early NBA stars. That file led me to Bill "Tosh" Tosheff, and eventually to Dave Minor, who spent hours with me on the phone. Dave died suddenly in March 1998, on the eve of his long-overdue recognition as a basketball pioneer. I hope my portrait of him captures his courage and his warmth. Librarian James Hibbard, from the Indiana Room of the Gary Public Library, arranged the interlibrary loan for copies of the *Gary Post-Tribune*. I am also indebted to the *Post-Tribune*'s Richard Grey, whose stories on neglected stars such as Davage Minor helped me keep my athletic faith in an era of men with orange hair and attitudes.

Les McCreery found George Senesky for me, and George led me to Joe Fulks Jr., who in turn directed me to this country's best authority on Joe Fulks, Judge Bill Cunningham of the Fifty-Sixth Judicial Circuit in Kentucky. For three days, despite the press of his bench duties and research for books of his own, Bill found time to shepherd me around Lyon and Marshall Counties. He generously shared with me his tapes of his interviews with Martha Defew Wallington, Herb Hurley, Joe Fulks's sister Barbara Nell McKinney, Birmingham resident Mark Clayton, Dr. Ray Mofield, and Arlet Jones. Bill was kind enough to let me read his own stories on Joe Fulks, as well as his manuscript on the history of Old Birmingham. Joe's Kuttawa teammates Douglas W. "Carrots" McQuigg and W. T. "Teeter" Martin gave me a sense of the fever of Kentucky basketball, particularly in Old Kuttawa. Without James Defew's recollections, the history of Birmingham basketball during Joe Fulks's days also would have disappeared beneath the Tennessee River. Jimmy Griffin passed along his personal observations of Joe Fulks in the South Pacific, as well as a scrapbook of Joe's basketball career. Kentucky State Trooper Ron Anderson gave me his recollections of the fateful night of Joe's murder in 1976. Diane Smith, custodian of records for the Kentucky State Police, provided me with an official report of the investigation into the shooting. James Campbell, clerk of the Lyon County Circuit Court in Eddyville, made trial records available. Odell Walker of the Lyon County Historical Society supplied pamphlets on Lyon County history. Elvira Lewis of the Marshall County Historical Society directed me to Ernie Collins for anecdotal history of life in Birmingham. Warrior teammate Gale Bishop shared with me some of his recollections of Joe, and Dr. Warren Perkins and Johnny Ezersky recalled the difficulties of defending against his jump shot. I am indebted to Philadelphia's Prism Sports cable channel for a video copy of Jim Barniak's "Sports Scrapbook" on Fulks. Finally, critical parts of the Joe Fulks story were reconstructed from selected articles from the following periodicals and newspapers: *Philadelphia Inquirer, Paducah Sun-Democrat, Louisville Courier Journal, Saturday Evening Post, Lyon County Herald Ledger*, and the *Murray State Alumnus*.

For recollections on Johnny Adams, Curt Gowdy's memory proved as sharp and clear as his distinctive voice. I am grateful to O'Neale Adams and Gladene Adams Mask for enduring my pesky phone calls and what must have seemed like interminable interviews so that I could gather the story of Johnny's boyhood in El Paso and Beebe. Johnny's Beebe teammate Wilson Deese, as well as Lloyd C. Flynt and Bill Flynt, contributed valuable stories and anecdotes. Johnny's wife, Louise Adams, shared with me recollections of Johnny's professional life and his tragic death. Johnny's Arkansas teammate R. C. Pitts took pains to photocopy numerous *Arkansas Gazette* articles that helped me recreate the Razorbacks' 1941 run for the national title. I also relied upon clips from the *Kansas City Star* and the *Arkansas Democrat*. Judy and Rev. John Back researched additional issues of the *Gazette* that covered Beebe sports. Orville Henry, veteran *Gazette* writer, passed along memories and stories. Roy Simmons's fond memories of his friendship with Bro Erwin were critical. Finally, Bro's daughter Dr. Anita Erwin Jones and her son Clifford Jones filled in additional details.

Hemie Feutsch of the original Baltimore Bullets remembered trying to stop an early NBA star with the unusual name of Belus Smawley. Once again, it was Les McCreery who found him for me, and I am grateful to Joyce and Belus, not only for welcoming me into their North Carolina home for interviews, but for arranging for me to meet with Fred Smawley, who gave me additional information on Smawley family history, as well as a guided tour of Ellenboro and the site of the old railroad depot. E. G. Freeman, one of the original Sunshine Basketball Boys, spent an afternoon telling tales of mountain basketball and walking me around Sunshine. L. C.

"Izzy" Davis covered Belus's Spindale playing days; Willie Norville gave me a few more anecdotes on Sunshine; and Richard Pierce shared with me his recollections of Belus at Appalachian State. Julia Hensley of the Rutherfordton Library put me in touch with Nancy Ellen Ferguson, Rutherford County's premier historian, whose intrepid research uncovered a picture of the relocated depot. Charles Brown of St. Louis's Mercantile Library found relevant stories for me from the *St. Louis Globe-Democrat*. Paul Buck recalled Belus's first days with the St. Louis Bombers, and the late Bones McKinney could remember every detail of Belus's unique shot. Intrigued by the possibility that he was a distant relative of Belus, Prof. Emer. Bob Smawley of Washington State University helped me chase down early leads.

Kenny and Bud Sailors together provided the stories for the picture I have tried to recreate of their mother, surely as heroic as any of the basketball stars in this book. I am grateful to Boky Sailors for letting me monopolize Kenny for an entire day, and then having the patience to give me her recollections of Kenny's playing days, both collegiate and professional, at a wonderful Chinese dinner in Wickenberg, Arizona. Writer Lew Freedman's articles in the *Alaska Times* were essential. Coach Marv Harshman gave me his observations on both the running one-hander and the jump shot. Additional information was drawn from *Life Magazine, The Arizona Republic, The Cheyenne Tribune-Eagle, The Denver Post, The New York Times*, and the *New York Sunday News*.

Several books and magazines were important reading in preparation for this story. Neil D. Isaac's *Vintage NBA: The Pioneer Era, 1946–1956* (Masters Press, 1996) contained essential background. Bob Peterson's *Cages to Jump Shots: Pro Basketball's Early Years* (Oxford Press, 1990) was proof that basketball history could be compelling. I found Dr. Walter E. Meanwell's fascinating "little black book," *The Science of Basketball for Men* (Democrat Printing Company, 1922), deep in the stacks of Stanford's Green Library. The university's Cubberly Education Library made old copies of *The Athletic Journal* available.

There were numerous spiritual contributors to this story. Evan

Lee and Larry Miller kept asking me, "Who was the first?" My good friends Fenwick and Red took time out from our search for the perfect piece of pecan pie to give the manuscript a critical read. My wife Peggy's affectionate attentiveness is the source for my belief that there might be somebody *else* out there willing to listen to me tell stories. I am grateful to the University of Nebraska Press for believing in the story's importance, and to Patricia Shelton for helping me to tighten and polish it. Finally, I want to acknowledge my college coach Paul Rundell, who did not discourage my often errant jump shot, and whose brilliant and patient coaching contributed to my love of basketball.